NO WAY BUT THIS

Jeff Sparrow is a writer, editor, and broadcaster, and an honorary fellow at Victoria University. He writes a fortnightly column for *The Guardian* and contributes regularly to many other publications, as well as being a member of the 3RRR Breakfasters radio team. Jeff is the immediate past editor of the literary and cultural journal *Overland*, and the author of several books, including *Communism: a love story* and *Killing: misadventures in violence*.

Also by Jeff Sparrow

Radical Melbourne: a secret history
(with Jill Sparrow)

Radical Melbourne 2: the enemy within
(with Jill Sparrow)

Communism: a love story
(finalist for the Colin Roderick Award)

Killing: misadventures in violence
(finalist for the Melbourne Prize for Literature)

Left Turn: political essays for the New Left
(co-edited with Antony Loewenstein)

Money Shot: a journey into porn and censorship
(finalist for the Manning Clark House Cultural Award,
Barbara Ramsden Award, and John Button Prize)

JEFF SPARROW

NO WAY BUT THIS

In Search of Paul Robeson

SCRIBE
Melbourne • London

Scribe Publications
18–20 Edward St, Brunswick, Victoria 3056, Australia
2 John St, Clerkenwell, London, WC1N 2ES, United Kingdom

First published by Scribe 2017
Reprinted 2017

Printed and bound in the UK by CPI Group (UK) Ltd, Croydon CR0 4YY

Scribe Publications is committed to the sustainable use of natural resources and the
use of paper products made responsibly from those resources.

9781925321852 (Australian edition)
9781911344292 (UK edition)
9781925548143 (e-book)

A CiP record for this title is available from the National Library of Australia and British Library.

scribepublications.com.au
scribepublications.co.uk

For my father

CONTENTS

PART THREE: REVELATIONS

PRELUDE

'This morning the Committee resumes its series of hearings on the vital issue of the use of American passports as travel documents in furtherance of the objectives of the Communist conspiracy.'

It's 12 June 1956, and the House Un-American Activities Committee is once more in session in the Caucus Room of the Cannon House Office Building in the United States Capitol Complex, Washington, D.C. Three-tiered crystal chandeliers illuminate a raised bench where Francis E. Walter, HUAC's chairman, sits alongside congressmen Clyde Doyle, Bernard Kearney, Gordon Scherer, and their staff director, Richard Arens. The room is closely packed with politicians, lawyers, journalists, and anyone else able to wrangle a seat. This, they know, is no ordinary occasion.

Arens stares down at an FBI report, compiled from hundreds of hours of covert surveillance. It contains information about the secret aliases supposedly employed in communist circles.

He leans forward to the much larger man standing in the witness box. Have you, Arens asks, ever been known under another name?

The witness gives a rich, velvet laugh.

'Oh, please! My name is Paul Robeson, and anything I have to say, or stand for, I have said in public all over the world.'

He gestures defiantly at the proceedings around him, so reminiscent of a criminal trial.

'That,' he says, 'is why I am here today.'

INTRODUCTION
Sydney, Australia

I've watched the clip of Paul Robeson singing on Bennelong Point a dozen times or more.

There are many things that make the grainy footage so memorable, not least the glaring gap when the camera pans and you see, just for an instant, Government House and the Harbour Bridge. But where are the white sails of the Opera House?

The film dates from 1960 and, of course, the Sydney Opera House did not yet exist. This was Robeson's first and only trip to Australia. A news crew had accompanied him to Bennelong Point to visit the Opera House site. He came to sing for the workers, the men labouring on what would become a universally recognisable music venue.

In the clip, Robeson wears his beret and his big winter coat. We watch him move through a forest of scaffolding to a jury-rigged microphone and then launch, without accompaniment, into 'Ol' Man River'.

The song was composed by Oscar Hammerstein and Jerome Kern for their musical *Show Boat*. Robeson first played the role of the stevedore Joe in the London stage show of 1928 and then reprised it for the movie of 1936. After that, 'Ol' Man River' became Paul's signature tune, a reminder of his stature as, in one reporter's words, 'the best known American in the world'.

Certainly, in the clip he looks every inch the star, even in blurry black and white. At sixty-two, he's still striking: huge and solid, with

1

his beret — so different from the hardhats around him — providing a certain raffish glamour. He should, I think every time I watch the scene, be completely out of place: a celebrity black artiste performing on a rough building site to white men puffing on cigarettes and brushing away flies.

Yet see their rapt attention! They stare, fascinated, at Robeson's giant frame and let his voice, so rich and so warm, envelop them.

'*Tote that barge!*' Robeson sings. '*Lift that bale! Show a little grit, an' you land in jail.*'

Hammerstein wrote the words as '*git a little drunk, an' you land in jail*', a sentiment more befitting the shuffling Negro of the white theatrical imagination. But Robeson did not shuffle, not for anyone. By 1960, he'd been a key FBI target for decades; agents from the Australian Security Intelligence Organisation had filed a report as soon as he landed in the country. But he'd neither apologised nor repented, and, by changing the Hammerstein lines, he transformed a slight lyric of phlegmatic — almost comic — resignation into a song of defiance.

In its original form, 'Ol' Man River' had continued:

Ah gits weary
An' sick of tryin'
Ah'm tired of livin'
An' skeered of dyin',
But ol' man river,
He jes' keeps rollin' along.

That version offered Joe's suffering as something to be endured meekly, a natural phenomenon as inevitable as the Mississippi's ebb and flow. In the Bennelong Point footage, Robeson sings instead:

But I keeps laffin'
Instead of cryin'

I must keep fightin'
Until I'm dyin'

When he mouths the word 'laffin'', his lip curls in scorn; at 'fightin'', he punches his fist in the air, a gesture that makes clear to the listeners he has in mind their shared enemies: the employers and politicians who consider an uneducated labourer no better than a Tennessee 'nigger'. Suddenly, viewers feel that what's inescapable is not resignation or oppression but human dignity — the yearning for freedom that persists, and will prevail, just like the mighty river itself.

In 1960, construction workers were not respectable. Concert halls did not cater to labourers, whom few considered deserving of fine music or sophisticated entertainments.

So, with this gesture at Bennelong Point, by transforming — if only for a lunch hour — their worksite into the musical venue it would eventually become, Robeson makes a statement characteristic of his life and career. You aren't, he says to them, simply tools for others; you're not beasts, suitable only for hoisting and carrying, even if that's the role you've been allotted. You're entitled to culture, to music and art and all of life's good things — and one day you shall have them.

By the time the last resonant notes have died away, some of those on the scaffolding are weeping.

'Paul Robeson!' exclaimed the Canadian union leader Harvey Murphy in 1952. 'That name! What that stands for is what every decent man or woman in the world stands for.'

But that was long ago.

During my childhood, the name 'Paul Robeson' had signified little to me. If I knew of him at all, it was as the voice in the crackly song I tuned past on the radio, the star of a movie on afternoon television when I stayed home from school with a cold.

But in the late 1990s, I began working in a trade union bookstore in Melbourne, and it was there that the Robeson legend seized hold of me.

That shop was a co-operative, a perpetually impecunious venture that staved off insolvency by retailing secondhand books from deceased estates. A sympathiser — a unionist or a peace activist or a veteran feminist — would die and, when their family disposed of their possessions, someone called us. Often the library would be donated in toto, as a way of clearing the property. My job was packing the thousands of yellowing paperbacks into recycled wine cartons and loading them into a car boot.

It could be terribly sad. A book collection documents the evolution of an individual soul, and hauling away those libraries — each one a map of someone's intellectual development — seemed, at times, like winking at murder. Yet, as I sorted and packed, I became intimately acquainted with the enthusiasms of the recently dead: the ticket stub from a long-ago concert; the copperplate dedication in a tissue-thin flyleaf ('*In the hope that you will find Whitman as precious a companion as I do*'); the marginal exclamation marks that grew more emphatic as the grand, Romantic rhetoric of the *Manifesto* reached its climax; the clipped article from a socialist newspaper, yellowing within the pages in which it had been pressed many decades earlier. And over the course of several years, I absorbed the preoccupations of a certain cohort of progressives, a generation slowly passing away.

They'd read so very, very widely. Our donors were, in most cases, men and women who had not attended university (and very often never finished school). Their knowledge came from elsewhere: from union conferences and kitchen study groups and workplace arguments, from self-produced pamphlets and the cheap volumes pumped out by small, radical publishers.

The political engagement I knew sometimes brought a utilitarian narrowing, it seemed to me, as activists cultivated a focus on ideas most immediately useful, and impatient scorn for everything else. The libraries of those stalwarts of the Old Left, though, were different: crammed with texts about astronomy and ancient history and gardening and poetics and mathematics and ornithology.

On the shelves somewhere, there would always — always! — be books about Paul Robeson. I'd run my fingers along the dusty spines — Paul's memoir, *Here I Stand*; or his wife Eslanda's book, *Paul Robeson, Negro*; or Philip S. Foner's *Paul Robeson Speaks*; or the early biographies, such as Ron Ramdin's *Paul Robeson: the man and his mission* or Marie Seton's *Paul Robeson* — and I began to greet the man like a friend.

That was how I absorbed Paul's story: in dibs and dabs, a chapter here and a few pages there, from books balanced on my knees in a cluttered apartment or an old study, surrounded by half-packed boxes and the sad remnants of someone else's life.

Paul Robeson's father was a slave who, after escaping his owner, transformed himself into a minister of religion. Paul grew up in Jim Crow America, subjected to discrimination that limited almost everything that a black man did. Against all odds, he won a scholarship to Rutgers. Against all odds, he graduated with honours and prizes from an almost completely white institution, forcing his way into its elite fraternity.

Robeson played basketball professionally, while on the football field he dominated so completely that the iconic coach Lou Little dubbed him the greatest athlete in the history of the game. He won ribbons for oratory; he graduated from Columbia with a law degree. His phenomenal linguistic gifts meant he could perform in more than 20 languages, including Chinese, Russian, Yiddish, and a variety of African tongues. He became one of the first black box-office draws in Hollywood and among the finest Shakespearean actors of his age, a man who met with presidents and romanced movie stars and was adored from New York to Johannesburg for having the richest, purest voice of the twentieth century.

But, more than anything, Robeson was a man of commitment, who made personal and political choices that today seem almost unimaginable.

———

In 2014, I went to Sydney for its writers' festival, the glitziest book event in Australia. I was there to hustle, to drum up publicity for the small literary journal I edited. In the sessions I attended, authors spoke with great confidence about the importance of literature and the power of the arts.

But in the corridors afterward, and at the hotel bar in the evening, the mood was far more sombre. The conservative Liberal Party had regained office the previous year, pledging to turn back asylum-seeker boats at sea. After that victory, the secrecy imposed on the detention facilities in Nauru and Papua New Guinea, in which the government housed its refugees, had intensified. Still, we'd all heard the grim stories: the epidemic of self-harm; the sexual abuse; the utter desperation of men and women assessed as genuine refugees and then subjected to indefinite imprisonment without charge or trial by one of the wealthiest countries on earth.

In the midst of our despairing conversations about these events, I found myself thinking about Paul Robeson.

'The artist must take sides,' he had famously declared. 'He must elect to fight for freedom or slavery. I have made my choice. I had no alternative.'

The speech was given during the Spanish Civil War, a conflict sometimes called 'the poets' war' because so many authors became embroiled in its battles.

'I am […] your decision,' wrote W.H. Auden. 'Yes, I am Spain.' The reactionary poet Roy Campbell jeered in reply, 'The Sodomites are on your side / The cowards and the cranks.'

In Spain, George Orwell was shot through the throat; in Spain, Arthur Koestler waited for the executioner in a fascist death cell. The list of writers who died for the Republic included John Cornford, Ralph Fox, Christopher Caudwell, Charles Donnelly, and many, many others.

By comparison, the contemporary literary scene seemed strangely hollow. We were an isolated coterie scrabbling for crumbs of recognition while the forces of barbarism gathered around us. What did taking sides mean — what could it possibly mean? — when so few knew or cared what writers or artists thought?

Or perhaps I was just jaded.

Whatever the reason, the next day I decided I needed a break. I left the hotel and the festival for a walk, ambling without purpose or goal along the ocean's foreshore.

I arrived, naturally, at the Opera House.

Sydney presents as a Teflon city, made from sunbleached chrome and steel, with no fissures for the past to grip. The poet Judith Beveridge remarks how, near the harbour, 'the light spills intemperately and as wantonly as honey', and her words capture something fundamental about the place: a sensuality, a certain hedonism that eschews introspection.

Beige steps now covered the earth where Robeson once sang among the scaffolding and wheelbarrows. I clambered up the stairs, hoping in a vague way that, by standing where Paul had sung, I might experience a faint echo of the emotions he'd stirred. But there was nothing, other than the clamour of international tourists. It was only when I pushed through the crowd and walked down the promontory that I felt the presence of the past, as a much older story tugged at me.

The famously tortured construction of the Sydney Opera House dragged on until 1973, with politicians and the press mocking and undermining Jørn Utzon's remarkable design. But if you focused away from that building and onto the landscape — the land and the water — you could place that recent history in the context of a human occupancy stretching back tens of thousands of years.

The Eora, the Indigenous inhabitants of Sydney Harbour, called the promontory 'Djubuguli'. They used it for meetings, for ceremonies, and for great feasts of shellfish. Even the modern name Bennelong Point took its name from a warrior known variously as Wollewarre, Boinba, Bunde-bunda, Baneelon, and Bennelong — an Eora man ordered kidnapped and then befriended by governor Arthur Phillip, before living, for a while, in a little house at the very tip of the point.

That day, standing where Bennelong's brick hut must have been constructed, I remembered how the Indigenous activist Faith Bandler had contacted Paul Robeson in the Hotel Australia. Bandler knew that Robeson wanted to meet Indigenous leaders, and so she screened him a documentary about government neglect of Aboriginal people in the Warburton Ranges: footage of emaciated and ill children, too weak to brush the flies from their faces.

Paul had watched the film intently. When the projector ceased its whir, he threw his cap on the floor in rage. Tears in his eyes, he asked someone for a cigarette, even though he rarely smoked. He finished, ground the butt out, and told Bandler that he would do whatever he could to help her struggle.

You can glimpse his anger in another clip from the tour: a snippet from a television program called *Spotlight*. The footage captures Paul being interviewed by a panel of local journalists, who treat him, this controversial foreigner, with a very Australian mix of obsequiousness and belligerence, as if they're intimidated by his fame and are overcompensating for that unease.

One of them asks whether he considers himself an American.

'Unquestionably, I am an American,' Paul replies, with his easy courtesy. 'Born there. My father slaved there. Upon the backs of my people was developed the primary wealth of America, the primary wealth. You have to have accumulated wealth to start, to build. You did it another way here in Australia. You had to build your accumulated wealth too — you just came and took it ... That's what you Europeans did, you just came and took it.'

He chuckles, and the panellists join the laughter — but their mirth sounds decidedly nervous. That whispering in our hearts, the historian Henry Reynolds calls it: the nagging awareness, in a colonial settler state, of foundational injustice embedded in the earth itself.

'He was so angry,' Faith Bandler said of Paul's response to the film she'd played him, 'and he said to me, "I'll go away now, but when I come back I'll give you a hand."'

He didn't, of course, since not long after he left Australia, Robeson's own life fell apart, in a spectacular and awful fashion.

Nonetheless, as I looked out across to Kirribilli Point, I was struck by just how remarkable the exchange with Bandler had been. Robeson's insistence on performing for blue-collar workers was extraordinary enough. But his offer of practical solidarity with Indigenous Australians, a gesture made entirely without patronage or posturing, felt almost unthinkable in the Sydney of today.

It was then I decided to write this book.

In a famous passage, the father of psychoanalysis, Sigmund Freud, applies his formidable intellect to an analysis of ghost stories. Freud wonders what gives the tales their eerie power. The uncanny — the spookiness we sometimes sense — stems, he argues, from the propensity of the repressed to re-emerge from wherever we store it. Ghosts, Freud says, are *what return*, psychic injuries making themselves felt as the history we've buried clambers from the grave and stakes its claims on the present.

The narrative of Paul Robeson — his dizzy rise and his crushing fall — involves, it seems to me, more than the life of one individual. It's about the successes, and then the failure, of a particular dream — one that, at the midpoint of the last century, had moved millions upon millions.

Robeson's extraordinary career intersects with some of modernity's worst traumas: slavery, colonialism, the Cold War, fascism, Stalinism. These are wounds covered over and forgotten, but never fully healed. Not surprisingly, the paths Robeson walked remain full of ghosts, whose whispers we can hear if we stop to listen. They talk of the past, but they also speak to the future.

Here, to tell Robeson's story, I visit the places that he went, in search of what's haunting the landscape.

I begin in the American South, since the searing experience of slavery shaped so much about Paul Robeson, just as it continues to challenge the

United States today. I shadow Robeson from his childhood in New Jersey to the New York of the Harlem Renaissance; I follow him to London, where he became a superstar, and to Wales, where he forged an intense and remarkable relationship with the men and women of the mining villages.

Much of the time, I walk in Paul's footsteps. But I also go places that, as far as I know, he never visited, but that nevertheless illuminate the key themes in his story: questions of historical memory and contemporary injustice. While Robeson did, famously, visit Spain, on my journey there I am less concerned about retracing his itinerary — though I do that, too — than in finding the traces of the civil war that prod uncomfortably through the skin of a modern, democratic nation. In Russia, I try to examine that which Robeson didn't (or wouldn't) see: the ghastly repression and violence that the Old Left scarcely acknowledged and that remains central to any honest accounting of the Cold War.

I present Robeson's own narrative mostly (though not always) in chronological order, sufficiently so, I hope, to give readers an appreciation of the sweeping grandeur and tragedy of his life. Nonetheless, this is not a conventional biography. I think of it more as a ghost story, shaped by places where particular associations form an eerie bridge between then and now.

That day on the building site, Paul Robeson had performed, through the rough-and-ready sound system, another of the songs with which he was indelibly linked.

Alfred Hayes published the words to 'Joe Hill' in 1934, and Earl Robinson penned the melody two years later. The song emerged from the vanished world of international socialism, of which both men were part. It tells the tale of an unjustly executed agitator, whose musical immortality foreshadows a future in which the outcasts and the dispossessed finally receive their due.

'*I dreamed I saw Joe Hill last night*,' Paul croons in the Sydney footage. '*Alive as you or me.*

Says I, "But Joe, you're ten years dead."

10

"I never died," says he.'

The real Joe Hill was framed for murder in Salt Lake City and put before the firing squad on 19 November 1915. Yet, in that flickering film, Robeson presents Hill as a spectre, a revenant who somehow manifests wherever 'working men defend their rights'.

The dead do come back, the song tells us, though not necessarily how we expect.

The libraries I unpacked have long since been dispersed, and the owners who cherished them are no more. Paul Robeson, too, died decades ago, and the memories of him have faded, so much so that a new generation barely knows his name.

Nevertheless, let's see, in the landscapes of the twenty-first century, what ghosts we might raise.

PART ONE
GENESIS

1

A PECULIAR INSTITUTION
Williamston and Greensboro, North Carolina

It was a long way from Melbourne, Australia, to Williamston, North Carolina. But the distance I was crossing was more than merely geographic.

I parked my rental car in the yard belonging to a dilapidated oyster bar in Washington Street, near the Roanoke River. The building, like the surrounding neighbourhood, had known better days, with the discarded shells littered about the only sign of recent custom.

I was here to meet a woman called Phyllis Roebuck. I'd come because her ancestor had owned Paul's father as a slave.

Williamston lay in Martin County, in the midst of the Black Belt — a term originally referring to the dark soil of fertile land, but later denoting the presence of the African Americans upon whom American agriculture had traditionally depended.

In 1963, Williamston had briefly made national headlines when the desegregation campaign of the Freedom Movement became a cause célèbre during the struggle for civil rights. The town was a stronghold of the Ku Klux Klan, and the protesting African Americans were regularly presented with evil little cards reading *KKK is watching you*. Later that year, 250 Klansmen, in full regalia, gathered in a field on the outskirts of Williamston to raise and burn a 30-metre cross, in a different but no less sinister warning.

The very extremity of American slavery rendered the 'peculiar institution' (the euphemism preferred by Southern ideologues) so distant as to seem almost incomprehensible to me. The Romans had owned slaves — and they had crucified criminals and staged gladiatorial battles for sport. Slavery in North America felt like that: an unimaginable practice from a different epoch, separated from the contemporary by deep, nearly geological, time. Yet Paul Robeson, alive when I was born, was the son of William Drew Robeson, a man kept in bondage on the tobacco farm of the Robason family near Robersonville, North Carolina, a few kilometres from Williamston.

For a researcher, the biographies of African Americans living under slavery remain notoriously difficult to reconstruct, since the enslaved were generally forbidden education and thus left few written records. Often, the only information comes from the white owners documenting the ages and histories of the individuals who were considered their property. That's why, when the ex-slave Frederick Douglass addressed abolitionist meetings in the North, he would begin by saying: 'I appear before you this evening as a thief and a robber. I stole this head, these limbs, this body from my master and ran off with them.'

In any case, my difficulties were more than merely archival. Paul's visit to Sydney mattered so much to Faith Bandler because of the parallels between his life and her own. Her father had also been a slave — an Islander man kidnapped from the New Hebrides and forced to work the sugarcane plantations of northern Australia. Bandler shared the institutional segregation directed at the Indigenous people with whom she allied herself, a discrimination recognisably similar (though by no means identical) to that enforced in the American South. But I was white and raised in a metropolitan centre, and my experiences were very different. I'd come to the United States to study a racism I'd never endured personally, a stranger trying to bridge a gulf of history and culture in a country not my own. But if I wanted to understand Paul's life and its meaning, I felt I had to try.

Martin County, I knew, was where Paul's story began.

———

The Inn at Moratoc was a family-style restaurant, with a buffet of candied yams, chicken and dumplings, and banana fritters, and a daytime clientele consisting mostly of retirees.

Phyllis was clutching a photo album, sitting at a table next to two women of a similar age. She introduced her companions as Becky and Joyce.

The three were cousins. They'd all been raised in Williamston, but their friendship had grown through their shared research.

'George Outlaw Robason is my great, great granddaddy,' Phyllis said, pulling out her scrapbook. 'Do you wanna see a picture of him?'

She handed me a photo of a severe-looking, rather whiskery nineteenth-century gentleman. The appellation 'Outlaw' came from his Scottish ancestry: George had belonged to the MacGregor clan, which had been disbanded ('outlawed') in the seventeenth century, and his insistence on the name a hundred years later suggested a propensity for long-term grudges.

She passed around images of other relatives and then of the house George had lived in. It wasn't precisely a plantation but it was, as she said, multi-storied, and so would have been substantial for the time and the place. North Carolina was never particularly wealthy, certainly when compared with other slave-owning states.

'He made and shipped wine, high-quality wine, up north. He had a lot of Yankee contacts. When the war broke out, he became a special emissary for Robert E. Lee. Because he had so many contacts, he was able to get supply and arms for the Southern campaign. My half of the Robason side all became merchants as well as landowners. They set up the first grocery stores. We grew as the area grew.'

I'd already visited Robersonville, where George and his father, William Robason, had established that early shop on the corner of Roberson Street and Railroad Street. The place was tiny — a school, a Baptist church, a public library, and not much besides.

The African-American memoirist Mary Mebane had taught in Robersonville in the 1950s. '[I]t was easy to tell,' she wrote, 'when you were in a black neighbourhood: the pavement stopped ... The dirt singled the beginning of the black neighbourhood.' Little seemed to have changed. Where there was bitumen, it was cracked and splitting, and weeds sprouted along the edges of the sidewalk. The town was more than sixty per cent African American, inhabited by far more descendants of slaves than of slaveholders. Such was the consequence of the South's peculiar institution — a persistent poverty, handed down through the generations.

But I wasn't sure how to discuss that with Phyllis.

In his book *Slaves in the Family*, Edward Ball writes of tracing the slaveholding legacy of his ancestors. He recalls a saying of his father's: 'There are five things we don't talk about in the Ball family: religion, sex, death, money, and the Negroes.'

In fact, Phyllis mentioned slavery before I did.

'When I look at this Civil War stuff,' she said, still leafing through her photo album, 'I remember how I asked my grandmother at some point: Nanny, did George O. ever own any slaves? She said no. And I said, why not? And she said, because we didn't believe in that.'

All three women laughed, and I did, too, though I wasn't sure of the joke.

'Because of course he did!' she said, looking to check I was catching on. 'She'd cleaned that up, you see! She just created her own belief system.'

Ball describes a similar 'cleaning up'. His relatives had taken pride in their ancestors, in their vanished wealth and influence. They all recalled, almost lovingly, the extent of the family plantations. But they compartmentalised their recollections, avoiding questions that might shatter that fantasy.

'My father didn't own slaves,' snapped Ball's cousin. 'And my grandfather didn't own slaves. To do this [write this book] is to condemn your ancestors! You're going to dig up my grandfather and hang him!'

And I could see a sense in which that was true.

An hour and a half south-west from Williamston lay the town of Smithfield. On 21 May 1937, a white woman called Mary Hicks arrived there. Hicks was employed by the Federal Writers' Project, a New Deal scheme paying jobless authors to collect the tales of ordinary Americans.

On this occasion, Hicks was interviewing Cornelia Andrews. Mrs Andrews was eighty-seven years old, and as a girl she'd been enslaved, at about the same time as Paul's father.

Hicks asked the old woman if she'd been mistreated during slavery. 'Was I ever beat bad?' Mrs Andrews replied. 'No ma'am, I wasn't.'

But Mrs Andrews' daughter intervened. 'Open your shirt, Mammy, and let the lady judge for herself.'

Eventually, the old woman slowly (she seemed 'ashamed', wrote Hicks) loosened her shirt so as to expose her back and shoulders. The flesh was 'marked as though branded with a plaited cowhide whip. There was no doubt of that at all.'

'I was whipped public,' she said tonelessly, 'for breaking dishes and being slow. I was at Miss Carrington's then, and it was just before the close of the war. I was in the kitchen washing dishes and I dropped one. The missus calls Mr Blount King, a patteroller [a patroller, a man charged with disciplining slaves], and he puts the whipping you see the marks of on me.'

No, you couldn't dig up the family and hang them — but the knowledge of Mrs Andrews' treatment brought about a different kind of execution. For how could the tale not change your attitude to the historical Carringtons? How could the story not define them for posterity? They might have been cultured and intelligent people, they might have cared for their children and showed kindness to their neighbours, but they'd ordered a young slave girl thrashed to the bone because she dropped a dish.

'The glory of my boyhood years,' Paul had written, late in his life, 'was my father. I loved him like no one in all the world.'

William Drew Robeson was probably born in 1845. His mother was a woman called Sabra (pronounced *Say-bra*). His father, Paul's grandfather, was called Benjamin. We know that, alongside William, Sabra had two other children in slavery: Ezekiel and Margaret. Of course, others might have perished in infancy. The rate of mortality for slaves was dizzyingly high — twice that of white babies. The slave diet was poor (corn bread, pork, and molasses, supplemented by meat from possums, raccoons, rabbits, and other game), and slaves were usually supplied with rough clothes and wooden-soled shoes only once a year, leaving many wearing rags most of the time.

Throughout his life, William avoided discussing his past in the South. To his children, he divulged nothing about his enslavement. We can't know what William endured. But the historian Edward Baptist notes the centrality of violence to the slave system. 'Every modern method of torture was used at one time or another,' he writes, 'sexual humiliation, mutilation, electric shocks, solitary confinement in "stress positions", burning, even waterboarding.'

In his memoir, Paul remarked on his father's symptomatic silence. 'I am sure that had my father ever spoken about this part of his life, it would have been utterly impossible for me as a boy to grasp the idea that a noble human being like my father had actually been owned by another man — to be bought and sold, used and abused at will.'

But, of course, that was an aspect of adulthood for Paul: realising that his dignified father had once been treated as an object — and recognising that he too might be reduced to the less than human.

Phyllis had never given much consideration to her family's involvement in slavery. But during her genealogical research, she'd uncovered, she said, documents in which the social relations of the past became shockingly apparent.

Becky nodded agreement. 'In the wills, the slaves were left like property,' she said, something like wonder in her voice. 'Every will we have in the family history, they would leave people in their wills. Like, they would say, "I'm gonna leave Bessy to Joyce," "I'm gonna leave Laura to Becky." And it was only first names. The slaves never had last names.'

I explained to them how William had escaped in the early phases of the Civil War, when the Union captured the strategic Fort Hatteras, and slaves from all over the state rushed to join the Northern soldiers. William's brother, Ezekiel Roberson (the spelling of both the black and the white version of the name varies between Robeson, Roberson, and Robason), fled to New Bern, a town about ninety-six kilometres from the Robason plantation — and, most probably, William accompanied him, possibly with their sister Margaret.

On that trip, William and his siblings had been forced to leave Sabra behind, I said. Family lore held that during the Civil War, William had twice, at great risk to himself, crept back to the fields to visit his still-enslaved mother. The church where William had ministered in Princeton still contained the stained-glass window he'd built, inscribed *In loving memory of Sabra Robeson* — a reminder of that heartbreaking separation.

Phyllis' face lit up in recognition. 'Oh, Sabra! Oh, I've got her here.'

She leafed frantically through her folder until she came upon a will. In 1845, William Robason left to George O. Robason what the notarist described as 'one Negro boy named Arden, one cow and calf [and] one feather bed', while to his daughter Caroline he bequeathed 'one Negro girl named Sabry during [Caroline's] natural life and then to her children'. If Sabry was William's mother Sabra — and that seemed almost certain — somehow she (or perhaps just William) had eventually become George's slave.

Phyllis was still staring at the paper. 'Oh, this is giving me the creeps. You know, I thought when I saw it, that's a real beautiful name.'

The three women were completing high school during the Williamston Freedom Movement, and they told me of the changes wrought by it. Phyllis recalled being outraged when her parents declared she'd be pulled from class if a single black student attended. Becky said that when she went to college, she'd recognised, with a sickening jolt, the injustice the older generation had accepted without question. 'Wait a minute! We owned people? Like livestock? What makes that right? Why would you do that? Why would you treat people that way?' she remembered thinking.

Becky had only recently returned to Williamston, after forty or more years away. The prolonged estrangement made her more conscious of the racial attitudes still prevailing in the town. 'It's like going back in time,' she said, and all three of them laughed. She continued, 'Some white people do feel an extreme privilege because of the past. They feel more entitled.'

'But that entitlement comes from both sides,' said Phyllis.

They all nodded.

'When I grew up,' Phyllis said, 'the black folks that lived on the farm, there was an obligation to take care of them and look after them. And I know my granddaddy and my daddy paid for many babies to be born that were not their babies. When they went to the hospital, they put the landowners' name on the record and then the landowner got whatever medical or baby bills. You were just expected to do that. Many of the older people that I was in contact with, older black people, they were called Aunt or Uncle.'

'Though they weren't really our aunts or uncles,' added Joyce.

'It was a title of respect,' said Phyllis. 'We treated them with respect. If we needed them, they were there; if they needed us, we were there.'

I didn't know what to say. Phyllis, Becky, and Joyce seemed lovely women, and they'd been very kind to me. Other members of the Robason clan flatly refused to meet once they'd learned of my project, whereas Phyllis and her cousins had gone out of their way to help. But I also knew that, during the struggle for civil rights, the Williamston Freedom protesters had specifically demanded authorities use 'courtesy titles' such as Mr and Mrs when interacting with African Americans. The campaigner Willis Williams explained: 'Blacks never became mister. They were "boy" until they got so old they couldn't walk and then they became "uncle".'

For the activists of 1963, the appellation Phyllis called as a gesture of respect was a belittling diminution — and they were willing to risk their lives to say so.

After more talk, I refused the offer of lunch and walked back to my car. As I drove away from Williamston, I was thinking about a curious passage in Paul's memoir in which he recalls an encounter with a descendant of those who had owned his father.

In a nightclub in New York in the 1940s, he'd been approached by a white man who introduced himself as a Robeson from North Carolina. The Southerner explained his mother's particular attachment to Paul's career, how she'd kept a scrapbook documenting the honours Paul had brought to their shared name.

He suggested all three of them get together for a chat. It would be, he said, a kind of family reunion. 'You see,' said the stranger, 'your father used to work for my grandfather.'

An angry Paul snapped back: 'You say my father "used to work" for your grandfather. Let's put it the way it was: your grandfather exploited my father as a slave!'

Needless to say, the proposed reunion did not occur.

So goes one version of the story. There are, however, two other accounts of that incident.

The second variant comes from the actress Uta Hagen, Paul's co-star in *Othello* and lover. In her account, the Southerner was drunk and deliberately baiting Paul. 'Your daddy was probably one of my daddy's slaves,' the man yelled. 'You probably belong to me.'

In this telling, Paul responded by shouting, 'You bastard!' and had to be restrained from attacking his namesake.

Robeson's son, Paul Robeson Jr (nicknamed 'Pauli' by his mother), recounts a third version, in which a slightly intoxicated white man approached Paul. The stranger wasn't aggressive so much as nervous, awed by the proximity of a global superstar. He referred to their shared surname while asking for an autograph, in a clumsy attempt to make a personal connection. 'My grandfather gave your father his name,' he stuttered.

Pauli describes his father as momentarily stiffening. But then Paul recovered, and scribbled the man a personalised message with a broad smile. 'Let's just say my father worked for your grandfather.'

In this version, it's Pauli who becomes angry. He demands to know why his father wasn't more militant. Why not put the white man in his place?

'It is far better to educate than to humiliate,' Paul says. 'Save your anger for the real enemy.'

From our vantage point, there was no way of knowing exactly how the encounter played out. Yet the psychological plausibility of all the scenarios demonstrated something, I thought, about the institution and its legacy. Slavery left its imprint on the oppressor as well as the oppressed, even as it marked the interactions between them. Those accounts hinted at the complexity of America's great and unhealed wound.

My next stop was Greensboro, North Carolina, where I stepped from the train carriage into a building dedicated to the vanished glory of rail. The J. Douglas Galyon Depot had been constructed for the old Southern Railway network back in 1927. The elegant curve of the interior hinted at the distant and glamorous horizons to which a Jazz Age traveller might once have been conveyed; the ionic columns supporting the exit added an aura of almost Athenian sophistication.

It was only later that I understood the building's incongruous grandeur. Once, the Greensboro station had marked the gateway to the Jim Crow–era transport system of the South. Not only had the waiting room been segregated; its luxury was also, in a sense, a celebration of segregated travel for its white patrons.

I'd come to Greensboro looking for a man called Robeson Logan. He was a descendant of William's siblings, the Robesons who'd stayed behind in North Carolina.

In 1866, William had moved to Pennsylvania and enrolled in Lincoln University, where he'd eventually earn a BA, an MA, and a degree in theology. That meant mastering Ancient Greek, Latin, Hebrew, geometry, chemistry, geology, trigonometry, mineralogy, political economy, and the myriad other components of a nineteenth-century classical education. It was an astonishing achievement, given William had almost certainly lacked any schooling at all when he escaped.

Paul always knew how lucky he'd been. 'I have cousins who can neither read nor write,' he said in 1941, at the pinnacle of his fame. 'I have had a chance. They have not. That is the difference.'

Indeed, the census of 1870 showed the Robesons who stayed in Martin County — Ezekiel and his family; Benjamin (then fifty and working as a farmhand), Sabra, and their three youngest children — were all still illiterate.

Logan was a big man: tall and solid and friendly. The resemblance to his ancestor was apparent as soon as I looked. They had the same stature, the same musculature, the same easy smile.

'My grandmother's maiden name is Roberson,' he told me. 'She would be —' He hesitated, thinking through the relationship. 'Paul's second cousin.'

I nodded. My genealogical research had brought me to the same conclusion. 'Her father was Ezekiel, and he and William were brothers.'

We'd met in Scuppernong Books on Elm Street, a charming bookshop where indie rock played softly on the stereo and where the cold-drinks menu was titled 'To Chill a Mockingbird'. A bearded man cut cakes on a counter bedecked with signs advertising organic coffee and locally sourced wine. Near the couch where we sat, a shelf featured reviews of works by local poets and novelists.

Logan had inherited a little parcel of land near Robersonville, a patch he could trace back through his grandmother's line to when his family worked as sharecroppers. But he didn't like the town. 'The land was predominantly owned by the slave owners. I'm not gonna say that the mentality is still alive today, but I just see how defensive they are. They own the town, practically. Wilson, Williamston, Robersonville. I am lucky enough to have something in my name. But, as far as the areas that are more profitable, downtown, well, they're owned by the same people.'

He paid the small amount of tax owing on the land almost as a matter of principle, even though he knew he'd never become a farmer. 'Every year I go back and remind myself: my father, my grandmother, Paul's father — all my relatives, all the way back to the days when we were slaves — they all walked across those fields. I just can't sell it.'

Logan was born in Raleigh and raised in Greensboro, places where, he said, racism mostly remained hidden. During his childhood, it was entirely unexceptionable for African-American kids and white kids to be friends, to socialise and hang out. Sexual relationships, though, were more problematic. 'No one would directly say anything, but you see it. We don't make it such an issue, but we know what lines not to cross, you know.'

I asked him to explain.

'Well, for example, the parents might slip up and say something if I was with a white girl. See, it's mostly an older generation who would react — I'm thirty-three, so it's the generation before me. They're mostly the ones who might have a problem.'

Greensboro was the site of the famous 1960 sit-in at Woolworth's segregated lunch counter, in a building now restored as a civil-rights museum. The student protest spurred imitative actions all throughout the South, the great eruption of civil disobedience that toppled the Jim Crow system.

Logan also came from a family of activists. His mother had worked for the Equal Employment Opportunity Commission. His recently deceased father had been a life member of the National Association for the Advancement of Colored People (NAACP), the senior pastor of the Johnson Chapel Missionary Baptist Church in Elm City, and the treasurer of the Baptist State Convention of North Carolina.

Just a few days before I met with Logan, the teenager Michael Brown had been killed by police in the town of Ferguson, and so inevitably we talked about that and the resulting protests that had spread from Missouri across America.

A similar killing could, he said, easily take place in Greensboro. The previous year, a policeman had been captured on camera throwing a young African-American man to the ground outside his house and handcuffing him, for the offence of 'running off his mouth'.

That was why, as a youth, Logan had been given 'the talk', with his parents advising him to avoid becoming a statistic. 'I recognise I have to be careful. It's just the nature of it. I'm a threat, I'm six foot four, 270 pounds — I fit the profile.'

Paul had sat down with his own son in the early 1940s for a very similar discussion, warning the sixteen-year-old that he'd make a likely target for the state police. The language he'd used was almost identical.

'I know my place,' Logan said again. 'I make myself known in my community. There's maybe four black families in my neighbourhood. And I'm aware of that. I get myself involved being on the housing association, not because I want to, but for my own safety. That was something my parents said: "It might be a good idea that you get involved." I make myself visible, I make myself known. If it's a nice day, I do yard work. Make sure I wave to everyone. That way I can avoid —' He hesitated. 'Well, something that might happen.'

Listening to him, I was reminded of my visit to the Civil Rights Museum further down Elm Street, where, earlier that day, I'd tagged along behind a group of children from a school in Raleigh. I'd been with them as they'd entered a room depicting racial atrocities of the past. The famous picture of Thomas Shipp and Abram Smith dangling from a tree in Marion, Indiana, after being taken from jail and beaten by racists. A burning cross in North Carolina. Dogs mauling marchers in Birmingham, Alabama. The charred corpse of worker Will Brown, burned by a mob in Omaha, Nebraska, in the 1919 race riot. Emmett

Till — a fourteen-year-old brutalised in Money, Mississippi, after allegedly flirting with a white girl — lying in his coffin.

For the most part, they'd seemed unmoved by the images around them. They were kids, after all: more intent on jostling one another and fidgeting than paying attention to their teachers' instructions.

But every so often, one of them stared with sudden intensity, as if a particular image had confronted them as a real event, a representation of extraordinary violence inflicted on someone who looked very much like them.

Then, on their way out, the children shuffled past a long list of names: a roll call of those arrested in the struggle for civil rights.

I was struck, walking down that hall, by how a discussion of race in America necessarily overturned all the assumptions of liberal civics. In the Greensboro exhibit, the heroes were those who stood against their own government and its police — because the government and police were wrong.

Logan couldn't tell me much more about Paul. He knew his own heritage — his mother had urged him, he said with a laugh, to produce as many kids as he could to carry on the lineage — but he also confirmed what I'd already suspected: that few of his peers even recognised Paul's name. At school, he'd sometimes prompted his teachers to discuss Paul Robeson. Invariably, they'd reply that the topic wasn't part of the curriculum.

Still, there was something satisfying in the evolution of the name: once the appellation of a slaveholder, it had become, for Robeson Logan, a designation of pride and a reminder of resistance.

I was thinking about that all the way to Princeton.

2

IN MY FATHER'S HOUSE
Princeton, New Jersey

I was staying on Independence Way, about seven kilometres from the town centre. A car setting off down US Route One would make New York City within the hour. Yet as soon as I walked along to the Ridge Road turn-off, the landscape became, quite suddenly, almost bucolic. Here, the houses were slender and white and elegant, tastefully screened from the traffic by a fringe of trees.

In 1952, Paul had visited Albert Einstein when the great scientist was living and working in Princeton. 'You were born here, really. Imagine that!' Einstein said. 'I didn't know anyone was ever *born* here. I thought that Princeton was only a place where people *died*.'

For his part, Paul didn't object to Princeton's staidness. He hated the town — or, at least, parts of it — for different reasons. It was, he claimed, a northern outpost of the white supremacist South: a place 'spiritually located in Dixie' where 'Bourbon and Banker were one ... and ... the decaying smell of the plantation Big House was blended with the crisper smell of the Countinghouse'.

I walked down past the canal and across a bridge, where a sign explained how Washington's men had forestalled Lord Cornwallis during the revolutionary war. Main Street ran parallel to the Millstone River, where the homes became grander still, and plastic-wrapped editions of *The New York Times* glittered with the dew from the lawns. Birds warbled in the cold; frozen puddles exploded underfoot with a sound like cracking glass.

These were the Bourbons and Bankers, I thought. Well, perhaps. Certainly, some of the more opulent houses looked like they might belong to financiers with patrician sensibilities. But if there were hints of Dixie in the white pillars and broad verandahs, in other respects the street was unexpectedly urban, especially as I came closer to central Princeton. For a modern university such as Princeton ('Practically all there is in the town,' said Paul, rather sniffily) brought with it a globalised college culture: the organic cafés, the bookshops, the boutique bars, the vaguely countercultural sensibility.

Witherspoon Street ran north-east from Nassau, at an intersection near some of Princeton's grandest old buildings, with Nassau Hall, the historic university compound, looming over the corner like a sprawling medieval keep. I turned down Witherspoon and walked a little further, past an organic bakery and a cigar bar, and saw, with a strange burst of excitement, the green street sign advertising Paul Robeson Place.

This was where Paul was born.

'I always tell people that if I ever write my memoirs, the first sentence would be, "I was born coloured." Because when I was born, we were coloured. When I was at high school, we were negro. Through college, I was black, and today I'm African American. We are the only race that's been changed so many times.'

The Princeton Historical Society had recommended Shirley Satterfield to me as an expert on the town's African-American history. She lived in Quarry Street, in the Witherspoon-Jackson area, a cluster of streets once known as African Lane. A bust of Paul sat outside the exuberantly modern Arts Council of Princeton building, near the corner of Witherspoon and Paul Robeson Place.

Most of the houses, though, were significantly older. The Wither-spoon Street Presbyterian Church was a small wooden building opposite the Princeton Cemetery. A historical marker by its entrance commemorated Betsey Stockton, the slave who'd helped found the church in 1840.

'My grandmother and all her siblings were born in Princeton,' Shirley said. 'They were baptised by the Reverend Robeson, and my grandma's older sister played the organ in the church during William Robeson's time.'

Paul was born in 1898, the youngest of five surviving children: William D. Robeson (Bill), nearly seventeen; John Bunyan Reeve (Reed), twelve; Benjamin Congleton, six; and Marian Marguerite, four.

In Princeton, as the nineteenth century came to an end, the opportunities for African Americans, who made up about twenty per cent of the population, remained cripplingly narrow. William's flock took menial jobs, as labourers or domestic servants or cleaners or cooks, and they lived in the ghetto near the church in which they worshipped. As a minister, William was a pivotal figure, a leader in matters earthly and spiritual. He was not wealthy — theirs was always a poor congregation — but his profession allowed him a dignity denied to his neighbours.

Shirley brought out an old photograph belonging to her grandmother. 'Somewhere in there is Paul Robeson.'

The image showed neat little children all sitting in a row. The young Paul stood out immediately in most of the photos from his childhood, simply because he was a head taller than everyone else. She turned it over. 'See, here's a list of all the pupils — and here's Paul's name and his address.'

When the adult Paul Robeson returned to Princeton to see his relatives, he would also visit Shirley's family. 'I remember him telling me stories, but I didn't know who he was because I was too little. I just knew he was this wonderful man with this big deep voice. My mother said he was a great man, but he was just Paul to me. But he became very soured against Princeton because of how his father was treated and how people here were treated, for this was a segregated town.'

It was segregated when Paul went to school and it was still segregated during Shirley's education in the 1940s. She grew up, she said, in a place where blacks and whites inhabited two different realms, much as Paul had described a generation earlier. 'We had a coloured school, a coloured Y [YMCA], a coloured cemetery, and a coloured church. Every other store around here was either a candy store or an ice-cream parlour or a beauty parlour or a restaurant because we couldn't go to stores on Nassau Street — we weren't welcome there.'

So much had changed. When I explored the neighbourhood, I stopped at Labyrinth Books on Nassau Street, where the window displayed a selection of titles by Naomi Klein. Further down, a big organic grocery co-op sold carob and kale; at the Small World café, the bathroom graffiti advised, *Riot, don't diet.* It was difficult to connect Shirley's story to such places. Obviously I knew, on an intellectual level, about American history — and, of course, about Princeton's specific past. But there was a difference between that abstraction and her description of everyday Jim Crow: say, the prohibition on a little girl entering a shop a few blocks downtown purely because of her skin colour.

Shirley had left Princeton after graduating from college to teach elementary school in Las Vegas, Syracuse, and elsewhere. But she returned with her daughters in 1981, working as a guidance counsellor at Princeton High School for many years. It was then that she became invested in local history. 'I actually started with the history of my church. But then I realised that our community was prime property in Princeton and that we were likely to lose a lot of the historic community. I became a member of the Historical Society of Princeton in 1990, and they were just talking about white history in Princeton. Being on the board, I said, I'm going to start a tour in this community — because when they do historical tours of Princeton, they stop at the Witherspoon-Jackson area. Nobody was talking about this community! One of the things we want is to make the area recognised as historic so that the developers who are coming in don't destroy it. Like the house where Paul was born.'

The old Robeson house was on the corner of Witherspoon Street and Green Street, just down from the church. When William had been residing in the parsonage, he'd been surrounded by relatives. His brother

Benjamin and family lived almost next door; his other brother John lived in Green Street with his wife and children.

The building was now owned by the Witherspoon Street Presbyterian Church, and Shirley and I went into the church office — another original house on Witherspoon Street — to organise a visit. An elderly white woman was inside, typing beside a small radiator throwing out moderate warmth. She and Shirley discussed an upcoming church meeting while the woman rustled up the keys. 'The door sticks,' she said, as she handed them over. 'Be careful with it.'

Once we got there, her warning made sense. The church had purchased the decrepit parsonage to prevent its destruction, intending eventually to create a Robeson museum. An architect had been commissioned to assess how the crumbling structure might be stabilised. But as yet no renovations had proceeded — and the old place was only barely standing.

In most Robeson biographies, William's house is described as a relatively prestigious address, a home befitting a man honoured and esteemed by his community. But when Shirley managed to get the stiff lock open, the place just seemed small and rundown.

'It's not very big, is it?'

'No,' she agreed. 'It's not. And it would have been smaller than this, too. Later, they merged it with the house next to it. In William Robeson's time, the parsonage was just the one building.' Each house must have been tiny.

We walked into the lounge, the floor bending under our weight. I tried to picture the layout of the original building, attempting to mentally strip away the various additions. It was not easy. In their decay, the various elements of the house had come to seem as old as one another, crumbling together as one.

Shirley pointed to a pile of newspapers from 1934. The architect had found them under the peeling linoleum, where they'd been used to keep out the cold: a form of home-made insulation employed by the poor. 'After William Robeson moved out,' she said, 'a woman whose name was Mrs Taylor lived here for many years, and she ran it as a rooming house for African Americans who couldn't stay anywhere else.'

'Why not?' I asked, and then realised. 'Oh ...'

She nodded. 'Most of the hotels wouldn't allow African Americans. So all around this area were boarding houses. Just so folks had somewhere to sleep.'

That was why the Robeson place looked as it did. We climbed an unsteady staircase and, upstairs, the rooms had been divided and divided again so as to offer as many little sleeping spaces as possible.

'You can go up to the attic if you like.'

Sensibly, Shirley didn't follow: the stairs here were even less safe. But the attic, too, had been transformed with cheap wood into monk-like cells, each barely long enough to lay down a bed. It was a legacy of segregation, a memory of racism embedded in the fabric of the house.

Later, walking around the block, she pointed to another old building. 'See this house down here? I have a picture of Booker T. Washington sitting in front of this house. It was another boarding house, for people who couldn't get accommodation anywhere else.'

Washington, the former slave who'd become the great apostle of gradualism and black self-improvement, had dined in the White House with President Roosevelt in 1901, an event of such symbolic power that North Carolina's vicious Senator Tillman declared: 'The action of President Roosevelt in entertaining that nigger will necessitate our killing a thousand niggers in the South before they learn their place again.'

Even a man sufficiently famous to sup with the President couldn't take a room in Princeton.

We came back downstairs and through to the kitchen.

'You can see what disrepair it's in,' she said, somewhat redundantly. 'We do sometimes use it for meetings, but the last person to stay here was David.'

'David?'

Then I grasped who she meant. I had attended a service at the Witherspoon Church, and the Reverend Burroughs, the current minister, told me the story while we chatted over coffee and cake after the Sunday worship. David Bryant was an African-American man. He had been arrested in 1975, when he was eighteen, charged with the rape and murder of an eight-year-old girl. He spent thirty-eight years in prison before investigators re-examining the case found that semen discovered on the girl's body didn't match his blood type.

The charges against him were dismissed. But, by the time he was released, all of his family were dead. 'I don't have a mother or brother or sister,' he'd told the press. 'I don't have any place to go. I don't have a dime to my name. What am I going to do?'

The church had assisted him. That was why one little room in that dilapidated building contained a mattress and a few posters and some other signs of recent occupation. Where else could a newly released prisoner go as he awaited the outcome of his appeal?

'There's a tradition of this house being a place of refuge,' Shirley said. 'And we're trying to continue it.'

Bryant had spent fourteen months out of jail, accustoming himself to an America changed almost beyond recognition — and then a higher court had upheld the prosecution's appeal, sending him back to prison.

The Witherspoon-Jackson area might no longer be poor, and the Jim Crow laws might have been abolished, but in 1850, there were nearly 900,000 adult men enslaved in America — and in 2013, almost 1.7 million African-American men in the United States were either in jail or on parole. To put it another way, more black people were deprived of their liberty in the twenty-first century than at the height of slavery, a comparison absolutely astonishing and deeply depressing.

Shirley was still looking around the ruined walls. 'We need more money. Now, have you seen enough here?'

I nodded.

'Alright,' she said. 'Let's go to where the Robesons had to move.'

'Even while demonstrating that he is really an equal (and, strangely, the proof must be superior performance!), the Negro must never appear to be challenging white superiority. Climb up if you can — but don't act "uppity". Always show that you are grateful. (Even if what you have gained has been wrested from unwilling powers, be sure to be grateful lest "they" take it all away.) Above all, do nothing to give them cause to fear you, for then the oppressing hand, which might at times ease up a little, will surely become a fist to knock you down again!'

When, in his autobiography, Paul explained the lesson that, he said, every African-American child was forced to learn, he was probably thinking about 1901 — the year in which William was sacked and the life he'd built came tumbling down around him.

William's position had always rested upon the benevolence of white Presbyterians, who exercised ultimate control over what they described as the 'coloured church'. In effect, he was a go-between for the two communities — Paul called him a 'bridge between the Have-Nots and the Haves' — representing the interests of his African-American constituency to the churchmen of Nassau Street and embodying a Presbyterianism governed by whites to the black worshippers of the Witherspoon-Jackson area.

On 22 February 1898, a fortnight before Paul's birth, a white mob in Lake City, South Carolina, set ablaze their post office and the house attached to it. Frazier Baker, the postmaster, died, shredded by bullets, and his baby, Julia, was killed in her mother's arms. The Bakers were, of course, black.

Ben Tillman, the senator who later found Booker T. Washington's White House visit so abhorrent, described the killings as understandable. No one could expect, he said, 'the proud people' of Lake City to 'receive their mail from a nigger'.

Later that year, white supremacists in Wilmington, North Carolina, burned down an African-American newspaper and ran the democratically elected African-American leaders out of town. Scores of black Americans died in the violence, and the demography of Wilmington was fundamentally changed.

The Wilmington coup came at the end of a decade of atrocities, with lynchers killing an average of two people every week, a slow stream of murder eroding the social gains African Americans had made since the Civil War.

Most of the African Americans in Princeton had relatives in the South, and something needed to be done, they agreed, some opposition registered. The Reverend Robeson was one of the few in the community with authority and prestige. Naturally, when a meeting was called, it took place in his church. Naturally, he spoke from the platform, standing alongside those other representatives of black Princeton who could be induced to appear. Naturally, he was, in due course, selected as a delegate to a subsequent protest in Philadelphia.

Paul always maintained that his father's insistence the government protect black citizens provoked his sacking by the white Presbyterians, a few years later. The churchmen wanted a minister who kept 'coloured folk' in line, not a man who attended indignation meetings and called for racial justice.

The Reverend Robeson's dismissal was catastrophic for his family. William was fifty-six years old and suddenly unemployed. His wife, Maria, was ill. They had five children — and, all at once, no house and no income.

Shirley and I left the parsonage and walked around the corner to Green Street, a brief journey, even on the slippery, slush-covered sidewalks, but one that traversed the depths of the Robesons' fall.

'This is the house that they went to,' she said, 'after they were thrown out. The woman who lives there now teaches violin. If I'm doing a tour, she'll usually come out and speak to them about Paul Robeson.'

This place, too, was white, but much, much smaller than the parsonage. Again, the building had been substantially renovated over the last century. Even from the outside, I could see that the verandah wasn't original. In its current form, the house looked pleasant enough — not big, but compact, and comfortable for its size. But those were not words that anyone would have used in 1901. Back then, when William installed his family, Green Street was notoriously poor, even within an impoverished neighbourhood. The building at number thirteen was usually described as a 'shack'; Paul later said it was 'so bad it should have been condemned'.

But what else could they do? Where could they go? Without his church, William had no accommodation, no profession, and little chance of finding other employment. What vocation awaited a former pastor?

No longer a young man, he scrabbled for whatever work was available. Occasionally, he filled in for other ministers elsewhere, offering a sermon when they were ill or indisposed. But that was scarcely a regular income.

He bought a horse and wagon, and, whenever he could, hired himself out to white students seeking transport around the town. Most of the time, he worked as an ashman — that is, he went to the houses of Princeton's wealthy, scooping up the debris from their fireplaces and adding the ashes to the huge pile accumulating in his own yard.

Paul remembered his father's frock coat — the uniform of his respectability — becoming gradually stained with filth and charcoal. Yet he never heard his father complain. 'Not one word of bitterness ever came from him. Serene, undaunted, he struggled to earn a livelihood and see to our education.'

Worse was to come.

'It was in here that Paul's mother died,' Shirley said.

In the early years of the twentieth century, the Robesons were buffeted by a succession of misfortunes, each more grievous than the next. By 1904, the Reverend Robeson had scrimped to see Bill through Lincoln University and managed to enrol Reed, the next oldest, there. The other children were studying, too, with Paul taking lessons from Shirley's grandmother. But funding the education of five children on an ashman's pitiful stipend was never easy. In the past, William had been secure in the church and anchored to the parsonage. Now, he was travelling, accepting any work available, wherever it could be found.

On 19 January, he was away on business in the town of Trenton, New Jersey. The children were at school, apart from Ben — who, at age eleven, had been kept home to help Maria. They were tending the stove in the parlour together when a falling coal lodged in her dress. Her clothing caught flame, and she succumbed to her burns the next day.

Maria's accident plunged the family deeper into crisis. With his wife's death, William hadn't simply lost his life partner and the mother of his children; he seemed also to have confirmed the worst expectations that others had harboured about him. For when he wed Maria, in 1876, he'd married — or, at least, so Maria's relatives had felt — way out of his league. The Bustills could trace their ancestry back to the Revolution — an almost unparallelled feat for African Americans, whose family trees were usually truncated by enslavement. For generations, the Bustills had played a prominent role in black public life, fighting against slavery and agitating for civil rights. They were keen to maintain their hard-won respectability.

Maria had received as good an education as a black woman might obtain at the time. She was very light-skinned, sufficiently so as to pass for white, and her family expected a great match, preferably with a man from an equally respectable family. They did not anticipate she'd settle upon a dark-skinned former slave, a fellow still in the process of raising himself from rural obscurity.

The Bustills barely acknowledged the marriage. Later, they blamed William for Maria's illnesses, particularly after Paul's birth, and they were even more furious after William's dismissal. By losing the trust of the white Presbyterians, he had, they thought, brought disgrace on the entire clan. Maria's death in the broken-down slum in Green Street confirmed all their worst fears. Their no-good son-in-law had first shamed his wife, and then killed her through neglect.

William himself must, in his darkest hours, have wondered about the course he'd taken. His insistence that his children receive the best education available reflected the philosophy upon which his own life had been constructed. Yet, somehow, his progress had been reversed. Where once he'd risen, he was now falling, gradually coming unstitched, with everything that education had provided dropping away in stages: his profession, his home, his family.

Why, then, did study matter? Why master Ancient Hebrew and theology and complex mathematics if, in your late middle age, you found yourself suddenly living a life no better, and in many ways worse, than that of your illiterate neighbours?

William never posed those questions, as far as we know, but Paul's brother Reed certainly did. Unexpectedly, Reed dropped out of Lincoln and returned home, enraging and disappointing his father. Yet in response Reed could point to William's own situation and ask: why did college matter? The plain fact was, one of the most scholarly men in black Princeton hauled ashes for a living.

Soon Reed, too, was driving a carriage — earning just as much (or as little) as his highly educated father. Not only did he reject all the accommodations William had made, but he also urged his younger brother to do the same. Paul recalled Reed carrying a bag of rocks in the back of his cab as a weapon against the often rowdy (and invariably racist) students who hired him. 'Stand up to them,' he told his brother, 'and hit back harder than they hit you.'

The philosophical clash between father and son soon came to a head. As Reed's inflexibility brought him into more and more trouble with the authorities, William demanded the boy leave Princeton, worrying that Paul would follow Reed's example.

But he needn't have feared.

'Paul loved his father,' Shirley told me. 'He adored him. William was old enough to be his grandfather, but that didn't matter. Paul just loved him.'

Paul's absolute faith in William was soon vindicated. In 1906, when Paul was eight and still at the Witherspoon School, the Reverend Robeson abandoned Presbyterianism for the African Methodist Episcopal Zion Church: one of the oldest black denominations in the country. Shirley suggested that the conversion reflected his bitterness at how the white Presbyterians had treated him. But the affiliation also offered him a professional future, for under the auspices of the new denomination, he could take up a small pastorate in the town of Westfield.

In 1907, he relocated his family about 80 kilometres to begin building a congregation and a church in which to worship. Even at the Witherspoon Church, the Reverend Robeson had never been wealthy, but in Westfield, he — and hence his dependants — barely managed to survive.

'I never remember us going hungry,' Paul's sister Marian later said. 'Pop always had a garden and we ate good.' But her response, in itself, spoke of the subsistence conditions in which they lived, without the close community support they'd relied on in Princeton. They might not have gone hungry, but they had few luxuries — a friend recalled Paul's school lunch as two buttered slices of bread sprinkled with sugar — and little security while William struggled to reconstruct his life.

Yet within a year or so, the Reverend Robeson had, once again, established a church, a following, and a parsonage. To his son, it must have seemed a miracle: a kind of secular resurrection.

Shirley continued her tour, taking me past the house where John Robeson, William's brother, had lived, just down the road from Paul's place. The street was almost entirely empty — it was a cold morning, and the sidewalks were slick with ice — but you could imagine the narrow space crowded with noisy children and their games.

I said as much, and Shirley nodded. 'When I was coming up, that was what it was like. Everyone knew everyone. Everyone was related. You couldn't talk about anyone without thinking about who they were related to. It was a poor community, but it was tight like that, a friendly place.'

As a girl, this solidarity had insulated her from the worst of the town's racism, so much so that it was the abolition of segregation that first made her feel the gulf between her community and her white neighbours. 'Integration came in 1948. When we left the Witherspoon Street School for Colored Children, I left behind the friends who lived in the neighbourhood. The teachers were from our community. They were part of our families as much as they were part of our schools. When we went to the Nassau school, I was in second grade: that was when I realised I was different, because the teachers taught us differently. They basically told us that we couldn't learn like the white kids. We got on fine with the kids themselves; it was the teachers who weren't ready for integration. That's when I realised that we were different — because the teachers treated us different.'

The Princeton cemetery was just across the road from the church. It, too, had been originally divided by race. By far the largest graves belonged to the white founders of the town. Interred in here were vice-president Aaron Burr, Jr; president Grover Cleveland; US Senator Richard Stockton; clergyman Henry Van Dyke; and a long list of other notables. But Shirley was a member of the cemetery committee (along with, it seemed, almost every other committee in Princeton), and she had insisted that the official tourist guide to the tombstones should include some African Americans. Accordingly, the cemetery brochure now listed the jazz musician Donald Lambert, the painter Rex Goreleigh, and a man called Jimmy Johnson, an escaped slave who'd become a well-known fixture of Princeton life in the nineteenth century.

We walked to the tombs of William and Maria Robeson, in a plot marked with a large granite slab. The stone had been erected by Paul's sister, Marian, long after the deaths of her parents. Because of that, it looked somewhat incongruous, disconcertingly modern among the old graves nearby.

After his success in Westfield, William had been transferred to Somerville, a town with a bigger African-American congregation in the already existing St Thomas AME Zion Church. It was a promotion, to a post at least as prestigious as the one in Princeton. For the second time, William Robeson had created a rich life by sheer force of will.

Paul, too, began to display the range of his abilities. Bill had identified Paul's musical talents during the family's parlour entertainments, in the course of which he invariably sang.

During Paul's concert years, critics searched for superlatives to describe his vocal timbre: 'all honey and persuasion', wrote one admirer in the late 1920s, 'yearning and searching, and probing the heart of the listener in every tiniest phrase'. But that was much later. Bill's early praise merely meant that Paul added the church choir to an ever-growing list of activities, with sport very much the priority.

The commencement ceremony after Paul's first year in the local coloured school was held in William's church: the local paper praised Paul's speech there as a 'rendition whose excellence has seldom been surpassed by a public school pupil'. He entered Somerville High School, becoming one of a handful of African-American students in a sea of whites. Enrolment in the college preparatory course meant that he followed William's footsteps with a largely classical education, focusing on Latin, German, and English, as well as mathematics, the sciences, and ancient history. He played baseball, basketball, and football, quickly becoming the star of the high-school football team. He edited the school paper, he acted with the drama group, he sang with the glee club, he spoke in the debating society. Every so often, when his father was ill or absent, he preached at the church.

Later, pupils from Somerville High remembered Paul with great affection. He was universally liked, they said, easygoing and kind, modest about his achievements. The teachers cherished his courtesy and intellect; the students hailed him as an athletic hero, the school's best player in every sport. Yet, at a white institution, a barrier always remained. Paul rarely attended school social events, for instance. It was safer if he didn't: as he said, 'There was always the feeling that — well, something unpleasant might happen,' especially since the principal, a certain Dr Ackerman, was an overt racist.

In another circumstance, an African-American boy so athletically talented might have been channelled exclusively into sports. But William cherished education, never expecting less from his son than academic perfection. If Paul returned home with a test score in the nineties, William would ask why he hadn't obtained one hundred — and then help him practise to ensure improvement.

Paul graduated top of the class his first year in Somerville. 'Pop was pleased by that, I guess,' he wrote, 'though it was only what he expected of me, and his attitude never allowed for feelings of exaggerated self-esteem.'

Looking down at William's grave, I remembered how Pauli speculated about William's tutelage and its consequences for Paul.

'My father was always extremely reluctant to talk to me about [William's] personality,' Pauli wrote, 'as if some painful memories were associated with such recollections. Reverend Robeson was often silent and remote at home, rarely dispensing praise and unlikely to demonstrate affection. Though he was a devoted family man who was respected and loved by all the Robeson children, he was also feared. Quick to anger and short on humour, he could not have failed to demand excellence from each of them.'

In public, however, Paul always defended William's methods. Certainly, they produced results. In his last year of high school, Paul learned of a scholarship to Rutgers. He crammed furiously, spurred on, he said, by the good wishes of his friends and the ill will of Dr Ackerman — and, most of all, by a sense that 'Pop's quiet confidence had to be justified'. He later described winning a place at Rutgers as a defining event in his life, an achievement by which he proved to his own satisfaction that he was not inferior to the whites who denied him equality.

And that was his father's point. William's insistence on individual accomplishment was a political strategy as much as a pedagogic technique. Paul wrote that he didn't know where his father stood in the great debate between 'the militant policy of W.E.B. Du Bois and the conservative preachments of Booker T. Washington'. But Du Bois and Washington were as one in arguing that talented black men needed to achieve their potential, thus giving a practical demonstration of what African Americans could accomplish. And it was an attitude that William shared.

At Rutgers, the Reverend Robeson watched his son accumulate academic and other trophies, triumphs that were never within William's own reach. Paul won fourteen varsity letters; he headed the debating team; he joined Phi Beta Kappa, an honour accorded to those deemed the best representatives of the college's ideals.

In 1918, the old man took sick, with his son scheduled to compete in yet another oratorical prize. From his deathbed, Reverend Robeson delivered a final command. 'I don't care what happens to me. I want you to go and give your speech, and I want you to win.'

Paul did, and his father died, true to his stern code until the end.

Shirley's voice snapped me back to the present. 'Let's keep moving.' I followed her further into the enormous cemetery, where she pointed to headstones in an area once known as 'the coloured section'. 'This woman here, her father owned two buildings on Green Street. His daughter also had a shop where she made her own hair products. But she only catered to white women. When I was little, I went to her to get my hair washed. She washed my hair out the back so that white women would not know that she had someone coloured in her shop.'

I tried to imagine how that must have felt. 'How did you react?'

'I didn't understand. Back then, I didn't really know about segregation. Our parents never spoke about it ... We knew that we lived in an area that was all coloured, but we just thought that was what we did. We went to the Playhouse movie theatre and we went to the back and sat on the right-hand side. No one told us that's where we had to sit; we just knew that was where we always went. But once I went to school and we were treated differently, that's when I knew what segregation was. And it was hard. It was hard.'

'When you think back on that, are you bitter?'

'Sometimes. Because it has continued. When I think of things like Ferguson, like the man [Eric Garner] who was choked to death for selling cigarettes in New York, saying "I can't breathe" while they choked him, I am bitter. But I wasn't bitter growing up because I had a good childhood. That's why, now that the old community is breaking down and people are dying, I'm trying real hard to keep all this history before I pass.'

She gestured elsewhere, waving at one grave after another. 'Right there, those are my relatives. That's my mom, and I'm waiting for her tombstone to come. That's my uncle, and that's my grandma who taught Paul Robeson, and I'll be buried behind her.'

The last was a matter-of-fact statement, expressed in the casual tone one might explain a luncheon engagement. For Shirley, community extended even to mortality, so that being interred with one's family was a source of comfort and security, and death almost a homecoming — a reunion with those she loved. Listening to her, I remembered how deeply Paul had treasured his community. He'd once commented that, while he recognised the scholarship to Rutgers as an achievement, he'd never really wanted to go there. He'd have preferred Lincoln, for at a black institution he'd have been among friends.

In a birthday message to Paul in the 1940s, at the peak of his success, the African-American educator Mary McLeod Bethune called him 'the tallest tree in our forest'. The tribute, encapsulating what he meant to so many, was often repeated by Paul's admirers. But few recognised the essential loneliness of the image.

After farewelling Shirley, I walked back the way I'd come, heading up Witherspoon Street towards the university. Nassau Street took its name from Nassau Hall, which dated from 1756. In 1783, the hall briefly served as the temporary capital of the nation, when the Confederation

Congress met there after fleeing Philadelphia. The vast Georgian Colonial structure had been substantially refurbished since then, fitted out in an ostentatious Italianate renovation in the nineteenth century. Nevertheless, it remained at the heart of the campus, as it always had — an imposing embodiment of Ivy League prestige, with three sweeping paths cross-sectioning at its entrance.

I paused at the wrought-iron FitzRandolph gates, named after the man who'd donated the college's original land. It struck me that William Robeson must have walked here, making his way between the columns when he came to convince Woodrow Wilson, the university's president, to enrol Paul's brother Bill.

Princeton regulations provided no legal basis to bar pupils on grounds of colour. But that didn't matter. Such exclusions were often a result of racialised etiquette rather than statutory bans. Wilson understood that the 'racial purity' of his institution mattered greatly to Southern students. A reputation for upholding white supremacy made Princeton the only Yankee university they trusted.

Though Bill was undeniably clever, for Wilson and the university administrators, the Reverend Robeson's insistence on pushing his son's case was insolence — so much so that it probably contributed to William's dismissal from the Witherspoon Church.

To the right of the gate, I could see the Nassau Presbyterian Church — the impressive Greek Revival building that traditionally housed the white counterpart to William's little congregation. Paul had spent his childhood looking up Witherspoon Street at the churchmen who ruined his father, and the college from which he and his siblings were forever excluded.

That was why his Rutgers scholarship mattered so much.

Paul was just seventeen when he jogged out onto the Rutgers football field for the first time. At 188 centimetres and 87 kilograms, he wasn't particularly huge by today's standards. In 1915, though, those figures made him a giant.

'There's a big darky on the field,' the Rutgers football coach, George Foster Sanford, had warned the other players. 'If you want him, OK; if not, OK.'

'Send him out,' said one of them. 'We'll kill him.'

Paul was well acquainted with the intricate web of restrictions by which segregation was enforced. He could not eat in restaurants with his classmates. He could not stay in certain expensive hotels. He couldn't even order alongside white patrons in a drugstore.

Whether he could play football in an almost completely white competition remained unclear.

Ominously, none of the other players spoke when Paul greeted them. Then, when the whistle blew, they fell upon him.

In 1915, American football was brutal. A decade earlier, the deaths of eighteen students in a season had prompted a few rule changes, most notably the introduction of forward passing. But the game remained unabashedly violent.

The white players tried to hurt Paul however they could. When the whistle sounded, he could barely walk. His nose was broken, his shoulder thrown out, and his body stippled with cuts and bruises. It took ten days for him to recover.

Not surprisingly, while recuperating in bed, Paul decided he would abandon college football. All through high school, he had endured similar violence — and the same indifference from the coaches and referees. As he told his older brother Ben, he was weary of being brutalised by white people.

Many years later, Paul remembered what had changed his mind. 'I didn't know whether I could take any more. But my father … had impressed on me that when I was out on a football field or in a classroom or just anywhere else, I wasn't just there on my own. I was the representative of a lot of Negro boys who wanted to play football and wanted to go to college and, as their representative, I had to show that I could take whatever was handed out.'

For that reason, he dragged himself back.

The second session began like the first. The white players didn't acknowledge him before the game, and then they pummelled him on the field whenever they could. At the end of the play, Paul was lying on his back, desperately catching his breath, when a student called Frank Kelly stomped on his hand to break his fingers.

Suddenly, an enraged Paul no longer cared about the ball or the game or the team. As the players rushed at him, he knocked three of them over — and then he lifted Kelly into the air.

'I wanted to kill him and I meant to kill him,' he explained later in an interview. 'It wasn't a thought, it was just a feeling, to kill. I got Kelly in my two hands and I got him over my head — like this. I was going to smash him so hard to the ground that I'd break him in two, and I could have done it.'

But Coach Sanford, seeing what was about to happen, yelled, 'Robey, you're on the varsity,' a call that snapped Paul out of his rage.

He'd won a kind of acceptance — but only a kind.

During his university career, Paul proved himself one of the greatest American footballers of a generation, so much so that Coach Sanford designed Rutgers' game-day tactics specifically to exploit his star's manifold talents. Paul could run. He could throw. His weight and size made him almost impossible to stop; his tackle took down opponents with emphatic finality. At the time, college football (rather than the professional code) was the game that counted, and Paul's role in Rutgers' upset win over the Newport Naval Reserves in November 1917 attracted national attention.

'Robeson of Rutgers', the press called him, 'The Magnificent Robeson', a 'super-man of the game'. Yet, even as he was twice named in the College Football All-American Team, Southern players made a point of snubbing him, sometimes insisting that they would not run out while he remained on the field.

William, of course, had instructed his son that, as a black player in a white competition, he could not break any rules. Paul remained faithful to the letter of that injunction — if not quite the spirit. 'I can honestly tell you,' he later said to his friends, 'that never, I mean *never*, not once while I was playing college football, did I use my hands illegally. And, as you know, most players always use their hands illegally if they can get away with it. I *never, never* did. But I'll tell you what I did do: I practiced breaking orange crates with my forearm.'

I walked through the gates and onto the neat lawns frosted by snow in search of Stanhope Hall, the third-oldest building on the campus. Once known as the Geological Hall, it now hosted the Center for African American Studies.

In a basement room, I found Keeanga-Yamahtta Taylor sitting behind her computer, a desk jumbled with books and papers. She was much younger than Shirley, and in a long shirt and jeans, with close-cropped hair. Having grown up in the South and then lived in Chicago, she lacked Shirley's emotional investment in the town's history. 'It's incredibly wealthy here,' she told me, with evident distaste, 'and it's incredibly white: it's like old, aristocratic, affluent America. That's part of the reason why I live in Philadelphia and commute. Princeton's the furtherest south of any of the Ivy League universities, and people talk about an ethos of Southern gentility, which gets expressed as a passive-aggressive, buttoned-up culture.'

'The theology was Calvin; the religion, cash,' Paul had quipped about Princeton. Keeanga-Yamahtta's disdain came from a similar register.

Still, something like six per cent of those currently enrolled were African American, and I'd read that the campus was seeing vocal protests against police killings from Black Lives Matter activists. Princeton's Center for African American Studies had its own building and the capacity to hire its own faculty, which was, as Keeanga-Yamahtta said, a significant departure from the usual academic attitude to a discipline often dismissed as marginal.

By the time of my visit, overt segregation had long vanished from Princeton, just as it had been abolished everywhere else. But it was difficult for an outsider like me to understand how integrated America was in practice. Would a young African-American man today still encounter the white world as something foreign, a sphere entirely separate from his own experiences?

'It's an interesting question,' Keeanga-Yamahtta said. She thought for a minute. 'According to the census, there are more biracial relationships than ever, more biracial marriages, and more people who declare themselves biracial ... But that's not necessarily reflected in [patterns of] where people live and thus where people go to school. For wealthy blacks, there's much more integration in terms of school and social life than for the majority of working-class and poor African Americans. There's a significantly larger black elite today.'

Chicago, for instance, remained largely divided on racial lines, with almost thirty kilometres of solidly black areas where working-class kids could go most of their lives without interacting with a white peer. In fact, she said, often the only white people they encountered were policemen or other authority or administrative figures. 'So it is also about residential segregation. American cities are either as segregated or more segregated than they were forty or forty-five years ago, during the last period of sustained social movements. Schools are supposed to be neighbourhood-based and so, when you have this intense segregation in neighbourhoods, the schools reflect that.'

At Rutgers, Paul's life was structured like that of any other privileged young gentleman at an elite institution. He was expected to dress and speak well; he was inducted into the various rituals of college culture; he studied a classical syllabus. Yet he was also barred from much that his peers took for granted. He couldn't attend student socials, since a black man dancing with white girls was unthinkable. He was never invited to join the glee club (even though he occasionally sang at Rutgers concerts), for many would have considered his participation in a tour an embarrassment. Only once was he asked to the traditional celebrations for the football team in which he starred, and that seems to have been by error. As one of his teammates remembered, 'coloured people were not accepted in hotels and public restaurants, so whenever there was a banquet for the footballers, Paul always arranged, gracefully, to have some other place to go.' When the squad played an away match, Paul invariably told the manager he'd organise his own food and accommodation — for, if he had not, he would have become a liability, since there was no prospect of him eating or staying with the others.

All of this meant that, even as Paul won academic and sporting accolades at Rutgers, he did much of his socialising in the largely separate African-American community, where he was already gaining a public profile. The local Somerville paper reported regularly on his accomplishments and achievements, and African-American parents held him up to their children as an example to be emulated. Whenever he felt too great a pressure to live up to their expectations, he visited friends in Princeton, Trenton, Philadelphia, Newark, and New York: places where he wasn't so well known as the preacher's son. He also played semi-professional basketball for a Harlem team, an activity that brought him much-needed cash and the opportunity to interact with teammates in a setting that could not be more different from the Rutgers football field.

Both Paul and William expected that Rutgers would guarantee him a life of upper-middle-class respectability. Today, though, Keeanga-Yamahtta said, the African-American middle class felt increasingly under pressure. The economic crisis of 2008 hit black communities first, before it crashed the national economy, with something like half of the African Americans who had recently purchased houses losing their homes. It was, she said, the most catastrophic loss of wealth since the collapse of the Freedman's Savings Bank in the aftermath of Reconstruction in the nineteenth century.

The economic crisis had also taken place in a context where traditional African-American institutions no longer seemed nearly as relevant to their constituency. Keeanga-Yamahtta shook her head violently when I asked whether religion was as central to the African-

American community as it had been during Paul's youth. 'Oh no! No. Look, there are many reasons why the black church was central in the earlier twentieth century, many of which have to do with the institutional instability of everything else. It was one institution that could not be manipulated by whites in quite the same way. Today, though, the church — and religion in general — are simply less of a factor in all of American life.'

There was, she said, a deep generational divide when it came to the church, something that had become obvious in the 2014 protests in Ferguson and after other police shootings. 'There's been a much more conservative reaction from those in the civil-rights establishment with deeper roots in the church compared to young people, who are, after all, the ones who are being subjected to this police terrorism. That hasn't helped the stature of the black church in the eyes of many young people.'

She quoted statistics from *The Guardian* showing that police had killed an astonishing 928 people a year over eight recent years, a number more than twice as large as the official toll. Most experts regarded that tally as an underestimate, since, until 2016, authorities simply didn't keep accurate figures about so-called 'law enforcement homicides'. 'And if we know that the police are twenty-one times more likely to be shooting young black men than white men, then we know the majority of those who are being killed. It's no wonder we're seeing a reaction from black millennials. These are people who have come of age in a time of endless war, economic crisis, and police murder, and they're the fulcrum of all of this.

'Police brutality, police murder: it's getting worse. And it's one issue about which there's really no way to register a complaint, for not only do the police exist above the law but they're a protected class about which no politician will ever complain, no public figure will ever say a single disparaging word about. There is literally nowhere to go if you want to complain about the police, other than to take to the streets. In Ferguson, you already had a very corrupt police force — about which everyone knows now — but the murder of Mike Brown was really transformed when they left his body out on the street for four and a half hours. That transformed the death from a typical police shooting to something like a lynching. It was a signal to people in Ferguson, a signal that the situation could still get worse in terms of brutality.'

I found myself thinking, listening to her words, of an incident during Paul's college years.

On 2 April 1917, Woodrow Wilson had announced the United States' commitment to war with Germany. The man who'd excluded Paul's brother from Princeton now said that the world 'must be made safe for democracy'. But there was a coda to his declaration of principles.

'If there should be disloyalty,' said the President, 'it will be dealt with with a firm hand of stern repression.'

Rutgers soon glimpsed what that might mean. On 23 April, a professor instructed his class to deliver speeches in support of the government's Liberty Loan scheme. One freshman, a youth named Samuel Chovenson, refused. The proposed oration implied a public endorsement of the war, something Chovenson wouldn't give. Accordingly, as the local paper reported, 'word of his seditious actions rapidly went the rounds of the student body, stirring up the patriotic young men, until every one was demanding that some action be taken'.

That action was a lynching.

The students seized Chovenson and imprisoned him in a dormitory for five hours. Eventually, he was dragged before a four-hundred-strong crowd, stripped, and smeared with molasses and feathers. His captors blindfolded him, tied him to a plank, and paraded him down George Street, carrying signs denouncing him as a 'Bolsheviki' and a 'pro-German'.

From the sidewalk, onlookers (including many soldiers) demanded what the paper called 'more severe punishment'. A public execution was eminently possible, not least because the name Chovenson sounded distinctly foreign. Eventually, the young man was released on the corner of George and Albany Streets, beaten and terrified but still alive.

Paul was not on campus at the time. But what he heard later — an incident so reminiscent of a KKK intervention — must have reminded him, once again, to be careful. If his fellow students would handle a dissident white man like that, what would they do to an African American who stepped out of place? Baker's death was a lesson; the Wilmington coup was a lesson; William's dismissal was a lesson — and Paul knew only too well how to read what had been done to Chovenson.

He was by no means a radical himself. The Russian 'Bolsheviki' did not interest him, for he fully supported the struggle against Germany. He served in the Reserve Officers Training Corps program, and the prize-winning speech he gave just after his father's death was titled 'Loyalty and the American Negro'. His situation was quite different to what Keeanga-Yamahtta described. He was on an upward trajectory, with every reason for optimism about the future.

Which didn't mean, of course, he was unaffected by the racism that surrounded him. His football teammates judged Paul 'a nice, placid, kind guy' who had 'great control of himself; he never blew his top, he didn't have a short fuse'. It would be more accurate to say that he kept his rage tightly in check — so much so that, during his acting career, whenever Paul wanted to portray anger, he would think back to what he'd endured as a college athlete.

In 1896, the African-American poet Paul Laurence Dunbar described the duplicity expected of black men, writing of the 'mask that grins and lies'. Paul adopted a similar strategy — except that for him, sport occasionally provided an outlet to strike back safely. In one match against West Virginia, Paul was allowed to start, against the objections of his opponents. When the players lined up for the whistle, the white youth opposite Paul leaned forward and hissed, 'Don't you so much as touch me, you black dog, or I'll cut your heart out.'

'Can you imagine?' Paul told friends later. 'I'm playing opposite him in a football game and he says I'm not to touch him. When the whistle blew, I dove in and he didn't see me coming. I clipped him sidewise and nearly busted him in two, and as we were lying under the pile I leaned forward and whispered, "I touched you that time. How did you like it?"'

For the most part, though, Paul cleaved to the strategy drummed into him by his father and then reinforced by his own experiences. Overt resistance would be crushed. You could only evade the restrictions of the white order if you achieved a position of respectability and prominence — and even then you needed to take great care with your response.

Keeanga-Yamahtta suggested that, for most young African Americans today, that kind of conciliation no longer seemed possible. The new activism was, she said, driven by desperation, a sense of grim necessity. 'The level of inequality now is so extreme, and this country is just crazy. That's why with policing, well, they've basically just unchained the police. There's an entire twentieth-century history of police violence and harassment and it's nothing like what we're seeing today.'

I needed to understand, Keeanga-Yamahtta said, that political lessons could go both ways.

That was something else Ferguson had shown. If the treatment of Michael Brown had been intended as a warning, it had failed, for the people in Ferguson refused to be cowed. They came onto the streets. They protested. They spoke out. And, through their courage, the climate had been transformed. 'Because of their refusal to let the issue die,' she said, 'Ferguson provided a model, one that others could use in response to police shootings. Which is what we've seen since.'

I pondered on that final comment during the bus ride to New York. Throughout Paul's childhood, his father had told him that his achievements would inspire others. That was why, for instance, William insisted Paul stick with football: there was more at stake than Paul's own preferences. Later, Paul downplayed the political significance of his individual accomplishments, conscious that his personal success might be used by conservatives to minimise the structural barriers holding back other African Americans. Besides, he'd come to reject his father's model of self-improvement as a means of social change.

Yet, in a way, William's point retained its validity.

The activists in Ferguson had forged a template for communities grappling with police violence. They had shown the possibility of defiance and shattered the fear on which impunity rested. Hadn't that always been the same? Didn't every struggle, no matter how spontaneous, depend on someone being willing to go first, to put their body on the line to prove the viability of resistance?

Despite all that had changed, I could still see a parallel. The stances that Paul took as an adult — his opposition to segregation and, ultimately, to capitalism — provided a model, a political example that others could (and did) imitate.

That was why it became so important to destroy him.

3

THE GREAT FUTURE
GRINDING DOWN
Harlem, New York

'So here we have Harlem — not merely a colony or a community or a settlement ... but a black city, located in the heart of white Manhattan, and containing more Negroes to the square mile than any other spot on earth. It strikes the uninformed observer as a phenomenon, a miracle straight out of the skies.'

On West 138th Street, you could understand what the writer James Weldon Johnson had meant, especially if you'd just toured Princeton's African Lane. In Witherspoon Street, William had raised his family in a narrow wooden dwelling. In Harlem, Paul began married life in a huge brownstone — a home, with its gabled windows and regal front steps spilling from a wide doorway, almost palatial by comparison.

It hadn't been as grand in the 1920s, of course. Paul only rented one floor, for a start: Pauli described his parents as living in an oversized studio apartment with 'a mahogany bed, dressing table and chest of drawers' at one end, and 'a handsome grey Sloane rug with a deep black border, large comfortable chairs, bookcases, a mahogany gateleg table and soft lamps' at the other. Nevertheless, there was a solidity and sophistication in the building quite different from the dilapidated homes available in most black neighbourhoods at the time.

The Harlem Renaissance — to which Paul Robeson both belonged and contributed — developed from an unlikely conjunction of factors. One was property speculation. As late as the 1880s, Harlem was barely settled. The land bubble of the 1890s spurred a construction boom aimed at people we'd today call gentrifiers. It seemed a plan that couldn't fail: attractive properties in such a central location would surely attract a cashed-up clientele. But the entrepreneurs hadn't anticipated the slump of the 1910s — and suddenly their top-notch real estate became unsaleable.

Or, rather, unsaleable to those for whom it was originally intended.

An African-American businessman offered a solution to the despairing developers: he would, he suggested, act as a broker, surreptitiously identifying African-American clients for the discounted properties. The timing was perfect. The glut of real estate coincided with the Great Migration of millions of African Americans, pushed out of the rural South by white violence and pulled to the cities by the prospect of better jobs. Harlem, as writer Rudolph Fisher said, appealed to them both as 'a land of plenty' and 'the city of refuge'.

For once, Jim Crow worked to advantage African Americans. The presence of a single black family in a neighbourhood invariably caused whites to move out, which, in turn, allowed more African Americans to find homes. As Johnson explained wryly, 'seeing that they could not stop the movement, [white residents] began to flee … Their conduct could be compared to that of a community in the Middle Ages fleeing before an epidemic of the black plague.'

Harlem became very black, very quickly: in 1910, African Americans numbered about ten per cent of the population; by 1930, the figure was seventy per cent. There were, of course, urban concentrations of African Americans elsewhere in the nation. Typically, though, black people were stuck on the fringes of cities. Yet Harlem sat in the very heart of New York, and allowed African Americans to occupy purpose-built houses rather than shanties. Not surprisingly, it was, as Cab Calloway said, 'the place for a Negro to be. [N]o matter how poor, you could walk down

Seventh Avenue or across 125th Street on a Sunday afternoon after church and check out the women in their fine clothes and the young dudes all decked out in their spats and gloves and tweeds and Homburgs. People knew how to dress, the streets were clean and tree-lined, and there were so few cars that they were no problem.'

But, for many, a black city in the middle of New York represented something more profound. In an influential essay, Alain LeRoy Locke — sometimes heralded as the 'father of the Harlem Renaissance', or at least its philosophical architect — lauded Harlem as providing African Americans a chance for self-expression. It was, he said, 'prophetic' — a geographical foreshadowing of what black Americans might yet become.

That was why the poet Langston Hughes declared himself in love with Harlem long before he ever arrived — and why so many others felt the same.

Paul, though, was different.

His final year in college had been marked by tremendous industrial upheavals, police repression, and racial conflict. Throughout the so-called Red Summer of 1919, whites sought to intimidate black soldiers returning from France to accept pre-war conditions through lynchings and other forms of violence, resulting in hundreds of African-American deaths across the nation. There was nothing out of the ordinary in that. What was new was that African Americans were fighting back — sometimes even taking up arms against their assailants.

In Rutgers, Paul was insulated from direct contact with the turmoil. When he graduated in June that year, the college yearbook celebrated him in verse:

> All hats off to 'Robey'
> All honor to his name
> On the diamond, the court or football field
> He brought old Rutgers fame.

Already, everyone knew Paul to be touched by destiny. He was young, breathtakingly handsome, and preternaturally good at almost everything to which he turned his hand. Claude McKay's poem about black America seemed written with Paul in mind: 'Mine is the future grinding down today / Like a great landslip moving to the sea ...'

Yet Paul himself had no idea what that future might be. If, when he moved to Harlem, he didn't embrace the city with instant joy, his hesitancy reflected that uncertainty. It wasn't simply that his father, the guiding force of his early life, was suddenly gone. It was also that the values of William's generation were being challenged by a different sensibility.

Locke and other intellectuals had identified the militant resistance to white violence as signalling the arrival of the 'New Negro'. The 'Old Negro' was now deemed cautious and ignorant and conciliatory; the New Negro was hailed as young and educated and fearless.

The New Negro sounded, in other words, a lot like Paul. But what followed from that? What did it mean to be part of a generation of African Americans who were making different choices? What did it mean to be black in the century of modernity?

When Paul enrolled in law at New York University, it was less from any passion for litigating than because the profession offered a logical progression for someone of his capabilities. In the interim, he supported himself as best he could, taking on various odd jobs while he waited to graduate.

A little way back east, down 139th Street, I came to a block that was even more spectacular than the Robeson apartment: an aggregation of beautifully restored houses shaped out of limestone and brick. On one of the gates, a sign instructed visitors, *Walk your horses* — a legacy, presumably, of a pre-automotive century. This was the iconic Strivers Row: built in the 1890s for upper-middle-class white families and then sold off at a reduced rate to African Americans in 1919. The elegant houses became homes for Harlem's most respectable inhabitants, including, in the years before she married Paul, Eslanda 'Essie' Cardozo Goode.

For many biographers, Essie occupies a somewhat ambiguous place in the Robeson story. The two spent most of their lives in partnership, even though their relationship was, at times, deeply strained. But Essie lacked Paul's sociability and charisma, and many of his intimates (including his brother Ben) never liked her. She was, they said, a snob and a social climber, ruthless and grasping and ambitious.

Yet the friends who only saw Paul with a woman with whom he had nothing in common failed to grasp how the two complemented each other.

Essie was ambitious, without doubt, but so too was Paul, underneath his disarming modesty. By the time he met Essie, he'd transferred his legal studies to Columbia. He was attending St Philip's Episcopal Church, the most prestigious black congregation in the city. He sang in its choir, acted in its amateur theatre, and played in the basketball team it sponsored, even as he earned a living through professional football.

He was, in other words, quite as much of a 'striver' as Esssie.

When I'd been travelling through the South, I'd visited Charleston, South Carolina, partly because of the Avery Research Center, an archival repository of African-American history and culture. The red-brick building had once belonged to the Avery Normal Institute, the first accredited secondary school for African Americans in the city. From the 1860s, the school had provided education, including teacher training, for African Americans. Essie's grandfather, Francis Cardozo, had been its second principal. He'd eventually become secretary of state of South Carolina in 1868 — the first African American to hold such a senior post anywhere in America — and state treasurer. His daughter, Essie's mother, grew a beauty parlour into a successful business, and her hopes for Essie were not unlike the faith William put in Paul. Essie was clever and confident and light-skinned; she broke through barriers of race and gender to study chemistry at Columbia and then to work as a chemist at the Columbia Medical Center.

From an early age, Paul had been attractive to women — and attracted by them. Despite his admiration for his father, the stern sexual morality of William's church had never appealed to Paul and, by the time he encountered Essie, he'd had several relationships, including an intense affair with a woman called Geraldine (Gerry) Neale. Decades later, Gerry explained to Pauli that she'd loved his father deeply but could not commit herself to the life she sensed he would lead. 'He would belong to the world, rather than to his family,' she said. 'He was wonderful to be with, and yet I couldn't live with a man like that.'

But the world didn't scare Essie. She knew herself to be extraordinary, and found the prospect of a big life with Paul appealing rather than frightening.

The early phases of their relationship illustrated their different personalities. Always decisive, Essie knew as soon as they met that she wanted to wed Paul. He, however, kept her at arm's length — until, all of a sudden, committing himself to marriage.

Essie's steel would be a key factor in Paul's success. In 1920, he was offered a lead part in a production staged by the Harlem Young Women's Christian Association. He hesitated. He'd never envisaged himself an actor, and had always considered theatre as, at best, an occasionally pleasant diversion, akin to the parlour entertainments in William's house. Besides, he didn't need more commitments on top of his work, study, and sport. But the director persuaded him — and his acting career was underway.

In another essay, Locke explained how the peculiarities of Harlem led to a concentration of African-American intellectuals alongside rural blacks migrating from the South. Rather than becoming isolated, writers, artists, and thinkers were thrown into renewed contact with the masses, in a way that encouraged solidarity and racial identification.

That YWCA performance illustrated the point. Because the group was in Harlem, where all the youthful innovators were thinking about race, the script they chose was a groundbreaking piece of African-American theatre: a play called *Simon the Cyrenian*, centring on 'Simon the Tiger', the African slave leader said to have carried Jesus' cross. The play's small audience contained theatre professionals from the experimental Provincetown Playhouse. They were astonished by the stage presence of the young man playing Simon, and offered him a paying role in the Eugene O'Neill play *The Emperor Jones*.

Yet Paul was still the son of the Reverend William Robeson. A biblical story was all well and good, but the Provincetowners wanted to cast him as Brutus Jones, an ill-educated murderer speaking in crude pidgin. 'I'll git de hide frayled off some o' you niggers sho'!' Jones shouted from the stage. All of Paul's education revolted against the idea. Play a criminal using the N-word? With some heat, he turned the part down.

Paul didn't act seriously again for some time. He and Essie married in secret in August 1921, moving in together on 138th Street that year. In the early days of their relationship, Paul was supporting himself through various odd jobs, including stints coaching football at Rutgers and playing for the Akron Pros and then the Milwaukee Badgers.

But professional football at that time was neither respectable nor particularly secure, not least because the game's violence regularly resulted in crippling injuries. Paul was still studying at Columbia, and his long-term plans centred on practising law.

Essie, however, had been ruminating about theatre and, when Paul was offered a part in *Taboo*, a vanity project written by a wealthy white socialite, she urged him to accept. Oh, the play was silly and unthinkingly racist, a nonsensical script about African voodoo rites, but the black actor Charles Gilpin had recently achieved great acclaim with *The Emperor Jones*, the part Paul had refused. Who knew what Paul might achieve if he backed himself in the role?

She made him an offer. She would, she said, keep them both financially afloat while he concentrated on an acting career. It was a tremendously generous proposal, necessitating the abandonment of Essie's own plans to study medicine. It also showed her clarity: she recognised, well before Paul did, that he'd be profoundly limited as a lawyer. 'This was America,' she later reasoned, with justifiable bitterness, 'and he was a Negro; therefore he wouldn't get far.'

In early 1923, that assessment was cruelly vindicated. Though Paul graduated, his legal career ended after a few weeks, when he asked a stenographer to take a note for him.

'I don't take dictation from a nigger,' she said.

Paul put on his hat and marched out, leaving the office and the profession.

His ability to defend himself on the football field, where the fans invariably chanted racist slogans while Paul fought off white opponents, led to an offer to retrain as a heavyweight boxer. Promoters and fight fans spoke quite seriously about a potential Paul Robeson–Jack Dempsey clash. But prize fighting was even less reputable than playing football for money, and Paul declared he'd rather do anything at all than enter the ring.

On Essie's urging, that 'anything' proved to be acting. He accepted a part in *Taboo*. While that show closed quickly, Paul's performance ('I knew little of what I was doing,' he remembered) brought renewed attention from the Provincetown Players. This time they wanted him for Eugene O'Neill's follow-up to *The Emperor Jones*, a new play called *All God's Chillun Got Wings*.

Essie had been taking her husband to serious theatre, consciously undermining the conservative ideas he'd inherited from his father. Paul had seen enough to understand that O'Neill was a playwright of national significance, and that the role being offered was a remarkable opportunity.

But he didn't expect that his first major performances would be so thoroughly controversial. *Chillun* dramatised the primal fear of American racists by depicting sex between a white woman and a black man. O'Neill wasn't exactly advocating interracial relationships. On the contrary, his play seemed as much a warning about miscegenation and its consequences.

Nevertheless, a press syndicate circulated a rehearsal photo captioned 'white actress kisses Negro's hand' — and then the yellow press did the rest. 'Riots Feared From Drama', ran the headline in the New York paper *The American*. The *Greensboro Daily News* said the play was 'inviting a lynching'. The KKK promised to bomb the theatre, and the authorities tried petty bureaucratic harassment to close the production.

In the midst of that, the Provincetown Players opted to briefly reprise *The Emperor Jones*, thinking that offering another play before *Chillun* might defuse some of the tension. The decision put massive pressure on Paul. He understood very little about theatre. He'd barely been on stage before. Suddenly, he was rehearsing simultaneously for two starring roles, both of which he knew would be scrutinised intensely.

Paul was nervous before *The Emperor Jones* and even more so prior to *Chillun*, particularly since the latter opened with police encircling the theatre and burly steelworkers protecting the dressing rooms. Yet in both roles, he was stunning, winning over the audience and reviewers with a combination of physical presence and the elocution he'd practised at Rutgers. 'Robeson,' wrote the critic George Nathan, 'with relatively little experience and with no training to speak of, is one of the most thoroughly eloquent, impressive, and convincing actors that I have looked at and listened to in almost twenty years of professional theatre-going.'

Essie's gamble had been vindicated.

In this site, Mr Marcus Garvey held his first public meeting in the United States in the year 1916.

When I saw the sign at St Mark the Evangelist church on 138th Street, I was struck by the lack of explanation, as if the authors assumed that readers would already understand. Yet Garvey's Universal Negro Improvement Association (UNIA) was largely forgotten in the developed world — even though, at one stage, he'd claimed an astonishing four million members.

In 1921, the flamboyant Jamaican orator had staged an international gathering of the UNIA in New York, during which he declared himself president of a 'redeemed Africa', a homeland to which the sons and daughters of slaves could be repatriated.

For other African-American leaders, Garvey's proposal to transport millions of people back to a continent they'd never known seemed like pure demagoguery — W.E.B. Du Bois snapped that the man was either 'a lunatic or a traitor'. Nonetheless, the very popularity of Garveyism boosted the perception of Harlem as an international 'black capital'; almost, in a way, a foreshadowing of the nation-state Garvey sought.

'One of the great measures of a people,' Paul told a journalist in 1924, 'is its culture, its artistic stature.' That was in an interview for *The Messenger*, a left-wing monthly founded by the socialists Chandler Owen and A. Philip Randolph. Paul's sentiments could equally have been expressed in the NAACP's magazine *The Crisis* (edited by Du Bois) or the National Urban League's *Opportunity* (edited by Charles Johnson). Though Harlem's intellectuals disagreed about much, a broad consensus had formed about the role of African-American art in elevating the race.

The centrality of black culture to the Harlem Renaissance helped explain the importance of the next building I visited, only a few minutes away from St Mark. The Harlem branch of the New York Public Library was a three-storey Italianate-style structure on 135th Street. Paul, like so many Harlem intellectuals, spent hours here: reading, discussing, and debating.

The importance of the library to Paul's generation suggested a certain continuity with the relentless self-improvement to which men like his father had been committed. But it also illustrated the changing times, for where William's focus had been on the European canon, the visitors here steeped themselves in black culture.

The Harlem library was one of the first in the city to employ African-American staff. It also housed a trove of black literature and art, including, from 1926, the collection belonging to Arturo Alfonso Schomburg, a Puerto Rican historian and writer. In school, Schomburg had been told that the world's black population lacked heroes, history, and accomplishments. He spent a lifetime seeking to prove his teacher wrong, amassing a treasury of items from Africa and the Americas.

The modern-looking Schomburg Center for Research in Black Culture was an annex to the older building, serving as both a museum and a resource for scholars. Its 'Curators' Choice' exhibitions displayed an astonishing range of photos and other images from its collection; its bookstore sold Claude McKay and Zora Neale Hurston and Jean Toomer alongside the works of contemporary African-American scholars and novelists.

The auditorium took its name from Langston Hughes, the writer most associated with the library. I'd been thinking a lot about how Hughes' career both parallelled and mirrored Robeson's. Each had won great acclaim when very young; each had embraced their blackness; each had travelled widely; each had been avowedly of the Left. But where Paul emulated his father and harboured a certain sense of ambivalence towards his mother's family, Langston rejected the self-hatred of his light-skinned father and embraced the race consciousness of his mother's ancestors (his great-grandmother married a man who fought with John Brown at Harper's Ferry). He'd overcome an unhappy childhood through reading — 'books began to happen to me,' he quipped — to become the most acclaimed writer in Harlem with his 1926 collection *The Weary Blues*.

In the main room of the Schomburg Centre, I walked on the red cosmogram beneath which the poet's ashes had been interred. The design was a graphical representation of his most famous verse, 'The Negro Speaks of Rivers', first published in *The Crisis* in 1921. 'I've known rivers,' it concludes. 'Ancient, dusky rivers. My soul has grown deep like the rivers.'

In the poem, Hughes uses elements of black history, with lines such as 'I bathed in the Euphrates when dawns were young', to laud the potential in what he called the black soul grown deep. He thus anticipated an argument that James Weldon Johnson, his sometime mentor, would go on to make. There was, Johnson insisted, a common idea that when the African slaves were brought to America, they were bereft of any culture or ideas of their own. But 'through his artistic efforts the Negro is smashing this immemorial stereotype faster than he has ever done through any other method he has been able to use'.

What stereotypes did *All God's Chillun Got Wings* smash?

'[I]f I do become a first-rate actor,' Paul had explained to the *New York Herald Tribune*, 'it will do more toward giving people a slant on the so-called negro problem than any amount of propaganda and argument.' Yet in O'Neill's show, he played Jim, a black man so captivated by an unhinged white woman that he fails his law exam so as to retain her love, eventually allowing her to destroy him. 'Nigger Jim Harris ... a full-fledged Member of the Bar!' says Paul's character near the end of the play. 'Why, the mere notion of it is enough to kill you with laughing! It'd be against all natural laws, all human right and justice.'

The sentiment cut very close for an actor recently driven out of the legal profession. Everyone recognised Robeson's charisma; everyone agreed he dominated the stage, but perhaps, in this play, his raw talent did more harm than good. Did not *Chillun* simply confirm the old racist canard about the sexual appetites and moral inadequacies of even the most accomplished African-American man? Was Paul not, with his remarkable performance, adding a veneer of legitimacy to such fantasies?

In the rancorous debate that followed, Du Bois defended *Chillun*, and Robeson's participation in it, arguing that O'Neill was at least attempting some subtlety in his writing of African-American characters, and in serious plays that addressed real issues. Others were far harsher. William Pickens from the NAACP denounced the play as a polemic against interracial relationships — essentially, propaganda for the KKK. Yes, he wrote, *Chillun* showcased Robeson as an African-American lead, but that just proved that actors would do anything for money.

Chillun did indeed make good money: it brought in consistent crowds over a long season, and it established Paul as an actor to watch. But Paul was deeply upset by the critical reaction, especially when Harlem heavyweights such as Marcus Garvey, Reverend Adam Clayton

Powell Sr of the Abyssinian Baptist Church, and Reverend J.W. Brown of the AME Zion Church endorsed Pickens' condemnation.

Essie, far less concerned by the response from reviewers, consoled him by reading out articles in white newspapers that blasted the play as an insult to the white race and then contrasting them with pieces in African-American papers denouncing it as offensive to the black population. But he remained disconsolate. Sure, he'd proved his talent. But art was supposed to elevate his people — and he seemed to be doing the opposite.

In North Charleston, South Carolina, a white policeman had been filmed shooting dead a black man named Walter Scott. By the time I arrived in Harlem, cell-phone footage was spreading all over the internet: video of a middle-aged African-American man jogging clumsily away from the policeman, who deliberately aims his gun and fires. How uncinematic real violence was, I found myself thinking. No explosion, no body flung through the air, just the soft *pop-pop-pop-pop* of a pistol, so muted that I struggled for an instant to recognise it, especially with Scott continuing to run until the last shot, which drops him, sprawling, to the ground.

'Oh, shit,' says the bystander holding the camera. 'Shit.'

The run-down park, the shaking lens, the officer's unhurried walk over to handcuff Scott's unmoving corpse — the peculiar horror of the clip came from the contrast between the prosaic and the grotesque, as we witnessed the casual extinction of a human life play out in such an everyday setting.

Lichi D'Amelio was a Harlem activist from the Black Lives Matter campaign. We were in the Lion's Head Tavern on West 109th Street and Amsterdam Avenue. 'Kind of like a dingy bar,' she'd warned me, when we'd made the arrangement. The place was full and noisy, so that our conversation took place at a volume only slightly lower than a drunken shout.

'A few months ago, two black women who had never been involved in politics put out a call on Facebook, calling for a day of anger, asking people to come,' she said loudly to me. 'Their Facebook page exploded — and there were fifty thousand people in New York. For a march that wasn't about one specific case so much as about the cops in general, that was big. It was multiracial and really angry, different from the past. In 1999, when Amadou Diallo was shot, the rallies were huge. You had celebrities — Susan Sarandon, whoever else. Of course, all the cops got acquitted. He's a Haitian immigrant and they fired at him forty-one times and they all walk away. But it's different now. It feels different.'

D'Amelio had been working with families of people shot by police, helping grieving relatives turn pain into anger. She told me about Constance Malcolm, whose eighteen-year-old son Ramarley Graham was pursued into his family's Bronx apartment by the narcotics unit. Graham had been seen adjusting his waistband; the officers concluded he was carrying drugs. Two policemen with guns drawn cornered him in the bathroom. Officer Richard Haste opened fire — he said, afterward, he thought Malcolm was reaching for a gun.

'It's something I think about a lot because these police murder cases happen all the time but it's only with some of them there's a political explosion. And that's something that families have to deal with. Someone else in another part of the country gets murdered and their case gets national attention, and you're left going: *Why them — why have they become important, and not my son?*'

Just before Paul moved to Harlem, the African-American soldiers sent to the Great War returned to New York. In Europe, the 369th Infantry Regiment, the so-called Harlem Hellfighters, had been assigned French commanders, so that white Americans didn't have to serve beside them. The American command even released a pamphlet warning French civilians about black soldiers' propensity for rape. Nevertheless, the Hellfighters endured heavy combat and distinguished themselves in battle. For their homecoming, they marched through white New York in tight formation — and, then, when they entered Harlem, their marching band struck up the jazz tune 'How Ya Gonna Keep 'Em Down on the Farm (After They've Seen Paree)?'

That was the sentiment of the Harlem Renaissance: a determination, after such profound suffering, to see change. 'We return,' said Du Bois in an essay for *The Crisis*. 'We return from fighting. We return fighting.'

Throughout his life, Paul identified Harlem as a centre not merely of black culture but also of black resistance. 'I am a Negro,' he wrote in his memoir in 1958:

> The house I live in is in Harlem — this city within a city, Negro metropolis of America … And it's so good to be back. For this is my community. Every street and landmark around here is rich with memories of the good times and dreams of young manhood … Harlem after the First World War. Here I met and married Essie; here life-long friendships began; here I started my career as an artist. Just a few blocks away, at the YWCA, I first walked on the stage in a play; and here I sang for fun, in the clubs and cabarets; here were the thrills of the big basketball games, the dances, the social life … Yes, here is my homeground — here and in all the Negro communities throughout the land. Here I stand.

In the passage, Paul identifies with Harlem and then uses it as a metonym for the African-American population throughout the United States. But that was a long time ago. D'Amelio expressed scepticism that the area played the same role today. 'I don't want to offend anyone or anything, but I'd say less and less so. It's not like it's been completely wiped out — I mean, there will often be rallies on 125th and Adam Clayton Powell. There's that area. I've been to lots of speak-outs and rallies that start there. But it's getting more and more …' She hesitated.

'Gentrified?'

'Yes.' said D'Amelio. 'Oh, yes. I mean, you walk down Frederick

Douglass or whatever, and it's all bourgie restaurants. They got rid of the Lenox Lounge, which is where Billie Holiday and Ella Fitzgerald sang. There's gonna be a Whole Foods around there now.'

Writing about the tourists coming to the Harlem of her day, Essie noted, with evident satisfaction, how for once it was whites that felt outsiders, who sensed they trespassed on a place belonging to others. By contrast, in her 2011 book *Harlem is Nowhere*, Sharifa Rhodes-Pitts describes sitting in a fashionable café that had opened near her Harlem apartment, eavesdropping on two white men, one of whom had clearly just moved into the largely black area. 'This is fabulous,' his visitor said. 'Really, you have to do something to get the word out. There need to be more people up here.'

But gentrification in Harlem was a complicated, even contradictory, process. As early as 1925, James Weldon Johnson pondered whether African Americans could 'hold this choice bit of Manhattan Island'. In a sense, of course, black Harlem had itself sprung from gentrification — that ill-fated attempt, just before the property crash, to move wealthy families into an impoverished Jewish area. But if economic crisis had made the Harlem Renaissance possible, economic crisis also brought it to an end, as the Depression destroyed the fragile African-American middle class upon which the hope of Harlem as a glittering 'race capital' had depended.

Johnson had nominated affluence — particularly, property acquisition by wealthy black individuals — as key to the maintenance of an African-American district. By a cruel irony, it proved to be poverty that kept Harlem black. When, in 1948, James Baldwin explained that his neighbourhood had changed very little in his or his parents' lifetime, he was referring primarily to the general destitution that condemned Harlem's infrastructure to slow decay. 'Now as then,' he said, 'the buildings are old and in desperate need of repair, the streets are crowded and dirty, there are too many human beings per square block.'

In the twenty-first century, Johnson's vision of a prosperous Harlem was being fulfilled — but not in the way he'd wanted. The spiralling price of New York real estate meant that these old buildings — or, at least, the land on which they rest — were becoming staggeringly valuable. Some Harlem landmarks had been knocked down; others, such as Paul's old apartment block and the buildings in Striver's Row, had been restored to their late-nineteenth-century glory. The rents were rising, rendering Harlem unaffordable to many who had previously called it home. According to some statistics, the proportion of African Americans in the area had fallen to its lowest level in a century.

'Don't get me wrong,' D'Amelio said. 'There's still some of the old residents. Most of the gentrifiers avoid 125th Street. It's the centre of Harlem; the Apollo is there, the people with African flags — the hardcore nationalists — with pictures up of slaves, selling knickknacks. There's still that history.'

And, of course, the history commemorated by Harlem remained different from that commemorated elsewhere. In Charleston, Essie's grandfather Francis Cardozo had been driven from public office in a violent campaign spearheaded by Wade Hampton, a man associated with the KKK–style group the Red Shirts. Hampton became governor in 1876; Cardozo resigned, and was then prosecuted on trumped-up charges of conspiracy and jailed for six months — essentially, for being black.

Hampton was honoured by Wade Hampton Drive, Wade Hampton High School, Wade Hampton Boulevard, and a score of other places. But during my visit to Charleston, I'd found no tributes to Francis Cardozo, America's first black secretary of state.

Instead, almost everywhere I went in the city, the plaques, streets, and sculptures honoured bigots and exemplars of white supremacy. I'd eaten lunch in Marion Square, dominated by a statue of former vice-president John C. Calhoun. Calhoun was best known for insisting that slavery was not, as some white Southerners apologetically claimed, a 'necessary evil', but a positive good, an institution to be cherished and strengthened. He was, in other words, a key propagandist for Southern slavery before the Civil War — and yet the city still commemorated him, high up on a pedestal overlooking a street that carried his name.

In Harlem, by contrast, the roads belonged — in name at least — to those who'd fought for freedom. The old 125th Street was now also known as Martin Luther King Jr Boulevard. It ran parallel to the street honouring Malcolm X. Adam Clayton Powell Jr had a statue; Marcus Garvey was honoured with a park. Harriet Tubman, the indomitable abolitionist, stood on the corner of St Nicholas Avenue and 122nd Street, while a leonine sculpture of Frederick Douglass guarded the boulevard that bore his name.

Douglass had once explained that to identify the vanguard of the people, you need only 'look to the uneasy dreams of an aristocracy and find what they dread most'. In Charleston, you could see what he meant. In 1996, civil-rights activists had begun lobbying for a tribute to a local resistance hero. Denmark Vesey had led a slave insurrection in the early nineteenth century, a scheme that may have involved as many as nine thousand African Americans. He'd been betrayed and was hanged alongside thirty-four of his comrades.

It was time, the activists said, for him to be honoured.

Charleston conservatives responded by denouncing Vesey as a terrorist, the moral equivalent of Osama bin Laden. After protracted debates, the monument was completed in 2014. But it wasn't erected in Marion Square. Instead, it stood a considerable distance from the main tourist area — in Hampton Park, a garden named after the racist Wade Hampton.

None of that surprised D'Amelio. But she was less certain when I asked her whether Harlem's commemoration of black leaders mattered. Did those street names and statues — the shades of old heroes — change anything in the present?

'Yes,' she said at once, before immediately amending her answer. 'Yes and no. It's important, but it's not the end of the question. But it's a remnant of something that hasn't been completely erased, and that matters.'

In the streets, you could trace, if you were so minded, the long arc of the freedom struggle in the United States: from the fight against slavery to the betrayal of Reconstruction; from the Renaissance to the civil-rights movement.

But that didn't necessarily mean that people did.

'Look, I'm originally from Argentina, which is a much more political country. I came here very early on because my parents fled, but when I go back, it's just fascinating to me. People discuss politics regularly. That's not true here: it's different. The movement doesn't have the same sort of political chops … We're starting from way behind the starting line. In the United States, there is a very low level of political engagement, not just with politics today but also with history. Yet the past still matters, and what people know about it is important.'

She told me about Constance Malcolm and her family, and how, when they'd begun their protest, they'd constructed a huge banner adorned with quotes from Garvey, a man still celebrated as a national hero in his native Jamaica.

Garvey was, of course, intensely quotable. 'Lift up yourselves, men,' he'd said, 'take yourselves out of the mire and hitch your hopes to the stars; yes, rise as high as the very stars themselves.' Even on the page, his words exuded some of the flamboyance, the sheer charisma, through which he'd built the UNIA into an international crusade.

Yet there were also good reasons why Du Bois thought Garvey little more than a crook. Garvey's insistence that African Americans should build their own civilisation sounded very radical. But, in practice, it meant accepting that blacks could do nothing to build a future in the United States, an argument sufficiently conservative that at one stage Garvey had held friendly discussions with the KKK (who, of course, shared his desire for a black exodus).

'So Harlem's history,' D'Amelio continued, 'the way it's remembered, has consequences. That being said — and I am sure there are people in the movement who would disagree — my opinion is that, these days, it's mostly a very superficial reference point. That's one of the difficulties. See, the movement really blew up around the non-indictments in the Mike Brown and Eric Garner cases, about a week apart. And that was a little while ago now. It's a perpetual problem for the US Left. It's very difficult to sustain a movement. You'll see massive explosions that flare up and then people will be like, *Now what do we do?* And there's not a clear answer. There's marches, there's anger, but there's no engagement with history. It's not like the movement then goes, *Well, what did we learn from the past? What did they do? What can we do? What's the difference and what's the same?'*

The lack of historical memory made determining clear strategies very difficult. Without a knowledge of previous struggles, without an assessment of what had worked and what had failed, every protest felt like the first protest. After a particularly egregious police killing, people took to the streets — as Keeanga-Yamahtta said, they had no other choice. But how did they continue the momentum? Where did they seek allies? What organisational structures — if any — did they build?

Similar questions had confronted generations of African-American radicals. In the 1930s, the Communist Party of America maintained an office on the corner of Lenox Avenue and 125 Street, campaigning for the 'Scottsboro Boys' (nine African-American teenagers wrongly accused of raping two white women in Alabama) and rallying against unemployment. When I went there, it was a tobacco shop.

In the late 1960s, the Black Panthers opened a branch on Seventh Street, before the entire local Panther leadership was charged — and later acquitted — of planning to bomb New York police stations. I found a grocery store on the site.

The questions posed in the contemporary context weren't exactly the same, of course. But there were obvious parallels. 'You look at the civil-rights movement: the cops were killing black people all the time. Think about the Panthers: their first real campaign was around police brutality, about the murder of a construction worker named Denzil Dowell who was killed by the police. That was in the very first issue of the first Black Panther newspaper, and local people were like, "Fuck, yeah." That's continued. It's just business as usual.

'The police and black America have had this relationship since Reconstruction. What's different is that there's more attention. Most of the time, white people are clueless to the lives of black people. They're fucking clueless. And I think this movement has given more white people a sense of it.'

She took a phone call and, while she talked, I went to pay for our drinks.

'You know,' she said when I returned, while gathering up her things, 'if you're interested in the history of Harlem, I should hook you up with Jazz Hayden. Do you know him?'

I didn't.

'The thing about Jazz is that he was in Attica for thirty years, but he has a real connection to Harlem and a memory of what it was like when it had more of a vibrant culture of black resistance. Jazz is seventy-five, but he's in amazing shape, and he might outlive us all. And he loves to talk. You really should meet with him.'

'Organised 1796', read the sign outside Mother African Methodist Episcopal Zion Church, just a few hundred metres away from the library. 'Freedom church. Where the difference is God.'

Mother Zion was more like a cathedral than the little AME Zion churches over which William had presided: a neo-Gothic edifice of white and grey stone, capable of holding a thousand or more people. The church traced its origins back to 1796, when black members of the John Street Methodist Church in New York rebelled against the racism of their co-religionists. The new denomination was based on a stipulation that 'no distinction should be made in the church on account of race, colour, or condition'. Sojourner Truth belonged to AME Zion; so, too, did Harriet Tubman and Frederick Douglass.

On 27 January 1976, Paul's body had lain in state here, as a huge crowd of mourners spilled out into 137th Street. Harry Belafonte attended the funeral, alongside Malcolm X's widow, Betty Shabazz, and a galaxy of other African-American stars. Delivering the eulogy, Bishop Hoggard explained that Paul had come home.

Certainly Paul had known Mother Zion well, even though the current building was still under construction as he was launching his theatrical career in the 1920s. His brother Benjamin was pastor of Mother Zion for many years; during the Cold War, Paul had found some respite from the pressure bearing down on him by temporarily living with his sibling in the parsonage.

Through the worst times, Ben and the church had been a link to another comfort. 'My brother's love which enfolds me,' explained Paul in 1958, 'is a precious, living bond with the man, now forty years dead, who more than anyone else influenced my life — my father, Reverend William Drew Robeson':

> It is not just that Ben is my older brother, but he reminds me so much of Pop that his house seems to glow with the pervading spirit of that other Reverend Robeson, my wonderful, beloved father.
>
> Next door to the parsonage is the church where on Sunday mornings I am united with the fellowship of thousands of my people, singing with them their songs, feeling the warmth of their handshakes and smiles — this too is a link with my earliest days, the congregations I grew up in as a boy in Princeton, in Westfield, in Somerville.

It was through that heritage, the black tradition that Mother Zion embodied, that he found a solution to the problems presenting him in the theatre.

When the intellectuals of the Harlem Renaissance discussed art, they meant, for the most part, high art — particularly literature. In respect of music, they praised African-American accomplishment in classical composition or concert-hall performance, but mostly eschewed popular genres. Alain Locke's influential anthology *The New Negro* made no mention of the blues, while its sole essay on jazz damned the form with faint praise: jazz was 'less harmful than drugs or alcohol', explained the writer, J.A. Rogers.

Paul had sung all through high school and college, both to entertain friends and to earn money. In 1922, when he'd needed funds, he'd seized the chance to fill a temporary vacancy in a four-piece vocal group called the Harmony Kings. That meant performing in the revue *Shuffle Along* — the first musical entirely written and performed by African Americans. Langston Hughes (who loved jazz and blues without reservation) declared *Shuffle Along* 'a honey of a show', while poet and critic Arna Bontemps described it as 'an overture to an era of hope', since it proved that black theatre could be financially viable. For Paul, though, it was just a gig. *Shuffle Along* still featured the tropes of racist vaudeville — comedians in blackface, 'Mammy' songs, and the rest of it. It scarcely felt like something of which he might be proud.

In 1925, the musician Lawrence Brown saw Paul at the corner of 135th Street and 7th Avenue. By then, Paul was already so popular in Harlem, first as a sports hero and then as an actor, that passers-by were stopping to shake his hand. But Brown knew Paul a little, and had earlier sent him an arrangement of traditional slave songs. He pushed through the throng. What had Paul made of the music, he asked.

Paul was on his way to a function for Jimmy Light, the Provincetown Players' director. He invited Brown to join him. They could try out the songs there, he said.

At the party, Paul sang 'Swing Low, Sweet Chariot' and 'Every Time I Feel the Spirit', with Brown providing a second voice. Applauding loudly, Light said, 'Why don't you fellows give a concert?'

More than twenty years earlier, W.E.B. Du Bois had praised 'the sorrow songs' of slavery as 'the singular spiritual heritage of the nation and the greatest gift of the Negro people'. But his was very much a minority opinion. For many educated African Americans, the spirituals were worse even than jazz: a crude music evoking stereotypes that Harlem's strivers wanted to dispel.

In his 1867 *Slave Songs of the United States*, the white scholar William Francis Allen described the unwillingness of freed black slaves to sing their old songs, even when asked directly. The people were, he said, too conscious of 'the dignity that has come with freedom'. The sorrow songs voiced the anguish of slavery; they were, in that way, the expression of a history from which free men were trying to awaken.

For this reason, news of the promised Robeson and Brown performance spread quickly throughout Harlem. Both men were sons of slaves; both were educated and successful. They'd won acclaim for mastering European culture, and yet they were advertising music composed on the plantation: the songs of the desperate, nameless inhabitants of America's slave camps.

Again, Essie sensed an opportunity. Others might have seen the event as a mere novelty, but she threw herself into making it a success, hustling their friends and acquaintances to make sure they attended. On the night of the first performance, the theatre was overflowing. Essie noted happily that 'the audience was very high class', a gathering of the fashionable and well heeled — white as well as black.

Symptomatically, Paul and Larry both wore tuxedos. Yet even before they sang a note, they were dripping with sweat. Someone later said that they'd never seen Paul so terrified. Nevertheless, he walked on stage beside the piano, nodded to Larry, and began.

There had been earlier popularisations of slave songs. But mostly the artists had presented the spirituals formally, almost as European art songs. This was different. Paul couldn't play an instrument, had never studied music. In his performance, he reached back to his experiences from church, his memories of the songs and singers of his father's congregation. His height, his physique, and his rich, deep voice contrasted with the peculiar tenderness of the lyrics.

'*Sometimes I feel like a motherless child,*' he sang, '*a long ways from home.*'

Larry's tenor perfectly complemented Paul's baritone. A talented composer, he'd won a scholarship to the New England Conservatory of Music and studied at Trinity College in London, and his sensitive arrangements drew out the intricacies and beauty of the melodies.

'*Sometimes I feel like I'm almost gone, a long ways from home.*'

The anguish in the lyrics expressed the Christian's separation from God and the heavenly land for which the sinner yearned. But that wasn't the only sorrow. After generations on the plantation, many slaves could barely imagine their homeland, but they'd been transported away from freedom, and they mourned everything that had been stolen. They sang, too, of the separations on which slavery depended, the casual removal of children from parents and the breaking apart of families.

The tears on Paul's cheeks might have come from his empathy with William, forced to leave Sabra enslaved in North Carolina, or from memories of Maria, burned in that little Princeton shack. If the audience cried with him, it was likely because the melodies reminded them of their own childhoods, the homes they'd left behind on the exodus to New York, the familiar places to which they'd never return.

The two singers were summoned back again and again for ovations. Reviewers were equally ecstatic. '[A]ll those who listened last night to the first concert in this country made entirely of Negro music,' said the critic for the *World*, '… may have been present at a turning point, one of those thin points of time in which a star in born and not yet visible — the first appearance of this folk wealth to be made without deference or apology.'

Brown's arrangements were both sympathetic and sophisticated, an intelligent treatment that took the music seriously. Though Paul sang with the enunciation of an educated man (thus rendering the performance palatable to concert-goers who might have been discomforted by the ecstatic hollering of black evangelism), the songs were still unmistakeably an expression of a distinctively African-American culture.

'The American Negro must remake his past,' Arturo Schomburg had declared, 'in order to make his future.' Paul Robeson and Lawrence Brown had done precisely that.

The spirituals — especially in Paul's emotional, untutored rendition — perfectly suited the white fad for 'Negritude'. They were an obvious product of a distinctly black experience that appealed to a white audience, too. As *The New York Times* declared, the songs 'hold in them a world of religious experience; it is this cry from the depths, this universal humanism, that touches the heart'.

Yet if the themes were universal, they were also particular, since the religiosity of the oppressed was very different from that of the oppressor. In 1831, a slave called Nat (better known as 'Nat Turner', after his owner) inspired his fellows to rise up in Southampton County, Virginia. Nat had understood that rebellion through scripture: '[T]he time was fast approaching,' he told his captors before they hanged him, 'when the first should be last and the last should be first.'

In that first Harlem concert, Paul performed a song called 'Go Down, Moses':

When Israel was in Egypt's land;
Let my people go,
Oppress'd so hard they could not stand,
Let my people go.

Ostensibly, the words presented a pious reiteration of Scripture. But, as its anonymous composer had surely known when he or she had hummed the tune in the fields, the lyrics could, with a certain emphasis, convey the spirit of Nat Turner, taking up arms against the pharaohs of America.

The spirituals were like that: simultaneously meek and militant, nostalgic but contemporary — and that complexity, those contradictions, made them an ideal expression of the Harlem of the 1920s, with all its competing imperatives. That's why, as another reviewer said, with this concert Paul became 'the embodiment of the aspirations of the New Negro'.

Very quickly, Paul secured an agent — and, unprecedentedly for a black singer, his agent was a white man. He booked more concerts; he signed a record contract, and ascended into a stardom that would remain unchallenged for almost twenty-five years.

Paul was becoming 'Paul Robeson'. He'd found the forms in which he could express his obvious talents and thus was more himself than he'd ever been. But people were beginning to recognise that he was also something else, even if they still weren't quite sure what. Even in the mid-1920s, he'd become more than a mere entertainer. The same argument that had been made about Harlem was increasingly heard about Paul: he represented black America not just as it was, but as it might be.

In 1939, at the absolute pinnacle of his career, Paul Robeson returned from Europe and took an apartment at 555 Edgecombe Avenue, in Harlem's Sugar Hill area. When I visited there, the place was still glorious — its lobby all marble and stained glass, with stunning art deco flourishes. The 'Triple Nickel', as it was known, had been segregated in its early years, but then went on to house a galaxy of black stars: Joe Louis, Count Basie, Coleman Hawkins, Thurgood Marshall, Duke Ellington, and others.

By then, though, the utopian elements of the Renaissance had faded.

'Harlem is a ruin,' wrote Ralph Ellison in 1945. '[M]any of its ordinary aspects (its crimes, its casual violence, its crumbling buildings with littered areaways, ill-smelling halls, and vermin-invaded rooms) are indistinguishable from the distorted images that appear in dreams and, like muggers haunting a lonely hall, quiver in the waking mind with hidden and threatening significance.'

Ellison shared Alaine Locke's conception of Harlem as an emblem, but on an entirely different basis. It was less a beacon, he argued, than a warning. 'Overcrowded and exploited politically and economically,' he wrote, 'Harlem is the scene and symbol of the Negro's perpetual alienation in the land of his birth.'

I was thinking about that quotation when I phoned Jazz Hayden.

He'd been expecting me. Yes, he said, Lichi had spoken to him, saying I might be in touch. 'I tell you what I'll do.' He spoke very slowly, so much so that I thought for a minute the line had dropped out. 'I've gotta go into Harlem this afternoon. There will be lots of people there you can talk about history with. Where you at?'

That evening, he picked me up on the corner of 97th and Lexington.

'Good to see you, man,' he said, as I climbed into the car. We shook hands. Jazz Hayden was small and dapper, with a neat grey beard. He was wearing an old-fashioned cap, and faint tattoos were visible on his muscular arms. D'Amelio had said he was in remarkably good shape, but I was still surprised by his vitality: he looked three decades younger than I'd expected.

'What's the event?' I asked.

'It's a service.'

'You mean, like a funeral?'

'Yes.' Another long pause. 'For Dr Ben.'

Yosef Ben-Jochannan was one of America's leading Afrocentric scholars, and the author of many books arguing for an African origin of Western philosophies and ideas. Dr Ben had been a follower of Marcus Garvey and an associate of Malcolm X; he'd spoken on stages with Amiri Baraka, Al Sharpton, James Brown, and Louis Farrakhan. An activist-scholar, some called him, a man hugely influential to a generation of African-American thinkers.

'Major figure,' said Hayden. 'Robeson-like.'

I was still absorbing the idea of the funeral. Surely I couldn't start interviewing at a wake, could I? 'Will people mind if I'm there?'

'Mind? Nah, man! They ain't gonna mind.'

I was not entirely assuaged — funerals made me uncomfortable at the best of times — but there was nothing to be done. We were in Harlem already, and he was circling to find a park. Every so often, a pedestrian would spot him and wave, and he'd wave back or call out the window. It seemed as if he knew an admirably large proportion of the neighbourhood.

We ended up walking a block or two to the imposing Abyssinian Baptist Church. Established in 1805, it was one of the oldest black churches in the United States. Adam Clayton Powell Sr had been pastor there for twenty-nine years, from 1908 until 1936, and the church had been the base for his social and political projects. Paul had spoken and sung at the Abyssinian Baptist many times.

It was now early evening. I'd forgotten my glasses, and without them I could barely recognise anything in the dim light. I heard the queue before I saw it, for several of the men in the long line that began at the church and extended down 138th Street were beating congo drums. Almost everyone there was African American and, again, Hayden seemed to know just about all of them.

'What's happening, brother?' he said to a man in a kufi cap and African robes. Dr Ben had donated his personal library — a huge collection of manuscripts and ancient scrolls — to the Nation of Islam, and the besuited members of that organisation were in attendance in large numbers.

The previous Sunday, I'd attended the service at Mother Zion, where the church had been full almost to overflowing. But the majority of the attendees were white tourists, travellers ticking off an authentic service as part of their Harlem experience. Elderly African Americans worshipped, almost defensively, in the front rows, their old-fashioned Sunday outfits a striking contrast with the jeans and t-shirts of the interlopers.

This felt quite different. It reminded me of how, in the 1920s, Paul and Essie had come into contact with a coterie dedicated to African-American culture and achievement, in a way that never would have been possible had Paul remained in Princeton. Despite Harlem's significance, it was small enough that like-minded people still found one another. Paul and Essie attended the soirees hosted by Carl Van Vechten, the white patron of the Renaissance. They became friends with Walter White, the NAACP activist and writer, and the lawyer William L. Patterson, who'd married one of Essie's best friends and who would go on to become a senior communist leader. In particular, Paul came to know W.E.B. Du Bois, with whom he'd draw particularly close in the years to come.

'What's going on?' said Jazz.

'Some hold-up in the front.'

Jazz darted off to investigate and, not knowing what to do, I tagged along with him.

A young guy had been stopped at the entrance, where he was arguing with a large doorman wearing a bowtie. The doorman said politely but firmly, 'I am sorry, brother. That's the policy.'

'What's the problem?' That was Jazz.

'The church doesn't allow backpacks.'

'The brother just wants to pay his respects.'

After talking to Lichi, I'd read something of Jazz's story. I knew, for instance, that he was still politically active, videotaping police incursions in Harlem and posting the clips on his website, a project that was part-way between the Black Panthers' notion of 'patrolling the pigs' and the citizen journalism of the social-media age. He was, quite evidently, fearless.

'Brother, you can't be like that.'

'I am sorry,' said the doorman. 'But it's the policy.'

Fortunately, the dispute fizzled out as quickly as it began, when someone else in the queue agreed to hold the man's backpack.

The line was moving again and, before I knew it, it was our turn. The bouncer gave an expressionless nod, like bouncers always do, and we were inside.

The church's interior was constructed on a circular design, so that all the worshippers could view the altar. But we were stuck in the foyer — the press of the crowd meant that the queue in which we'd been waiting outside more or less continued inside.

'What happens now?' I whispered to Jazz.

'The viewing.'

The viewing? As in, the viewing of a dead body?

I'd never been to a wake in the United States — I'd hardly been to wakes at all — but I'd read, long ago, *The American Way of Death*, Jessica Mitford's exposé of the funeral industry, and I vaguely remembered the importance of embalming, in a culture where friends and relatives paid their respects to a cadaver on display. Dear god, was that what we were going to do?

Should I tell Jazz I'd wait outside? Presumably, many of those here had known Dr Ben. I didn't want to intrude on their grief, especially not with the man's corpse visible through an open casket.

Again, voices were raised in the queue up ahead; again, Jazz went forward to investigate.

This time I stayed put. I couldn't follow what was happening, but I gathered another dispute was taking place, more intractable than the last. When Jazz came back, he clearly was not pleased. 'It ain't right.'

'What's happened?'

'They already closed the casket.' He was annoyed, not only on his own behalf but because no one had told those queuing patiently outside. 'It ain't right. If they came to view the deceased, they came for nothing. Let's go. Ain't no point being here.'

As we walked back out, into what was now darkness, he spoke to the mourners he knew. 'You're wasting your time. It's already closed.'

We went in the direction of the car, Jazz still annoyed and me trying to hide my relief. He suggested that we instead find something to eat before we leave.

Noisy teenagers dominated the McDonald's on Adam Clayton Powell Jr Boulevard. We ordered burgers and found a booth. Above the hubbub, he told me about the Harlem in which he'd grown up. 'There was always politics. Revolutionary thought. You could see Malcolm X standing on the corner of 25th Street; Garveyites, Nation of Islam, Black

Panthers, everybody. The city was totally politicised. It was a vibrant community. It was all here. Pan Africanism, anti-Apartheid, everything. Before 1964 and 1965, there was Jim Crow everywhere in America. But it wasn't too bad in Harlem because here it was pretty much a homogenous community. It was only when you went out of Harlem that you'd come into contact with overt racism and segregation. It was only then that you came into contact with that reality.'

He took another bite of his burger and chewed slowly. After he'd swallowed, he said, 'But after the passage of the Civil Rights Act and the Voting Rights Act, the black and white middle class left Harlem. The only people left behind were the people who couldn't get out. Half of these buildings were empty, abandoned. You could buy real estate in Harlem for next to nothing.

'The middle class left, the whole economy of the Harlem community fled to the suburbs. We had high unemployment, lack of opportunity, and all that was left was the underground economy. Drugs. Gambling. Shoplifting. People had to survive, and they used whatever was available. This was the late Sixties, early Seventies. In response to the political activity of the Sixties — civil rights, anti-war movement, black power movement, and so on — politicians initiated the war on drugs, the war on crime, which was just a euphemism for a war on poor people and on people of colour.'

In the 1960s, as the old Jim Crow structures became increasingly indefensible, politicians shifted from arguing against civil rights on openly racist lines to defending law-and-order on a supposed colourblind basis. Hence the attacks on Martin Luther King: if initially conservatives attacked King as a race-mixer, later they accused him of fostering criminality by encouraging civil disobedience. Oh, of course segregation was a problem, they said. Still, they couldn't support the civil-rights campaign because it was eroding respect for the law.

After King's murder in 1968, riots broke out across America — and President Johnson responded with the Omnibus Crime and Safe Streets Act.

That bill created the Law Enforcement Assistance Administration, which, over the next decade, enabled the militarisation of American police. As a result, local police forces now possessed machine guns and drones and armoured vehicles and equipment you'd otherwise expect of an occupying army. Those massive arsenals on display during Black Lives Matter protests could be traced back to white fears of black riots in the late 1960s.

Later, Richard Nixon perfected what has come to be known as the Southern Strategy: the plan by which the Republicans, traditionally the party of the North, picked up votes in a South once solidly Democrat. Race was central to the scheme — but the new appeal to racial resentment was subtler than the old. As one Nixon adviser explained, the white politicians of the 1950s could openly promise their constituents that they'd keep the black population down, but by the end of the Sixties, that sort of language was no longer possible. Instead, Republicans spoke in code. When, for instance, Nixon spoke up for 'state's rights', he knew white voters understood him as pledging to defend the traditional bigotry of the South. When he promised to get tough on crime, they heard a promise to crack down on inner-city blacks.

Reagan used the same rhetoric in 1982, and for similar reasons. He also launched a war on drugs. At that time, less than two per cent of the American public identified drugs as the most important issue facing the nation. But right from the start, the war on drugs was presented as a war on urban — that is, African-American — drug-taking. The emergence of crack cocaine turbocharged the anti-drug rhetoric, which was reinforced by extraordinarily punitive legislation. The number of Americans behind bars skyrocketed.

'The prison population in this country was 300,000,' said Jazz. 'Today it's something like three million — and it all started back then. The money they were supposed to use for affordable housing, they built prisons.' He chuckled. 'That was their affordable housing.'

After Reagan, the Democrats embraced and extended the war on drugs. During the Clinton administration, for instance, Washington slashed funding for public housing by $17 billion while giving an extra $19 billion to the prison system. Not surprisingly, the criminal justice system became a central part of African-American life.

Jazz had been arrested in 1967, aged sixteen, for possession of heroin, the first in a series of run-ins with police that brought him to the notorious Attica state facility in 1970. Attica was hugely overcrowded, and the vast bulk of its inmates were African American. But in the politicised climate of the time, the prisoners were also running study groups and debating history and politics and theory.

Jazz became a leader in a prison on the cusp of an explosion. In August 1971, he was transferred to a different facility (where his conviction would be overturned). Two weeks after he left, on 9 September, the inmates in Attica seized hostages and demanded to negotiate.

We are men! read their manifesto. *We are not beasts and do not intend to be beaten or driven as such.*

On 13 September, the authorities abandoned negotiations, and used tear gas and state troopers to take Attica back. Hours of gunfire left thirty-nine people dead, including ten hostages — and many of Jazz's friends.

In the aftermath, guards revenged themselves on the prisoners, beating the wounded survivors and forcing them to crawl naked on broken glass. The official story held that the hostages had been killed by the inmates. In reality, they'd been shot dead by guards.

'I watched the whole place go up on television,' said Jazz. He shook his head. 'Today we have 2.3 million human beings in cages. Another five million on leashes. We're five per cent of the world's population, and we've got twenty-five per cent of the world's prisons.'

Attica, he said, was a premonition, a forerunner of what was to come. The contemporary statistics about criminality in the United States were extraordinary. In her book *The New Jim Crow: mass incarceration in the age of colorblindness*, Michelle Alexander notes that, in Chicago, the total population of black males with a felony record is the equivalent to eighty per cent of the adult black male workforce. In Ferguson, a 2015 Justice Department investigation in the wake of Michael Brown's death showed that police maintained outstanding arrest warrants for 16,000 people in a town with a population of 21,000. Quite literally, the police regarded the majority of individuals in a predominately black city as wanted criminals.

Across America, ex-felons were forbidden by law from seeking employment in a huge array of fields. Even where they could apply for jobs, bosses were entirely within their rights to turn away those with criminal records — and very often did. A felony conviction meant, in many places, that you couldn't vote, couldn't apply for public housing or welfare, and couldn't access free education. A huge number of African Americans had felony convictions; a huge number of the African-American population were thus excluded — quite legally — from public life.

'You have surplus population, surplus labour,' said Jazz. 'You gotta control it. That's social dynamite! It might blow up any time if people get together. So you have to maintain control over that population, and so you take one half of that population and put them in control of the other half of that same population. In the prison system, the poor rural whites are the keepers; the poor urban blacks and Latinos are the kept. The economy went from industrial to service, and capital fled the country in pursuit of cheap labour, and consequently there's nothing but poverty here. People are working for minimum wage and they can barely survive. American labour can't compete with Chinese labour, can't compete with Indian labour. What do you have? Social control and mass incarceration!'

The downward pressure on wages in places such as Harlem was accompanied by an upward pressure on rent. So where were the original inhabitants going, I wanted to know.

His look implied the answer was obvious. 'Homeless shelters.'

He put down the burger. 'The kids who go to college, they don't want to go back to the suburbs, they want this urban life. So they're coming here. And the black kids from poor backgrounds go to prison.'

Alexander argued that drugs were used by people of all ethnic and racial backgrounds at a very similar rate. Some surveys showed white professionals as the group most likely to take illegal drugs. But white professionals remained the least likely to be arrested. It was people of colour who were policed, the statistics showed, and it was people of colour put behind bars.

'Go to prison,' Jazz repeated. 'Meanwhile, wealth accumulates at the top; poverty and lack of opportunity accumulate at the bottom. Middle class is sinking down to the working class. So the prisons are a joint job program, like I tell you: for white rural communities and black urban communities. Put them together, make one the supervisor and one the prisoner. It's a job program. That's what these things are. The military is the same. In America, we see everything in terms of race, a whole narrative constructed to divide us.'

As Jazz picked up his burger again and we fell into silence, I thought of my brief visit to the South Carolina State House in Columbia. The extensive public garden, with its crisp lawns and carefully tended trees, could not have been more of a contrast with the surrounding grey concrete, so much so that the building and grounds felt like a compensatory fantasy: a colourful façade of heritage distracting from the neglected streets of the modern city. Near the main entrance stood a statue of Ben Tillman, the senator who'd defended the lynching of Lake City postmaster Frazier Baker and who'd claimed that Booker T. Washington's dinner with President Roosevelt would necessitate a thousand killings. Tillman was personally implicated in a lynching during the Hamburg Massacre of 1876. But in Columbia, a plaque lauded him as *loving and loyal, to the state steadfast and true for the nation.*

Elsewhere, I found a monument to J. Marion Sims, the pioneer gynaecologist who perfected his techniques on enslaved women he purchased specifically for research. A statue lauded Wade Hampton; a bronze sculpture honoured Senator Strom Thurmond, a notorious segregationist whose tribute had originally listed his four children from his marriage to wife Nancy before being amended in 2004 to include Essie Mae Washington-Williams: the daughter he'd fathered with his African-American household servant when she was just sixteen.

And, of course, I'd been confronted by the giant monument to the dead of the Confederacy. *Let their virtues plead*, read its text, *for just judgement of the cause in which they perished ...*

Just judgement on the Confederacy? On men who'd defended the right to sell African-American children at auction?

'Divide and conquer!' said Jazz, nodding his head. 'The poor whites get told: you're better than them. Meanwhile, the poor whites are living in shacks.'

I thought back to Princeton and those little rooms in Witherspoon Street, built during the days of Jim Crow. The new Jim Crow looked very different to the old Jim Crow that Paul had faced, even as it produced the same outcome: systematically perpetuating the marginalisation of the African-American population. But the mechanisms today were colourblind. The large number of young men who couldn't vote and couldn't run for public office weren't targeted because of their skin colour but because they were criminals — even if there were structural reasons for the overwhelming imposition of that criminality on black youth.

Alexander's book was, then, partly a polemic about affirmative action. Under the old Jim Crow, she said, the rise of individual African Americans to positions of power helped undercut the whole system, since it rested on the claim that black people were innately inferior. Today, the success of black individuals merely reinforced the logic of the new Jim Crow, which insisted that those with criminal records had chosen their own fate. For her, the elevation of a small number of African Americans did nothing to change the dire situation facing the rest of the black population, incarcerated in their millions.

To put it another way, even if the Harlem of Paul's youth could be rebuilt, it wouldn't alter anything. The solution, Jazz said, lay in radical political change. 'These young people, they have the passion, but a lot of them just want to vent. But politics is work, man. Strategy, vision, goals, tactics. That's what it takes. That's what we need. Look at the Tea Party in this country! They started out a bunch of raggedy-ass white boys.' Another chuckle. 'Next thing you know they shut the Congress down. That's the blueprint, but from the Left. Gotta take control of communities. Every struggle is about power — who has it and who doesn't. If the people woke up and organised themselves, we could take this country back.'

After our dinner, I caught the train back to the apartment where I was staying. All the way from the train station, I was thinking about another Langston Hughes poem — this time from 1938, when Hughes, like Paul, had been very close to the Communist Party. Called 'Kids Who Die', it had been rediscovered and circulated by campaigners for Black Lives Matter.

In it, Hughes addressed the murdered black youth of his day. 'Maybe, now, there will be no monument for you,' he wrote to the children killed by lynchers and other racists, 'except in our hearts.' But he pledged that, one day, a 'living monument' of love and joy and laughter would be raised: 'The song of the life triumphant, through the kids who die.'

That, I thought, was Jazz's message too. Harlem had changed utterly. Harlem was just the same.

PART TWO
EXODUS

4

AN ENGLISH GENTLEMAN
London, England

'I shall never forget arriving in Southampton,' Paul said, later in life. 'I thought I had never seen any land so beautiful — green and companionable. I longed to fling myself down on my face, and hug the cool earth.'

When I came to London, I thought I understood something of Paul's feeling: his wonder at English groves and meadows, and the history speaking to him from every alley and corner. If you'd been raised in a former colony, you absorbed a secret conviction that Britain contained the true, platonic form of your native landscape. An English tree was the real tree: the one you'd read about in books, the concept from which the prosaic shrubs of your childhood were distantly derived.

In central London, everywhere I walked looked realer than real — and then, because of that, strangely fake.

I was staying in an Airbnb in Newham, a little room in a crowded apartment, with the accents of the Caribbean and the subcontinent filtering through the walls all the night. The morning was damp, so I walked down streets that were greasy and cold and littered with fast-food cartons, next to buildings the sweaty grey colour of a man enduring a long illness. On the train, everyone seemed harried and overworked.

It was just like home.

Inner London, though, seemed fundamentally different, not least because of the dominance of the major tourist sites, which confronted the visitor like exhibits in a museum of Englishness. The Palace of Westminster sat by the river like a huge chocolate box, and while I squinted at Big Ben I realised I wasn't so much looking at it as comparing the tower with the much more vivid image already imprinted in my mind.

None of it felt real. Paul's education at Rutgers — and, more importantly, the authority of his father — predisposed him to an appreciation of English culture and sensibility. Later, he'd think very differently. But after he briefly toured in 1922 with an unsuccessful production of *Taboo*, he couldn't wait to return.

In 1925, following the breakthrough in New York, the Robesons went to London for an English season of *Emperor Jones*. Immediately, Essie searched out an apartment. She wanted, she said, to 'find a nice cozy place to put my Baby in so he could be free to do his best work'. That resulted, eventually, in a furnished flat in Chelsea's Glebe Place: two storeys of a three-storey building, complete with plush, tasteful carpets, a little garden out the back, and the services of a maid.

When I set off for King's Road in Chelsea, I'd been imagining Mary Quant and the swinging London of the Sixties, and then Vivienne Westwood and punk rock a decade later. But those fantasies quickly evaporated in the actual mannered and manicured streetscape. Chelsea was not punk. Chelsea was almost twee. With the iconic double-decker buses wheezing past me, I felt as if I were tiptoeing through a giant doll's house, stocked with fussy little shops and red London postboxes and other chintzy collectibles.

The Robesons' apartment stood in a long row of yellow-brick terraces with white trimming, fenced off from the street by no-nonsense iron railings. The current resident was watering her pot plants, and looked up inquiringly when I paused outside.

'I think Paul Robeson used to live here,' I ventured.

She put down the can, slightly friendlier. 'Really? Are you sure?'

'Yes, pretty much.'

'Well, how about that? You know, there's a plaque over there' — and she waved to the other side of the road — 'saying that Turner lived here. But I don't actually think that's true.'

For much of its history, Chelsea had been known as an artistic quarter, a precinct of writers and painters. The Chelsea Arts Club was located five minutes away, in Old Church Street. Arthur Ransome set his 1907 book *Bohemia in London* here: in it, he called Chelsea a 'bivouacking ground for art and literature', and Glebe Street 'full of studios'.

Had one of the studios belonged to Romantic artist J.M.W. Turner? I didn't know — but it was evident that no struggling painters lived in the neighbourhood now.

For Essie, the location was ideal: central but eminently fashionable, particularly in the slightly raffish circles in which the Robesons mixed. Lady Sibyl Colefax, one of the great literary hostesses of the day, lived almost on the corner of their street. The brothers Osbert and Sacheverell Sitwell, who, with their sister Edith, presided over another chic salon, were equally close, as were T.S. Eliot (Carlyle Mansions); Bertrand Russell (Sydney Street); A.A. Milne (Mallord Street), and David Lloyd George (Cheyne Walk).

The Emperor Jones puzzled London theatre-goers more than delighted them, possibly because O'Neill's preoccupations were so deeply American. But, even if they were lukewarm about the play, audiences and critics loved Paul. *The Daily Mail*'s review was typically enthusiastic, with a headline that read simply: 'Giant Negro Actor'. The exposure and the acclaim opened other possibilities, both professional (Paul sang on the newly launched British Broadcasting Corporation) and social (dinner parties, theatre invitations, even opportunities to watch Test cricket). Then, when the show closed in November 1925, the Robesons embarked on a long tour of the continent.

Back home in America, this pattern of Paul's career continued to repeat: even when shows fell flat, somehow he still emerged triumphant. His next play, *Black Boy*, deliberately exploited his athletic physique, in a drama loosely based on the tragedy of boxer Jack Johnson. Critics hated it — but they raved about Paul's performance. The recordings he made with Larry Brown sold well, and the new medium of radio took the songs to mass audiences, in a way that a previous generation of performers could never have imagined.

Still, despite Paul's success in his native land, the Robesons could not help but contrast the difference between an America where, during performances in Boston and Green Bay, Paul could be casually refused accommodation, and a Britain in which Essie could walk into the posh Ivy restaurant near the Ambassadors Theatre and overhear the fashionable assembly of ladies and gentlemen enthusing over her husband's talents.

It was not a coincidence that Paul's next breakthrough took place in London, when he played Joe in *Show Boat* in the Drury Lane theatre in 1928. Hammerstein and Kern had written the part with Paul in mind, but — against Essie's advice — he'd rejected the original Broadway production. It was the same old problem. The song 'Ol' Man River' opened with the line '*Niggers all work on de Mississippi*'. How could Paul sing that? He was not yet a militant by any stretch, but he had been schooled in the politics of representation well before he arrived in Harlem. Besides, the reaction to *All God's Chillun Got Wings* still stung. If, after all his successes, he clambered on stage and smilingly legitimised racial slurs, what message was he sending, both to white theatregoers and to all the African Americans locked out of the culture he was conquering?

Yet the Broadway *Show Boat* proved a monster hit — and that success changed Paul's mind. Essie's pragmatism seemed to have been vindicated. If you didn't compromise, you mightn't disappoint your audience — but, then again, you probably wouldn't have one. Perhaps it was better to bend, to compromise on some points to win on others. If Paul kept refusing the O'Neill plays, his theatrical career would falter before it began. Here was another opportunity to scramble one more rung, to ascend to a level at which he might, eventually, be able to pick and choose.

Paul did not speak in *Show Boat*. In fact, he featured on stage only for one brief scene in what was a very long musical. Yet, after the Drury Lane show in April 1928, Paul Robeson was all theatregoers talked about. 'People went out of their minds about him,' said the actor Bernard Sarron.

Some spoke about how, when Paul began 'Ol' Man River', his voice reverberating through the theatre like a church organ, they were transported beyond the silly narrative to an almost visceral experience of oppression and pain. While he sang, Paul used his huge frame, bent and twisted as he staggered beneath a bale, to convey the agony of black history while revealing the tremendous strength forged by centuries of resistance. 'A sorrow that seemed to know no end,' said the writer (and, later, Paul's friend) Marie Seton of that performance.

Paul was elated and overwhelmed by the audience response. He'd managed to have the racial slur changed to the marginally less offensive 'darkies', but he still worried about his decision. Yet he seemed to have successfully transmuted a commercial script written by white men into something authentic and true.

Soon, Lawrence Brown joined the Robesons in Britain, and he and Paul quickly scheduled some concerts to coincide with *Show Boat*. It was a clever move, since their presentation of the genuine sorrow songs shaped the reception of *Show Boat*, inducing audiences to see beyond the thinly sketched character of Joe to the real history from which it was derived.

Again, the response was almost ecstatic. 'They stomped, cheered and applauded all through the program,' Essie reported, with palpable and justified satisfaction.

In May 1928, the Robesons moved into a house in Carlton Hill, a place today only ten minutes walk from the famous Abbey Road recording studios. When I came out of the train station, I lost my bearings, and found myself, quite by accident, walking over the crossing where the iconic Beatles album cover was shot.

Essie, who located the Carlton Hill property, described it, with obvious pride, as 'charming, well-built English brick … furnished in rich, simple, comfortable taste'.

It was still pretty much that when I saw it.

This had long been one of London's most expensive postcodes, a place that wore its affluence with the confidence of well-established privilege. The Robeson house was five minutes from Lord's Cricket Ground, and not so far from the old St John's Wood Barracks, the traditional home of royalty's ceremonial troops. Daimlers and Mercedes lined the curb of a wide and quiet street, and a wall shielded the three-storey dun structure from rubberneckers like me.

The building's faux battlements were a fitting adornment for the place Essie had chosen as a base for their conquest of Europe. The Robesons had decided to stay in London, convinced that the British appreciated Paul in a way that race-conscious Americans didn't. He was bringing in remarkable amounts of money, both through *Show Boat* and his own concerts, with the proximity of the continent opening up additional markets. Accordingly, they needed, Essie had decreed, to live somewhere close to the theatres where Paul performed, and with central heating to ward off the colds to which he was susceptible. The Carlton Hill property came courtesy of an elderly countess who'd seen Paul in *Show Boat* and, like almost everyone, had been tremendously impressed. 'When we all returned to the garden for tea,' Essie recalled, '[the countess] said she had decided to let the house as it stood: silver, linen and servants — cook, maid and gardener.'

The inclusion of the staff in the rental agreement illustrated what the transfer meant: the Robesons' embrace of English respectability, just as respectable England seemed to be embracing them.

After his Drury Lane success, Paul was soon singing for the Prince of Wales, while Essie's outings featured in the society pages alongside the doings of London's socialites. Wealthy hostesses invited the glamour pair to parties; restaurateurs escorted them to the best tables.

If America was a nation divided on racial lines, in London, class trumped race — or, more exactly, race manifested through class. Many of the notables to whom Paul and Essie were now being introduced had previously imagined all people of colour to be illiterate and impoverished. The Robesons, however, were neither, and their evident education and rapidly mounting wealth made them presentable to the most elevated company.

These were the years in which Paul chatted with a future king (the Duke of York) and a future prime minister (Ramsay MacDonald). He hosted soirees with the film star Fred Astaire and the press baron Lord Beaverbrook; he conversed with James Joyce and George Bernard Shaw.

Standing next to all those luxury cars, I could understand the importance of the house, and the staff who came with it, to Essie and Paul. In London, Paul Robeson, a man who couldn't rent a room in many American cities, was living as an English gentleman.

But there were other reasons for Essie's particularity about their accommodation. In November 1927, she'd given birth to Paul Robeson Jr (later known as Pauli), their first and only child, and she was adamant that they would raise the boy in a respectable neighbourhood and in a property large enough for him to play.

But they didn't stay long in the rented residence.

I walked for nearly an hour from St John's Wood to reach Hampstead, the place where, in 1929, the Robesons bought a mansion of their own. The purchase reflected Paul's continuing ascension, his financial and critical success. *Show Boat*'s long run closed in February that year, but Paul had been performing constantly, in London, in smaller British towns and cities, and on a hugely popular European tour.

The new house was in another quiet street, very close to the famous heath.

All the way there, I'd been thinking about how, during Marx's residency in London, he and Engels had tramped up and around Hampstead Heath, thrashing out problems of political economy and taking in 'more ozone than in the whole of Hanover'. But, of course, the Paul of 1929 was more interested in the area's connection with Englishness than its association with German revolutionaries. Hampstead Heath had long been a haunt of writers and thinkers. Alexander Pope walked the Heath; so, too, did Shelley, Wordsworth, Keats, and Coleridge. Dickens drank in Jack Straw's Castle, the nearby pub, and wrote the area into many of his novels. It was, in other words, a perfect location for an outsider enamoured of English respectability.

The former residence of the Robesons was massive: I counted four levels in weathered grey stone surrounded by old oak and chestnut trees. I could understand how Paul's New York friends described a visit to the Robeson mansion as an overwhelming experience. They'd known him as an impoverished striver in Harlem, and now his parties were among the grandest in London. The five household servants, one friend noted, were particularly intimidating. The all-white staff didn't look down on African-American visitors because of their colour. Instead, they silently assessed them as belonging to a class subordinate to the Robesons, whom they treated with the deference owed to honorary aristocrats.

Walter Abel, one of the Provincetown actors, observed Essie's almost embarrassing pride in the house and its wealth: her exultation in the purpose-built nursery for Paul Jr, the tastefully furnished study for his father, and the white servants carrying out drinks. 'She was like a schoolgirl, just thrilled with things she never had before. As soon as we got there, she ushered my wife upstairs to show off her new dresses, all the latest fashion. And yet, it struck me all poignantly as not ostentatious but as an overstriving for something they had longed for in America but been unable to achieve.'

Though Paul was not as attached as Essie to the external trappings of success, he'd always enjoyed comfort — and, perhaps even more than his wife, he reveled in the deference that London seemed to be offering. 'The delight of it almost scares me,' he'd said when asked to sing for the BBC in 1926, a sentiment that expressed his general response to the critical and popular reception. By now, applause was familiar. Respect, however, was not.

Yet he remained uncomfortably conscious that the local enthusiasm for *Show Boat* hadn't been shared by African-American observers. The European correspondent of the African-American paper *New York Amsterdam News* wrote, for instance, that the play represented a 'deliberate attempt on the part of the White American to carry his anti-Negro propaganda into Europe'. He'd heard, the writer explained, 'many harsh things said against Robeson for lending his talent and popularity toward making it a success'.

It was the same issue that had bedevilled Paul in Harlem: his reliance on racially dubious material written by others — material that, despite his best efforts, still insulted African-American people. But what choice did he have? The limited roles that playwrights offered to black actors left Paul with precious few opportunities to display any range. He was invariably cast as the same kind of character, and as a result even his admirers ascribed his success to instinct rather than intellect, as a demonstration not so much of theatrical mastery but of an innate African talent for make-believe, within certain narrow parameters.

That's why the invitation, in 1930, to play Othello in a London production mattered so very much.

Later in his career, with his admiration for respectable Britain reduced to ashes, Paul specifically praised Soho, London's traditionally free-spirited centre of entertainers and musicians and sex workers. 'In Soho,' he said, 'I feel completely at home.'

When I arrived there, I could see only traces of the notoriety that Paul had been referencing, with the area's old impoverishment replaced by the cashed-up cosmopolitanism — bookshops and cocktail bars — of any modern entertainment district.

The entrance to Soho House was a plain door wedged between

expensive restaurants. I pressed the buzzer and was ushered up to reception, where an intimidatingly fashionable woman asked me whether Hugh Quarshie was expecting me. He was. She rang to check and, a few minutes later, I joined him in the private restaurant upstairs.

I'd seen Quarshie in the film *Highlander* many years earlier, and as Captain Panaka in the first reboot of the Star Wars franchise, *The Phantom Menace*. But when I sat across from him, as the staff brought us coffee, I was still taken aback by his presence. It was partly the symmetry of his face and his sculpted cheekbones and all the other elements that contribute to the striking looks of a professional actor. It was also the intelligence with which he spoke about the Royal Shakespeare Company's recent production of *Othello*, an easy erudition that transformed his handsomeness into a trait better described as charisma. Naturally, I thought of Robeson and the invariable accounts I'd read from those who had met him, even briefly — of how they remembered the encounter years afterward, as if he'd spoken to something deep within them.

Though born in Ghana, Quarshie had graduated from Oxford, and the imprint of that elite education — not so dissimilar from Paul's — probably contributed to the echoes I felt. But, of course, his experiences had been fundamentally different.

'When I first played Othello,' he told me, 'it was thought necessary to black me up.'

That was in high school. He still sounded incredulous as he remembered. 'In the rehearsal, someone decided that I wasn't black enough. I'm brown and Othello was black. To my shame, I went along with it, thinking: *Well, these guys know what they're doing; this must be the convention.*'

The grotesque episode came to an end halfway through the dress rehearsal, when Quarshie's kiss smeared makeup on his Desdemona, leaving her looking vaguely diseased. But the incident illustrated the tremendous anxiety attached, even in comparatively recent times, to the precise shade of Othello's pigment.

For black actors of Paul's era, no other play mattered like Othello. In one of his very early interviews, after his success with *All God's Chillun Got Wings*, he acknowledged that the subject always arose when an African American revealed any theatrical talent. 'Of course, I think about *Othello*,' he'd said then.

Shakespeare had described his character as 'a noble Moor in the service of the Venetian state', and the words made the script's significance to African Americans plain enough. Othello was not European, and he was also explicitly noble. The play thus provided the rarest of roles within the classical canon: a valiant high-ranking figure of colour, an African neither to be pitied nor ridiculed. That was why, during Paul's football career, sports writers sometimes dubbed him 'Othello', with the name a commonly understood shorthand for any African-American hero.

When the husband-and-wife team of Maurice Browne and Ellen Van Volkenburg offered Paul the part (and a sizeable salary to go with it), he seized the chance.

But he realised that it wouldn't be easy. Where Quarshie had been thought too pale to play Othello, Paul knew that he was too black.

In Shakespeare's theatre, white actors in the role of Othello had darkened their faces, and the custom continued until the early nineteenth century. But then American actor Edmund Kean started employing paler makeup for the role, a shift that corresponded with the legitimisation of plantation slavery. After all, the mere existence of a Shakespearean play with a black protagonist implied, contrary to the ideology of the slave owners, that black individuals were human, and deserving of respect. White critics were scandalised by the suggestion that Desdemona could be betrothed to a man resembling a field slave: 'It would,' said Samuel Taylor Coleridge, 'be something monstrous to conceive this beautiful Venetian girl falling in love with a veritable Negro.'

In 1930, the consensus was that Othello must be represented as Arab rather than black. The announcement of the Browne/Van Volkenburg production of *Othello*, with Robeson in the lead role, thus prompted immediate outrage, with a letter-writer to *The Daily Mail* expressing shock 'to find the part of Othello taken by a Negro' instead of a light-skinned Arab of North African descent.

The argument — and the passion it once engendered — seemed ridiculous in the modern age, not least because the position had been entirely reversed. No one queried whether a black man could play the part — in fact, Othello had become a taboo role for white actors. 'After Ben Kingsley did Othello in 1985,' Quarshie said, 'it was difficult for white actors to black up, indeed, to even think about it. Michael Gambon might have been the last, I think.'

'When was that?'

'The late Eighties. So quite late.' He laughed. 'I heard a story, which may be apocryphal, that Gambon looked himself in the mirror one day in his dark makeup, and said, "Nah, can't do it!"'

The question as to Othello's skin colour obviously pertained to a broader argument about the play's meaning. Shakespeare's plot runs like this: Iago, angered by Cassio's promotion to Othello's lieutenant, seeks revenge on him and Othello. He drops a handkerchief belonging to Othello's wife, Desdemona, in Cassio's chamber to convince Othello of her infidelity. Othello duly strangles Desdemona — and then, realising he's been duped, takes his own life with a dagger.

Quarshie quoted George Bernard Shaw's famous assessment that when judged by the ear, Shakespeare's language made *Othello* sublime — but when judged by the brain, the play was ridiculous. 'The reason it is ridiculous is that you have to believe that this wise and experienced and magnanimous man is persuaded on the evidence of a handkerchief that his wife is unfaithful. Not only that, he's persuaded he must kill her, and, not only that, he must strangle her in her own bed, rather than simply divorce her and send her home to her father in disgrace. It's frankly preposterous, despite those grand oratorical flights of verse.'

That was why, despite its appeal to black actors, the role of Othello could also be a trap. In the Elizabethan theatre, a Moor remained, first and foremost, an exotic: a figure of unfathomable otherness. The character was, Quarshie said, akin to a Red Indian in a John Ford movie, whose appearance meant that sooner or later the wagons would be circled. Shakespeare showed relatively little interest in Othello's psychology. He was a Moor: that was all the audience needed to know.

'It seems to me what he's doing is stretching the elastic slightly, by writing Othello against the grain of the conventional Moor, giving him a few more lines, saying: "Ah, this guy isn't just a murderer." And then when he releases the elastic, it springs back very violently.'

During the American Civil War, John Quincy Adams had even read the play as demonstrating that 'black and white blood cannot be intermingled in marriage without a gross outrage upon the Law of Nature'. For Adams, Othello killed Desdemona … because that was what black men did.

Quarshie's own recent performance as Othello had been preceded by a long brainstorming session, in which the key personnel of the Royal Shakespeare Company tried to negotiate through the play's racial issues. In their production, Iago was played by another black actor, so as to remove the suggestion of Othello being conned by a cleverer white man and to render Othello's belief in the charges against Desdemona more credible. They'd also reassigned and transposed particular lines to add a sense of psychological coherence they felt lacking in the original.

But in 1930, Paul hadn't been able to do anything like that. He'd always assumed that, if he ever played Othello, the part would be offered (as he said in 1924) as a 'kind of culmination': that he'd be eased into the most challenging role of his career, with support from an experienced director and cast.

That wasn't what happened. Not only could he exercise no control over the Browne/Van Volkenburg production, but also he received very little guidance from the inept pair. Browne, playing Iago, struggled so much with his own acting that he could scarcely advise others, while Van Volkenburg made strange cuts to the text, and then padded the action out with irrelevant dances and music.

'She can't even get actors from one side of the stage to the other,' said Essie, watching the rehearsals. 'Poor Paul is lost.'

In desperation, Essie convinced Paul to practise privately with an experienced Shakespearian actor. As if that were not stressful enough, he was also struggling to master English intonations, aware that the audience would sneer at any American inflection, particularly from a black man. To outsiders, Paul's talent seemed effortless. But as *Othello* approached, he was fighting to contain his anxiety — to the point where he contemplated withdrawing from the production.

On opening night, 19 May 1930, the Savoy Theatre was full to overflowing. The controversy had made the event a must-see in high society. But alongside the usual array of theatrical and literary personages, the audience included a disproportionate number of black people, whose investment in the play extended beyond aesthetic appreciation. They understood the ramifications of a poor performance by Paul. They knew, just as he did, that his failure would be seized upon as proof of a generalised racial inadequacy, a demonstration that coloured actors couldn't rise to serious drama. Black individuals weren't sufficiently intelligent for Shakespeare, the bigots would say; they weren't sufficiently analytical; they weren't — in the final instance — sufficiently human.

The play began badly, since Van Volkenburg had insisted on lighting so dim as to almost completely obscure her actors. To make matters worse, she'd clothed Paul in a long robe and equipped him with an Arabic-style beard and moustache (a concession to the argument about Othello's race).

When Paul spoke his first words, his nervousness was palpable. The lines sounded flat and awkward, leaving his friends and supporters braced for an embarrassing disaster.

But then he settled … and his distinctive interpretation emerged.

Why did Othello kill Desdemona? For Paul, the Moor faced in Venice the same struggle as an African American — particularly a famous or important one — confronted in Jim Crow America. Othello was tolerated because he was necessary, but remained more or less openly despised. 'As Othello I walk into the Senate,' he said later, 'among all those people who in their hearts hate me, but fear me and know they must use me.'

But where Paul had been trained not to respond to taunts, Othello came from a civilisation that had conquered most of Europe. He was a general, a fierce warrior, and he didn't smile obligingly when belittled or insulted. The disdain directed at him made him more determined to defend his honour — and that was the basis for his disproportionate fury at Desdemona's supposed infractions.

In other words, Paul presented the murder as a consequence not of race but of racism.

Othello's final plea — 'speak of me as I am; nothing extenuate / Nor set down aught in malice' — became a call for racial equality, a demand that whites see African Americans as they were rather than through the lens of prejudice. By placing the Moor's stature at the centre of the play, Paul transformed *Othello* into an affirmation of black achievement, while hinting at the rage that racism might yet engender.

As part of his preparation, Paul had visited London Zoo to study the big cats: his Moor, he'd told Marie Seton, would stalk the stage like a panther. With his athleticism, his prowling presence, he exuded an aura of restrained power, which was suddenly released into violence. 'The blow on Desdemona's face cut the house like a whip,' said a reviewer. The oratorical techniques learned from William and honed in Rutgers gave Paul's lines an almost prophetical force, a grandeur befitting the Moor's martial dignity. Above all, Paul tapped into his own suppressed fury at the taunts and snubs in his own life. His Othello was dangerous: a man who would be pushed no further.

When the curtain fell, the applause came like thunder, and Paul was dragged out for repeated ovations and an astonishing twenty curtain calls. According to one account, he was almost sobbing with joy and relief. 'I took the part of Othello with much fear,' he said. 'Now I am so happy.'

The Browne/Van Volkenburg production ran for six weeks and

toured briefly around the country. Thereafter, Othello became central to Paul's public persona. He performed the play twice more during his lifetime, on Broadway in 1943 and then in Stratford-upon-Avon in 1959; he often incorporated Othello's last soliloquy into his concert performances.

But he couldn't fully overcome the ambivalences inherent in the role.

'The original text,' said Quarshie, 'both in the folio and the quarter, reads, "Her name, that was as fresh / As Dian's visage, is now begrimed and black / As mine own face.' *Mine own face?* When we were brainstorming, I thought, *Um, would someone like Kofi Anan have said that? How can a conscious black guy justify that?'*

In other words, the textual politics of Othello remained, despite Paul's best efforts, distinctly ambiguous. After watching Robeson's 1943 version, the always-astute Langston Hughes complained (via his character Jesse B. Semple) that 'every time white folks see Art ... it is about a coloured man choking a white woman to death'.

Nevertheless, Paul's London triumph was, by and large, received as the anti-racist statement he intended. Even the critics who dwelled on the inadequacy of the direction and the ineptitude of the supporting cast acknowledged his achievement. 'There has been no Othello on our stage, certainly for forty years,' said the *Morning Post* reviewer, 'to compare with [Robeson's] dignity, simplicity and true passion.'

The emphasis on 'dignity' was crucial. If Paul's performance of the spirituals helped the reception of *Show Boat*, by 1930 his public persona — the general perception of him as urbane, educated, and sophisticated — shaped the response to his Othello.

At the same time, Paul's success with Shakespeare earned him fresh recognition as an artist, rather than merely an entertainer. Before I left Quarshie, he stressed how significant Robeson's achievement had been, how he'd paved the way for black actors who followed. 'For a black American like Robeson, *Othello* carried a lot more baggage than it does for me, as a black African. He grew up in a slave society, and the possibility of a black American taking on a major role that had historically been played almost exclusively by white actors — that had real significance for him. Besides, Shakespeare in general and *Othello* in particular: they are jewels in the crown of British culture. It obviously mattered that he should be allowed to take on this role.'

My exploration of London was interrupted by a short journey to Leeds, where the Nigerian-British actor Tayo Aluko was staging his acclaimed one-man show *Call Mr Robeson* at the Seven Arts Centre in Chapel Allerton. Aluko so effectively captured the Robeson charisma that it was only when I sat with him the next day in a café near the University of Leeds that I realised how little he resembled Paul. Aluko was much smaller, for a start, and less athletic: a gentle and well-spoken man whose careful enunciation recalled the architect he'd once been, in the days Robeson's story first caught hold of him.

He told me that he'd taken *Call Mr Robeson* to the Caribbean and Nigeria and Australia, and, almost every country he went, Paul's life was like secret lore: a subject about which the broader population knew very little, while a small minority shared Aluko's deep investment. 'Robeson's equally forgotten and remembered everywhere,' he'd said.

It was strange, then, to return to London and go hunting in the city's heart for the apartment where the Robesons moved in the wake of *Othello* and be confronted with the geographical evidence of Paul's deep entrenchment in British culture in 1930.

Coming out of the station, I stopped briefly at Trafalgar Square and then looked south from the monument to England's naval supremacy. To the southwest, the Mall would, I knew, take me past St James's Park and to Buckingham Palace. Alternatively, I could turn down Whitehall and make my way to 10 Downing Street.

Buckingham Street, where the Robesons had purchased an apartment at number nineteen, was ten minutes to the northeast down the Strand. The Theatre Royal in Drury Lane, where plays had been staged since 1663, was minutes away; the Savoy Theatre was closer still.

I was struck, thinking about this, with a renewed sense of just how far Paul had come, how extraordinarily successful he had been, even at this relatively early stage of his career. In 1930, Britain still ruled over a mighty dominion, controlling the subcontinent, the Caribbean, great chunks of Africa, and territories all across the map. Paul Robeson was the son of a slave, raised in segregated poverty. Yet in a few short years, he'd made a home for himself, right here in Empire's epicenter.

Buckingham Street ran from the Strand down towards the Victoria Embankment. The buildings dated mostly from the seventeenth century. Though they'd recently been renovated, I could see the Georgian sensibility in the grand windows looking down on the street.

The Robeson apartment was smaller than the Hampstead residence, but still enormous. Not surprisingly, when Essie decided to sell their house and buy here instead, her decision, made while Paul was away on tour, put the Robesons under a definite financial stress.

Again, she was thinking of Pauli. But on this occasion, she was motivated less by a desire to keep the baby with her than a need for some time without him. Her mother had recently arrived from Europe. Mrs Goode would, they had decided, live separately with the child, and the new apartment would be a retreat for Paul and Essie, a place in which they could be alone and — perhaps — repair their relationship.

The cracks in their marriage had been widening for some time, and the publication of Essie's first book earlier that year brought them, rather unexpectedly, into the public.

With Paul's career secured, Essie wanted to establish her own identity, making use of the talents overshadowed by her partner's achievements. During a visit to Switzerland, she appeared alongside Paul in an experimental silent film called *Borderline*. She'd enjoyed the experience, but she didn't see acting as a viable option. Journalism, though, was another matter — and she planned her biography of Paul to capitalise on the huge public interest in his Othello.

Much of Essie's *Paul Robeson, Negro* details, as might be expected, Paul's early life and successes. Yet the book also contains a dialogue in which Paul and Essie (she writes of herself in the third person) discuss Paul's infidelities.

In the book, a mutual friend called Martha asks Paul bluntly if he's been unfaithful to Essie. He refuses to answer, on the grounds that, even if he admitted adultery, he wouldn't be believed. She thought too highly of him, he says — she didn't understand his many flaws.

Essie comments: 'You mean that someone may have fascinated you and interested you tremendously, and that you consummated that interest. Let's suppose you did. Would it shock you to learn that I might have suspected as much?'

She then expresses a certainty that his love hasn't changed, that, if anything, he loves her more than when they'd first married.

It's a very odd and distinctly unconvincing dialogue. But it makes sense in context.

When Essie and Paul met, Paul was still quite socially conservative: a conventional product of a strict religious household. But in New York, he'd agreed to pose for the sculptor Antonio Salemme. During the sittings, he'd been introduced to the Greenwich Village art scene, in which he felt almost instantly at home. For Paul, the freedom of the Village was exhilarating: intellectually, emotionally, and sexually.

Essie, on the other hand, disliked the new environment intensely. She had always been more status-conscious than Paul, more worried about propriety and financial success. She wasn't interested in bohemianism and dissolute parties and long discussions about the avant-garde.

The artists adored Paul — and saw Essie as a prudish, money-obsessed snob. 'Everyone [in the Village] dated and slept with everyone else,' Salemme recalled, 'or at least talked that way. Certainly, no one would give it a second thought if Paul — black and married as he was — did the same.'

Which was, of course, what happened. From about the mid-1920s, if not earlier, Paul was regularly sleeping with other women, including, for a time, Salemme's wife.

Paul was never a seeker of conquests. He adopted the Village attitude to sex as one of life's pleasures, an experience to be savoured. 'Paul was adored by all the women he ever met,' said Salemme. 'Women absolutely swooned over Paul ... If a woman made it possible for him to go to bed with her, you never heard anything about it.'

Of course, his infidelities were tremendously unfair on Essie, who hadn't signed up for an open relationship of the kind Salemme and his wife maintained. Paul did tell a few friends in the mid-1920s that his marriage was unhappy and he was considering a divorce. But he made no move to formally dissolve the union, probably because, even by then, he and Essie had become co-dependent, with her identity wrapped up in his career, and his success depending on her sometimes ruthless focus.

Throughout the late 1920s, as they lived in London, Essie seems to have adopted a policy of 'don't ask, don't tell' about Paul and other women, which ended only when she discovered a note from an actress called Yolande Jackson — a letter that indicated that at least one of Paul's relationships had gone further than a fling. Her public insistence that the love between she and Paul had only grown was thus most likely a reassertion of her claim to their relationship and a warning to rivals.

But if the book was intended to shore up their marriage, the endeavour was undermined by the many passages in which Essie exposed, perhaps unconsciously, her dissatisfactions with Paul. In fact, in places her text reads less like an appreciation of her husband and more like a running critique. She writes, for instance, of walking beside Paul along the Heath and chiding him about the laziness deterring him from playing Othello. In her version of events, Paul is 'tremendously interested' in this assessment of his character and eventually agrees that he might be able to take on the role if he were to work hard at it.

'Attaboy!' she shouts encouragingly.

When she describes Paul's failings, she often — again presumably unconsciously — racialises them, discussing her husband in terms very close to the stereotypical image of the African-American man. 'He leaves a trail of friendliness wherever he goes,' she writes, 'this Paul Robeson, Negro, who, with his typical Negro qualities — his appearance, his voice, his genial smile, his laziness, his child-like simplicity — is carving a place as a citizen in the world.'

Paul only read the book after it was published — and was appalled. In particular, he found her patronising description of his father's community difficult to forgive, particularly when compared to her praise for the genteel Bustills, the relatives who had abandoned William when he needed them most. She'd even renamed Paul for the sake of respectability: the book discusses not 'Paul Leroy Robeson' but rather 'Paul Bustill Robeson'.

Such was the context for the Buckingham Street purchase.

The investment was perilously expensive, for though Paul was earning good money, the Robesons' lifestyle was not cheap. But Essie was determined to renovate their new apartment, to make it exactly right. The perfect home would, she thought, provide a setting in which their relationship might mend, while her ability to organise the refurbishment would demonstrate her mastery over the business of everyday life, something Paul tended to ignore.

Then, with Paul still abroad, Essie discovered another love note — this time from Peggy Ashcroft, Paul's co-star in *Othello*.

During rehearsals, Paul had struggled with his learned reluctance to show intimacy with a white woman. He was, he said, 'like a plantation hand in the parlour' — instinctively backing away whenever Ashcroft came close.

But the tension of the production had other consequences. Ashcroft subsequently wrote about their fling as 'inevitable', under the stressful, exciting circumstances in which they rehearsed. 'How could one not fall in love in such a situation with such a man?' she asked.

Essie was, understandably, both enraged and devastated by this new betrayal. Yolande Jackson was a largely unknown and not very successful actor, and many in their circle sneered at her. Ashcroft, however, was a beautiful, glamorous star.

Essie decided she could not ignore her husband's apparent infatuation. She wrote to Paul, confronting him with what she knew of his affair — and their marriage began to fall apart.

I left Buckingham Street and walked down John Adam Street and back onto the Strand. I was looking for The Savoy hotel, which was only a block or two away — just near the theatre where Paul's *Othello* had been staged.

Built in the late 1880s, The Savoy was one of the first modern luxury hotels in the city: a pioneer of air conditioning, elevators, efficient plumbing, and American cocktails. It quickly became a favourite for aristocrats and celebrities of all kinds. Oscar Wilde romanced Lord Alfred Douglas at The Savoy. Humphrey Bogart and Fred Astaire, Judy Garland and Al Jolson, all stayed there.

I found a man in livery and top hat standing by the door, next to two gigantic potted ferns. But the tourists were ignoring his pageantry of status. They'd gathered just around the corner to take photos of the Savoy Grill, The Savoy's restaurant, almost certainly attracted by the knowledge that it was now managed by Gordon Ramsay.

In our era, money and fame seem sufficient to gain entry anywhere. In Paul's day, hierarchies had been different. In 1929, he and Essie had been turned away from the Savoy Grill: informed by the management that black visitors were not permitted inside.

The snub, which would have been entirely ordinary, even expected, in New York, blossomed into something of a scandal. *The New Leader* fulminated about the introduction of American-style segregation into London: 'That Paul Robeson, that cultivated, sensitive spirit whose wonderful voice has sung itself into the minds and hearts of Great Britain, should be so insulted, ought to bring matters to a head.'

The publicity elicited a partial apology from an executive at The Savoy and a pledge from other London proprietors not to enforce a colour ban. 'If the Negro was a gentleman,' explained the manager of The Ritz, 'it would be unfair to refuse him.'

The episode provided, it seemed to me, a reminder of how race continued to shape Paul and Essie's lives, even so far from the land of their birth. Equally, you couldn't understand their marital turmoil in isolation from the bigotry by which their lives had been shaped.

Essie's pain-wracked diary entries, as she absorbed Paul's betrayal, illuminate some of the odder passages in her book about him. 'Paul is not any different from any other Nigger man,' Essie wrote in one entry, 'except that he has a beautiful voice.'

In the biography, when she'd described Paul's achievements, she had praised the positive traits generally ascribed to a 'Negro'. But now, in her anger, he became 'just one more Negro musician, pursuing white meat'. Essie was light-skinned but she was still black — and her husband seemed to be in love with a very fair white woman.

For his part, Paul was not at all abashed about being found out. In his letter of reply, he expressed surprise and a certain anger that she'd opened his mail and read Ashcroft's note. 'You will do these things,' he said. 'You evidently don't believe your creed — that what you don't know doesn't hurt you. It makes things rather hopeless.'

His response suggests that they'd already reached some kind of understanding: that, if their relationship wasn't exactly open, it wasn't precisely closed, either.

'I'm sure that deep down I love you very much in the way that we could love each other,' Paul wrote. 'It could never be wholly complete because we are too different in temperament.'

The letter thus marked the formal end of a conventional marriage. But Paul still signed off with a declaration of affection. 'I often feel extremely close to you,' he wrote, 'and want to see you and talk to you and perhaps weep in your bosom. Let's hope it will come out right.'

There didn't seem much chance it would. Not at first, in any case.

Contrary to what Essie thought, Paul's affair with Ashcroft wasn't particularly important, either to him or to her. His more significant relationship was with Yolande Jackson. Yolande might not have been famous, but Paul had fallen deeply in love with the person he described as 'a free spirit, a bright loving wonderful woman'. It was because of Yolande Jackson, not Peggy Ashcroft, that Essie and Paul began considering divorce towards the end of 1930.

In a horrible irony, the Buckingham Street flat, bought as a way of repairing their marriage, now contributed greatly to its stress. The expensive refurbishment put them into debt, at a time when they were also maintaining Mrs Goode and Pauli in a house in Switzerland. They couldn't afford a separate residence for Paul, and so they remained under the same roof, even as they tried to sort out their feelings for each other.

After some discussions, they agreed they would end the marriage, and then settled into what seemed at first an amicable companionship. As Paul spent more time with Yolande, Essie developed an intimate friendship with English playwright and actor Noël Coward, a relationship that Paul assumed was an affair. 'I had a talk with NC. We talked frankly as he said he knew all the facts,' Paul wrote to Essie. 'He was non-committal, and rightly so. After all, his business with you is your concern, not mine. He was very nice.'

Paul's matter-of-fact tone about his wife's relationship with Coward showed that he understood that sexual freedom went both ways. But, of course, negotiating a failing marriage wasn't as simple in practice as in theory, with Yolande's tactlessness in repeatedly calling the apartment in search of her lover angering Essie so much so that she decided to contest the divorce that now seemed imminent.

Their attempt to work through their complicated feelings for each other was not helped by the media interest in their relationship — an interest reflecting both Paul's status as an international star, and a prurient fascination with black sexuality. When Paul performed in New York, the papers reported that a 'beautiful English woman enamoured of Robeson [had] followed him'. The British press linked Paul to the shipping heiress Nancy Cunard; another article suggested he was romancing Edwina Mountbatten, Countess Mountbatten of Burma (in response, Essie quipped, 'She is just about the one person in England that we don't know.')

Paul knew what he was risking in a relationship with Yolande. '[Othello] was a general,' Paul had explained early in 1930, 'and while he could be valuable as a fighter he was tolerated, just as a negro who could save New York from a disaster would become a great man overnight … So soon, however, as Othello wanted a white woman, Desdemona, everything was changed, just as New York would be indignant if their coloured man married a white woman.'

But it wasn't merely white responses that Paul feared. He also understood the likely reaction of his black admirers to news that, once he'd become famous, he'd abandoned a wife from Harlem for a white lover from England.

But he didn't care. He loved Yolande; he wanted to be with her.

In 1932, just after appearing in a *Show Boat* revival in New York, he publicly acknowledged his separation from Essie and explained that he was in a relationship with an English woman — a white English woman — though he refused to mention her name. He told journalists that if there was a public backlash, he was quite prepared to leave America permanently.

The boldness worked.

The gossip about his private life barely dented the critical and popular acclaim he continued to win. His turn as Joe in *Show Boat* received as much applause in New York as in London, while the concerts in which he performed, for the first time, a selection of Russian-language songs proved a great success. To cap it all off, Rutgers awarded him an honorary master of arts, a tribute that, to his immense satisfaction, he accepted on stage alongside the president of Princeton — the very institution that had snubbed his father.

It seemed, then, that he'd stared down the opposition to his remarriage; that, by confronting his opponents, he'd cleared a path for himself. His success in England — his triumph in one of the greatest plays of Western culture — had freed him from the racial code into which he'd been born in America.

Even Essie had become more or less reconciled to their divorce. 'My husband and I have been exceedingly happy,' she told journalists. 'I think we are happier now than we have ever been. But we no longer wish to be married. Not to each other, that is. We want to be friends.'

Paul turned down several major offers in the United States to come back to Europe. He was determined to marry Yolande, to live openly with her in France — only to be utterly shattered when she simply did not arrive at their scheduled meeting.

What had happened? It seemed she'd decided that a life with Paul would be too difficult. Her conservative father had made clear his objections and she concluded, probably correctly, that his response was an anticipation of the broader reaction of her family and acquaintances.

A month later, she was engaged to someone else: Prince Chervachidze, a white Russian aristocrat. Essie later wrote that Yolande 'lost her nerve': 'It would be too risky an experiment to give up all her friends and stupid social life to marry Paul.'

Paul was devastated — almost suicidal, one friend suggested. It wasn't merely the collapse of the relationship for which he'd risked everything. It was bigger than that. He understood the basis of Yolande's decision: he knew she had rejected not just him but also his skin colour.

Walking back to the station after meeting with Hugh Quarshie, I had mused on a story Hugh had told me. We'd been discussing racism in the theatre today, and he'd spoken of all the times in his career when he'd been, as he'd put it, 'the only black face in the room'. 'You're always second guessing,' he said, 'trying to work out where you stand. Do you remember in *Annie Hall* where the Woody Allen character is invited to Thanksgiving dinner at her parents' house?'

He described the scene. The girl's grandmother is looking disapprovingly at Woody as he makes a joke, and then the camera cuts back to convey what he imagines to be her perception: Allen in a broad-brimmed black hat and ringlets like an orthodox Jew.

'I may have been guilty of that, in the past,' he said. 'There I am talking to a patron of the arts, expiating about Mozart and Buñuel, and then suddenly I wonder if what they are actually seeing are thick lips and a bone through my nose.'

All through the late 1920s, Paul, I thought, must have experienced something similar. He'd come to Britain as a self-trained vocalist, with little confidence in his acting ability. Somehow, he'd won the applause of the London elite. He'd dined with royalty; he'd conversed with the greatest intellectuals of the day. Yet he must have wondered if the mask would drop away and his so-called friends would reveal their true attitude to a man they saw as a racially inferior interloper.

Eventually, he thought that, by demonstrating his mastery of the best that English culture could offer, he'd put that anxiety behind him. '*Othello* has taken away from me all kinds of fear,' he'd said, after the favourable reviews came through, 'all sense of limitations, and all racial prejudice ... [i]n a word, *Othello* has made me free.'

But, of course, it hadn't — as Yolande's rejection showed.

In *Othello*, the Moor tells the Senate how he'd explained to Desdemona and her father his history and the travails he'd overcome to achieve his position. 'She loved me for the dangers I had pass'd,' Othello says, 'And I loved her that she did pity them.'

Yolande's change of heart revealed that the dangers Paul had passed — his rise from obscurity in Princeton to astonishing success in London — meant much less than he'd thought. He'd been prepared to abandon America for Britain, but now he realised that, even in London society, he was still an outsider. Despite its politeness, it seemed segments of respectable Britain still saw him as, like Othello, 'begrimed and black'.

For more than a month after Yolande jilted him, Paul remained in a deep depression, often staying all day in a darkened room, refusing to see anyone.

When he emerged, he had changed. He'd come to a decision, a new resolution to drag himself from his despondency. The end of the affair with Yolande meant the end of his infatuation with Englishness. London wasn't North Carolina but nor, he now understood, did it provide the solution that he'd sought.

Slowly, he and Essie achieved a kind of reconciliation. She'd been flirting with the French artist Marcel Duchamp, but the dalliance doesn't seem to have been very serious. In any case, with Paul no longer remarrying, there was no necessity for divorce. Essie and Paul were still friends and, more importantly, they needed each other. Essie knew that an ongoing association with Paul would provide her with a stature she'd lack without him, allowing her to write and speak and travel with a freedom otherwise not possible, while Paul continued to rely on Essie's judgement and practicality. He moved back into Buckingham Street and they recommitted to a partnership that worked, after a fashion, even if it wasn't a conventional marriage. They would remain together for the rest of their lives, yet each would be free to pursue other interests and affections.

'Paul and I understand each other,' Essie told her diary during this period.

'Am terribly happy at No 19,' Paul wrote, at about the same time.

Over the next few years, his career success continued. He toured, he recorded, he began acting in films. On the surface, all seemed as it had been.

But it wasn't.

5

PROUD VALLEY
Pontypridd, Tiger Bay, and Porthcawl, Wales

Pontypridd was a village carved out of stone. Grey terraced cottages, grey cobbled streets, and an ancient grey bridge arching across the River Taff. The sky was slate, too, a stark contrast with the surrounding hills, which were streaked with seasonal russet, teal, and laurel.

I was accustomed to towns that sprawled, as white settlers stretched themselves out to occupy a newly colonised land. Pontypridd, I realised, huddled. Its pubs and churches and old-fashioned stores were clutched tightly in the valley, in a cosy snugness that left me feeling a long way from home.

I'd come here to see Beverley Humphreys, a singer and the host of 'Beverley's World of Music' on BBC Wales.

'I have a strong feeling that we might meet in October!' she'd written, when I'd emailed her about the Paul Robeson exhibition she was organising. 'I know from personal experience that once you start delving into Paul Robeson's life, he just won't leave you alone.'

In that correspondence, she'd described Pontypridd as the ideal place to grasp Paul's rich relationship with Wales and its people.

I knew that, in the winter of 1929, Paul had been returning from a matinee performance of *Show Boat* when he heard male voices wafting from the street. He stopped, startled by the perfect harmonisation and then by the realisation that the singers, when they came into view, were working men, carrying protest banners as they sang.

By accident, he'd encountered a party of Welsh miners from the Rhondda Valley. They were stragglers from the great working-class army routed during what the poet Idris Davies called the 'summer of soups and speeches' — the six-month general strike of 1926. Blacklisted by their employers after the unions' defeat, they had walked all the way to London searching for ways to feed their families.

By then, Paul's stardom and wealth were sufficient to insulate him from the immiseration facing many British workers, as the industrialised world sank into the economic downturn known as the Great Depression. Yet he remembered his father's dependence on charity, and he was temperamentally sympathetic with the underdog. Without hesitation, he joined the march.

Some fifty years later, Pauli Robeson visited the Talygarn Miners' Rehabilitation Centre and met an elderly man who'd been present on that day in 1929. The old miner talked of how stunned the marchers had been when Paul attached himself to their procession: a huge African-American stranger in formal attire incongruous next to the half-starved Welshmen in their rough-hewn clothes and mining boots.

But Paul had a talent for friendship, and the men were grateful for his support. He had remained with the protest until they stopped outside a city building, and then he leaped onto the stone steps to sing 'Ol' Man River' and a selection of spirituals — chosen to entertain his new comrades but also because sorrow songs, with their blend of pain and hope, expressed emotions that he thought desperate men far from home might be feeling. Afterwards, he gave a donation so the miners could ride the train back to Wales, in a carriage crammed with clothing and food.

That was how it began.

Before the year was out, he'd contributed the proceeds of a concert to the Welsh Miners' Relief Fund; on his subsequent tour, he sang for the men and their families in Cardiff, Neath, and Aberdare, and visited the Talygarn Miners' Rest Home in Pontyclun.

From then on, his ties with Wales only grew.

Paul remained in Buckingham Street, London. He and Essie maintained a public profile as a celebrity couple, still mixing easily with polite society and the intelligentsia. But Paul was now aware of the labour movement, and began to pay attention to its victories and defeats. His frequent visits to mining towns in Wales were part of that newfound political orientation.

'You can see why he's remembered around here,' Beverley said. 'He was so famous when he made those connections, and the Welsh mining community was so very cowed. In the wake of the general strike, people felt pretty hopeless.'

She'd met me at the local station and then we'd gone to her sprawling house, in a street overlooking the village. The place was comfortable without being grand, with Beverley's taste evident in the elegant furnishings. An ancient cat, blind and painfully thin, purred and butted at my ankles. We drank tea in the airy kitchen; classical music played softly on the stereo.

Beverley, I'd realised not long after we began to speak, was a natural organiser. She was a woman of projects, a champion of causes. The elegant enunciation she'd developed on radio masked the steel of her personality, a determination that swept up others in her plans.

I liked her a lot.

The Robeson exhibition opening in Pontypridd in October 2015 was an echo of much grander presentation from 2001, which Beverley had assembled with Hywel Francis, the Labour MP for Aberavon, and Paul Robeson Jr. It was first shown at the National Museum at Cardiff and then toured across the country.

Staging that event had been a revelation for Beverley. She'd known that memories of Paul Robeson ran deep in Wales, but she'd still been astonished by the response. Every day of the exhibit, people shared their recollections, speaking with a hushed fervour about encounters with Paul that had stayed with them forever. 'Men and women who had only been in his presence for two minutes, who had been at a concert and heard him sing and then afterwards spoke to him. He would look at them and, in those two minutes, make them feel that they were the most important person in the world. Not just women; men as well. There was something about him that held people, that immediately made this very strong connection — and they just never forgot. You could see in their eyes and their way of talking … I've never known anything like it; I've never known someone to have such an effect after so many years.'

But memory was a physical presence in Wales.

As soon I had stepped from the train from Cardiff in the early evening, I'd been waiting, almost despite myself, for the clatter of heavy boots, the sound of the village men returning from underground. But, of course, there were no miners in Pontypridd, and no pits for them to emerge from, for the collieries had closed decades ago, leaving the architecture of the little community structured around a permanent absence.

Yet not so far from where Beverley and I were talking, 290 miners had been killed in 1894, when the old Albion Colliery exploded. Today, the capped mineshafts of those fields still protruded through the playgrounds of the Pontypridd High School in Cilfynydd, like hands reaching desperately for the surface.

Paul's interactions with Wales were shaped by the violence of mining life: the everyday hardship of long hours and low wages, but also the sudden spectacular catastrophes that decimated entire communities. In 1934, he'd been performing in Caernarfon when news arrived of a very similar disaster in the Gresford Colliery. The mine there had caught fire, an inferno so intense that most of the 266 men who died underground, in darkness and smoke, were never brought to the surface for burial. At once, Paul offered his fees for the Caernarfon concert to the fund established for the orphans and children of the dead — an important donation materially, but far more meaningful as a moral and political gesture.

That was part, Beverley said, of why Wales remembered him. He was by then among the most famous film stars of the day, the recording artist whose songs many hummed, and yet he was showing an impoverished and struggling community — people who felt themselves isolated and abandoned — that he cared deeply about them.

And the continuing affection for Paul was more than a recollection of generosity. 'The Welsh sensed the relationship was reciprocal, that he was deriving something from their friendships, from seeing how people in the mining communities supported one another and cared for one another. He later said he learned more from the white working class in Wales than from anyone,' she said.

Certainly, Paul discovered Wales — and the British working class in general — at just the right time.

He'd signed up, with great hopes, for a film version of *Emperor Jones* in 1933: the first commercial film with a black man in the lead. But the process played out according to a familiar and dispiriting pattern. Paul's contract stipulated that, during his return to America, he wouldn't be asked to film in Jim Crow states. Yet, movie star or not, it was impossible to be shielded from institutional racism. At the end of his stay, as he arrived at a swanky New York function, he was directed to the servants' entrance rather than the elevator. One witness said he had to be dissuaded from 'punching out the doorman', in a manifestation of anger he'd never have revealed in the past.

Emperor Jones itself was still very much shaped by conservative sensibilities: among other humiliations, the studio darkened the skin of his co-star, lest audiences thought Paul was kissing a white woman. Not surprisingly, while white critics loved the film and Paul's performance, he was again attacked in the African-American press for presenting a demeaning stereotype.

A few years earlier, he might have found refuge in London from the impossible dilemmas confronting a black artist in America. But he'd learned to see respectable England as disconcertingly similar, albeit with its prejudices expressed through nicely graduated hierarchies of social class. To friends, he spoke of his dismay at how the British upper orders related to those below them. Yolande, he said, had once tried to make love to him in the back seat of a car, ignoring his discomfort about the chauffeur's presence. It was only afterward that he understood: she didn't, he realised, consider the driver to be worth worrying about. Paul couldn't avoid a comparison with whites in the United States, blind to the humanity of the African Americans tending their most intimate needs.

As William Robeson's son, he'd always been aware of injustice — how could he not be? But, as William Robeson's son, he'd believed that he could win personal freedom through discipline and talent. Harlem had deepened his race-consciousness, even as it emphasised the liberatory potential of art. Yet in Britain, he'd done everything that could have been asked of him, as a singer, as an actor, and as a man. It still wasn't enough. It would never be enough. The problem was deeper, more systemic, than he'd realised, even if he didn't quite yet understand how.

He was ready, both intellectually and emotionally, for the encounter with the Welsh labour movement.

'There was just something,' Beverley said, 'that drew Welsh people and Paul Robeson together. I think it was like a love affair, in a way.'

And that seemed entirely right.

The next morning was Sunday. Beverley and I walked down the hill, beneath a sky that warned constantly of rain. Pontypridd felt ancient to me, but it wasn't — not by European standards. The town had been summoned into existence by the coal boom of the nineteenth century, in much the same way as contemporary China's booming economy had created new population centres to service its 'special economic zones'. But where the tech factories housed their labour in cheaply constructed barracks, the Welsh miners had built out of stone.

We made our way to St David's Uniting Church on Gelliwastad Road. From the outside, it seemed like a typically stern embodiment of Victorian religiosity: a grey, rather grim-looking legacy of the 1880s.

The parishioners greeting Beverley were familiar, too, in that they were mostly female and mostly older, as you'd find in congregations in Australia.

Inside, though, the traditional church interior — the pews, the pulpit, the altar — was supplemented by a huge banner from the Abercrave Lodge of the National Union of Mineworkers, hanging just below the stained-glass windows. *Workers of the world unite for peace and socialism*, it proclaimed, with an image of a black miner holding a lamp out to his white comrade in front of a globe of the world.

The walls held huge photos of Paul Robeson, glossed in English and Welsh: Paul in his football helmet on the field at Rutgers; Paul on a concert stage, his mouth open in song; Paul marching on a picket line. These were the displays extracted from the 2001 exhibition.

Beverley introduced me to Reverend Phil Wall, the minister. He was young and athletic, with a slight beard, and his English accent stood out among the sing-song inflections of the Welsh. We chatted with the parishioners, who were taking turns to keep the Robeson display open during the day for the entirety of Black History Month.

The service itself reminded me of my morning in the Witherspoon Street church, except that, where in Princeton I'd marvelled at the worshippers' command of the black vocal tradition, here I was confronted by the harmonic power of Welsh choristers: the old hymns voiced in a great wall of sound resonating and reverberating throughout the interior.

Paul, of course, had made that comparison many times. Both the Wesleyan chapels of the Welsh miners and the churches in which he'd worshipped with his father were, he said, places where a weary and oppressed people drew succour from prayer and song.

His movie *The Proud Valley*, which had brought him here to Pontypridd in 1939, rested on precisely that conceit. In the film (the only one of his movies in which he took much pride), Paul played David Goliath, an unemployed seaman who wanders into the Welsh valley, and is embraced by the miners when the choir leader overhears him sing.

Throughout the 1930s, the analogy between African Americans and workers in Britain (and especially Wales) helped re-orient Paul, both aesthetically and politically, after his disillusionment with the English establishment.

In London, Hugh Quarshie and I had talked about Paul's belief that Othello would set him free. Quarshie told me that, despite his own love for Shakespeare, he disagreed with the presentation of the Bard as the highest form of achievement. 'Look, there's a show called *Strictly Come Dancing*,' he'd said. 'Do you know it?'

The Australian version went by a different title, but I had a pretty good idea of what he was talking about.

'They go through an elimination contest in various stages, a rumba and a cha-cha-cha, and some of the guests can't dance and some of them can, and it's fun seeing whether they make fools of themselves or distinguish themselves. But you're forced to learn a convention that is not your own. I have absolutely no interest in learning how to do a rumba or a foxtrot. If the convention were the watusi or the funky chicken, that might be different — if the competition was "dance like James Brown", I'd say, yeah, I'd have a go at that. But the idea that these particular dances are evidence of your ability to dance in general is questionable, just like the idea that if you can master *Othello* that's evidence of your ability to act.'

Paul had never come around to precisely that position, even though by singing spirituals, he was implicitly making the aesthetic case for a previously despised form.

But during his early years in Britain, he'd worried about the reviewers who urged him to embrace classical music. Perhaps they were right. Perhaps he couldn't base an entire career on simple tunes composed by untutored musicians from the plantations. To placate the critics, he began adding classical songs to his repertoire.

But his contact with working-class communities in Britain provided him with an important reassurance. He told his friend Marie Seton about a letter he received from a cotton-spinner during one of his tours. 'This man said he understood my singing, for while my father was working as a slave, his own father was working as a wage slave in the mills of Manchester.'

That was in northern England, but he experienced a similar commonality everywhere, and it pleased and intrigued him. If the slave songs of the United States were worth celebrating, what about the music emerging from other oppressed communities? What connections might the exploration of distinctive cultural traditions forge between different peoples?

Significantly, it was in Wales where Paul first articulated this new perspective. In 1934, he gave a concert in Wrexham, in north Wales, between the Welsh mountains and the lower Dee Valley alongside the border with England. Yet again it was a charity, a performance staged at the Majestic Cinema for the benefit of the St John Ambulance Association. During the visit, Paul was interviewed by the local paper, and he told the writer he was no longer wedded to a classical repertoire.

He'd come to regard himself as a folk singer, devoted to what he called 'the eternal music of common humanity'. To that end, he was studying languages, working his way haphazardly through Russian, German, French, Dutch, Hungarian, Turkish, Hebrew, and sundry other tongues so as to perform the songs of different cultures in the tongues in which they had been written.

He had become, he said, a singer for the people.

The confidence of that statement reflected another lesson drawn primarily from Wales.

In African-American life, the black church had mattered so much, as Keeanga-Yamahtta had said, because religion provided almost the only institutional stability for people buffeted by racial oppression. In particular, because Jim Crow segregated the workplace, black communities struggled to form and maintain trade unions. Wales, though, was different. The miners found consolation in religion, with every village dotted with chapels. But they believed just as fervently in trade unionism.

The Gresford disaster showed why. As a song distributed anonymously after the tragedy put it: '*Down there in the dark they are lying / They died for nine shillings a day.*' In an industry such as mining, you relied on your workmates — both to get the job done safely and to stand up for your rights. The battle was necessarily collective. A single miner possessed no power at all; the miners as a whole, however, could shut down the entire nation, as they'd demonstrated back in 1926.

In particular, the co-operation mandated by modern industry might, at least in theory, break down the prejudices that divided workers — even, perhaps, the stigma attached to race. That was the point Paul dramatised in *The Proud Valley*, a film in which the solidarity of the workplace overcomes the miners' suspicion about a dark-skinned stranger. 'Aren't we all black down that pit?' asks one of the men.

In his visits to the Welsh villages and to other working-class communities during the 1930s, Paul grasped how, rather than just marking oppression, class also provided the basis for resistance, for social change. 'It's from the miners in Wales,' Paul explained, '[that] I first understood the struggle of Negro and white together.'

'To understand Paul's relationship with Wales,' Beverley told me, the following day, 'you need to understand Tiger Bay.'

We were back in St David's, waiting for a busload of children. As part of her mission to rekindle memories of Robeson, Beverley had been liaising with the local schools, who'd organised their pupils to write poems about the exhibition and to stage their own concert, before a performance of Robeson's music by the opera singer Sir Willard White.

It was, it seemed to me, an awful lot of work for a small-town exhibition, but Beverley was indefatigable.

The children burst noisily through the church doors and were shepherded by their teachers into the pews, until, eventually, they settled. With great patience, Beverley told them about Paul Robeson and his life, while the kids fidgeted and gaped at the huge pictures all around them.

Then she played them a CD of Paul singing 'Ol' Man River'. 'How would you describe that voice?' she asked, as the last notes died away.

A forest of hands.

'Loud!' said one child. 'It's very loud.'

'Yes,' said Beverley. 'Very good. It is loud — a loud voice. And what else is it? Do you know?'

Another little girl clearly did, as she was twisting herself into a pretzel in her determination to be called. 'Deep!' she shouted when called upon. 'It's deep!'

Beverley clapped. 'That's right! It is, isn't it? Very deep! And Paul Robeson said, "How can I use my lovely deep voice to change the world?"'

Paul, she told them, didn't like to see anyone get picked on. Did they know what it was like to be picked on?

I could see many of them nodding, their faces tremendously serious.

She talked to them about racism and discrimination and made a creditable attempt to gloss McCarthyism in a form suitable for primary-school students, before sending them off in pairs to fill in their worksheets with information from the panels.

As soon as she was free, she introduced me to Lesley Clarke, and to Harry Ernest and his son Ian, who'd slipped inside quietly after the kids. The three of them came, Beverley explained, from Tiger Bay, the centre of Wales' black community. They'd worked on the original exhibition in Cardiff, after Beverley had insisted that the National Gallery employ black guides, and now they'd come to Pontypridd to witness the new display.

At eighty-two, Lesley Clarke was thin but sprightly and alert. She spoke slowly and carefully, and her manner reminded me, almost at once, of someone else, though I couldn't quite put my finger on the familiarity. 'I hadn't realised there was a colour bar until I left Tiger Bay. When I went to grammar school, I realised for the first time that there were people who just didn't like coloured people. Didn't know anything about us, but didn't like us. I didn't know I was poor and I didn't know I was black: all I knew was that I was me.'

It came to me then. Lesley sounded like Shirley Satterfield, the woman I'd met in Princeton. The echo came not only in how she spoke, but also, I soon realised, in what she conveyed.

In the nineteenth century, coal exports transformed Cardiff into an international port. Inevitably, some of the mariners who visited chose to stay behind. By the early decades of the twentieth century, about seven hundred people from Africa and the West Indies lived in Cardiff — and most of them remained near the docks, in Butetown or Tiger Bay. During the First World War, Britain threw the entirety of its empire into the conflict, so that men from across the globe fought under English colours. Many passed through Cardiff and, again, some stayed. After 1918, the black population of the city had grown to about three thousand or so.

The echo of segregated Princeton was not coincidental. Well into the twentieth century, landlords would not rent properties outside Butetown to black people. Just as the Red Summer riots had devastated black America in 1919, Tiger Bay was forged by some of the worst racial attacks in British history. In June that year, returning soldiers encountered a group of black men walking with white women. Outraged, the troops, led by colonials (mostly Australians), rampaged throughout Butetown, attacking people of colour, destroying houses, and leaving four dead.

Britain mightn't have been Jim Crow but, for Lesley and Harry's generation, the colour bar was very real, especially in employment. Harry was impish and bald, and his eyes crinkled as he spoke, almost as if he took a perverse humour in the recollection. 'We'd ask if a job was open,' he said, 'and soon as they said yes, we'd say, "Can I come for interview right now?" To narrow the gap, because the minute you got there they would say, "Oh, the job is gone."'

'The minute they saw you were black, that was it,' said Lesley.

'And that was a common experience?'

Lesley nodded. 'You just took it for granted that it was going to happen. There were very few outlets, especially for girls. You either worked in the brush factory or you worked in Ziggy's, selling rags and whatnot, or there was a place just over the bridge that did uniforms.'

'I worked in the brush factory for a while,' Harry said. 'Oh, Jesus!' He shook his head and laughed in dismay. 'Jesus.'

But while Tiger Bay was known as a 'coloured' area, that descriptor took in a far wider racial and ethnic diversity in Wales than in the United States. In 1935, a report auspiced by the British civil-rights group League of Coloured Peoples found a remarkable range of cultures and faiths in Cardiff: Muslims and Catholics and Sikhs, West Indians, West Africans, Arabs, Malays, Somalis, Singaporeans, East Africans, and others, all trying 'to keep respectable homes under depressing conditions'.

Some of the Ernest family's ancestors were from St Lucia. Others came from Barbados. Lesley's story was similar. Her two grandfathers came from Barbados; her two grandmothers were born in Wales. 'And then I married a man from Barbados.'

That diversity reflected Britain's history as a colonial power, a history that meant that race played out quite differently to the pattern that Paul knew from America. In other words, in the early 1930s, even as he became interested in the labour movement, he was also developing and intensifying the engagement with black politics he'd begun in Harlem.

The intellectuals of the Harlem Renaissance tended to envision Africa as an abstraction, a symbolic negation of white society. In his poem 'Heritage', for instance, African-American author Countee Cullen describes his ancestral connection to the continent almost as an instinct, an exotic and perhaps dangerous cultural inheritance existing as much within the poet as the world. Paul had sometimes made similar claims, particularly when he discussed his music. But Britain brought Paul into contact with the reality of Africa, a place that many activists studying in London called home. Paul enrolled briefly in a PhD in philology, supplementing his growing familiarity with European dialects with

Hausa and Efik and other African languages. In the Buckingham Street apartment, he debated politics and history with the African students he met: men such as Nnamdi Azikiwe, Jomo Kenyatta, and Kwame Nkrumah, who would duly lead anti-colonial struggles in Nigeria, Kenya, and Ghana.

Paul's engagement with the labour movement was not, at this stage at least, shared by Essie. But she most definitely took an interest in Africa, embarking in an anthropology degree at the London School of Economics.

'So long, / So far away, / Is Africa', Langston Hughes had mourned. For the Robesons, that was no longer quite true.

Like many in Tiger Bay, Harry and Lesley had been tangentially affected by Paul's new enthusiasm for modern Africa.

'My mother actually took me to audition for the part of Robeson's child,' Lesley said. 'But I was too light-skinned.'

Harry nodded. He remembered his sister working as an extra on the set. 'She said that in six weeks of filming, she earned more money than for the rest of the year in her normal job.'

They were talking about *Sanders of the River*, a film made in 1934. Paul had agreed to play the movie's 'Chief Bosambo' character after the Hungarian-British director Zoltan Korda showed him an archive of footage recorded in Central Africa — a collection of music and dance that he said the production would showcase. At the time, Paul assured reporters that Sanders would 'do a lot towards the better understanding of Negro culture and customs'.

Of course, it did nothing of the sort, for the 'authentic' backdrops were merely used as the exotic setting for a traditional colonial narrative that, as the advertising puff explained, featured 'a million mad savages fighting for one beautiful woman'.

Though Paul disowned the movie, *Sanders of the River* was regarded with considerable affection in Tiger Bay, not only for the jobs created but also because it put so many locals on the big screen. Whenever the film screened in the Butetown area, cheers would erupt at the appearance of the witch doctor — universally recognised as Mr Graham from Sophia Street. Lesley's godfather featured briefly, capering about in a loincloth, and for years thereafter he kept the garment on his wall as a kind of trophy.

I thought, as she told me that, about Paul's filmography from the mid-1930s, the peak of his career as a screen actor. In 1936, he'd starred in the movie version of *Show Boat* as well as in a film called *The Song of Freedom*; the following year, he made *Big Fella*, *King Solomon's Mines*, and *Jericho*. Few of those movies have much to recommend them, since directors simply did not know how to employ a charismatic black lead. Nevertheless, Paul's fans found ways to enjoy his work, if only because a Robeson performance put an African-American man on a big screen otherwise almost entirely dominated by white people.

Lesley told me how, as a little girl, she remembered hearing that Robeson was visiting Loudoun Square in Tiger Bay. Naturally, the whole community rushed to greet him, in a reception that illustrated what he'd come to mean to them. One of the women who'd played a small part in *Sanders of the River* many years before asked: 'Mr Robeson, do you remember me?'

'Indeed I do, my dear. Indeed I do,' he replied — and whether the answer was true or merely a polite fiction, it confirmed for the community his ongoing affection.

On that occasion, he was visiting a relative — a man called Aaron Mossell, Robeson's uncle-in-law. Originally from Baltimore, Mossell had been the first African American to graduate from the University of Pennyslvania Law School, otherwise known as Penn Law. Like Paul, Mossell was a reader: locals remember that his room was always crammed with books. And, of course, he was a communist. 'There were a lot of communists in the docks at the time,' Harry said. 'Strong working-class area. Very strong! They called themselves the Colonial Defence Association. Most of them were seaman who were exploited by shipping companies, and they were very successful at organising.'

Ian, Harry's son, was stocky, with a shaved head and a much lighter complexion than his father. He was a generation too young to have had any direct encounter with Robeson. But he too remembered what it was like growing up in a politicised working-class area. He told me about his apprenticeship as a toolmaker and the education he received at work.

'Charlie, our shop steward, had left school at fourteen, but he was one of the most well-read people I have ever met. He could talk about anything, and I used to listen to him.'

He remembered Charlie confronting another worker who talked about emigrating to South Africa, explaining to the man that by moving there he'd be perpetuating apartheid.

'It was Charlie who told me about Paul Robeson. "Paul Robeson was the greatest man I have met in my life," he said — and he meant it.'

The conversation convinced me that I needed to see Tiger Bay myself. It was only a brief trip from Pontypridd back to Cardiff by train. But what I found there was not at all what I'd expected.

At the Butetown History and Arts Centre on Bute Street, I stopped for the paintings by Jack Sullivan, a self-trained artist who'd captured the street life of the 1950s: scenes of sailors coming home and streetwalkers plying their trade and cloth-capped men brawling under bridges.

But modern Butetown, I soon found, wasn't seafarers and drunks. It was the new Wales Millennium Centre and chrome office blocks and warehouse-style apartments and tourists in gourmet hamburger bars.

At the waterfront, I bought an ice-cream and looked out to the harbour. The very topography of Butetown had been reshaped. In the 1960s, slum clearance bulldozed much of the original housing. In the 1980s, the Bute West Dock became the focus of the Atlantic Wharf development, and then, in the 1990s, the Cardiff Bay Barrage transformed the mudflats into a huge freshwater lake and marina.

The solidity of buildings clearly intended for labour rather than recreation hinted at the past. I could identify the old warehouses;

I could see the places that once must have been hotels serving the thirsty dockworkers. Yet, often, the references to history in the redevelopments were sly, almost ironic: arch gestures towards a vanished lifestyle, reminiscent of how blue-collar culture was reappropriated in hipster bars once the workers themselves were excluded.

Ian had warned me, of course. 'That was the idea with Tiger Bay: to get rid of it, to erase it,' he'd said.

Lesley agreed. 'It was such a unique place.'

'They wanted to get everyone out of Tiger Bay. It's a very desirable area now.'

'When you'll see them is when there's a funeral,' added Harry. 'They are always big funerals, if it's an old dock family, black or white. It will be all the grandchildren and great grandchildren, coming back to Tiger Bay.'

From our first discussions, Beverley had assured me that Paul's relationship with Wales was reciprocal. To illustrate, she suggested a trip to Porthcawl, about forty minutes' drive from Pontypridd. It was there, she said, that the Welsh miners repaid their debt.

In the nineteenth century, Porthcawl had been an industrial port, used, like Cardiff, for the export of coal. But it had struggled competing with Port Talbot and Barry. By the first decades of the twentieth century, its docks were closed and the town began its reinvention as a beachside resort.

Traditionally, the mines in the Rhondda Valley shut down for two weeks every July and August. After the Second World War, the modern rail system enabled many Welsh families to enjoy a holiday, often for the first time in their lives. During the so-called Miners' Fortnight, Porthcawl swelled enormously, with thousands of miners, their wives, and their children taking caravans near the sands of Trecco Bay for two weeks of entertainment. It was a fortnight dedicated to the Coney Beach

Funfair, to brass band performances, darts competitions, dances, and similar amusements.

We drove down the M4, passing by the villages whose polysyllabic names ran through my mind like far-away music. *Pen-y-coedcae. Beddau. Llantrisant, Brynsadler, Coychurch.* When we reached Porthcawl, we parked the car on the Esplanade Avenue and walked down to the shore.

The town was charming, I thought, with its slate walkways and antique streetlights, but it was an anachronistic charm, evoking bathing belles and naughty seaside postcards. Or maybe that was my own cultural baggage. As an Australian, I couldn't imagine swimming in the rocky beach down from the Esplanade, particularly not in the perpetual greyness of a Welsh afternoon.

The Grand Pavilion dated back to 1932, when it had been constructed for miners' conferences, as well as the many social events once central to a resort town. It was a beautiful building but, again, from a different age: distinctively art deco, with its jazzy white pillars and dashingly curved frontage.

Beverley led me inside and we stared, somewhat doubtfully, into the building's innards. 'We need someone who can show us around,' she announced.

Within a few minutes, she'd hunted down a manager, a polite young man who, it transpired, shared her passion for opera, so that they bonded very quickly over a discussion of Spanish concert venues they both loved.

The main theatre was stunning: a wooden room furnished in red, with two tiers of stands, and circular tables on the old dance floor. Though it had been restored sufficiently to remain a functioning venue, you could still feel the aesthetics of a different time, a sense of what it must have been like to attend an event when all the miners came to town.

Eisteddfods were an old Welsh tradition. In the Middle Ages, bards had competed for honour and prizes, singing and reciting before judges and their public. The miners launched their own eisteddfod in 1948.

It was the only such event based on a trade union, a testament to the centrality of unionism to mining life — and one year it was largely devoted to help Paul Robeson win his freedom.

Paul had reached out to the Welsh miners when his career was at its height. They came back to him at his lowest ebb, almost two decades later, at a time when all he'd achieved seemed to have been taken from him. In the midst of the Cold War, the FBI prevented Paul from performing at home. Worst still, the US state department confiscated his passport so he couldn't travel abroad. He was left in a kind of limbo: silenced, isolated, and increasingly despairing.

On 5 October 1957, the Porthcawl Grand Pavilion filled with perhaps five thousand people for the miners' eisteddfod. Will Painter, the union leader, took to the microphone. After welcoming the delegates, he announced that they would soon hear from Paul Robeson, who'd be joining them via a transatlantic telephone line.

When Painter spoke again, he was addressing Paul directly. 'We are happy that it has been possible for us to arrange that you speak and sing to us today,' he said. 'We would be far happier if you were with us in person.'

Miraculously, Robeson's deep voice crackled out of the speakers in response. 'My warmest greetings to the people of my beloved Wales, and a special hello to the miners of South Wales at your great festival. It is a privilege to be participating in this historic festival.'

He was seated in a studio in New York. Down the telephone line, he performed a selection of his songs, dedicating them to their joint struggle for what he called 'a world where we can live abundant and dignified lives'.

The musical reply came from the mighty Treorchy Male Voice Choir, the winners of that year's eisteddfod, and a group that traced its history back to 1883. Paul joined the choir in a performance of the Welsh national anthem, 'Land of My Fathers', before the entire audience — all five thousand of them — serenaded him with 'We'll Keep a Welcome on the Hillside.'

'*This land you knew will still be singing*,' they chorused. '*When you come home again to Wales.*'

Paul had performed a similar stunt the previous year, singing through the telephone for London's St Pancras Hall. But the Porthcawl event was special, not least because it came from such a small place — a gesture of solidarity not from a capital city but from the ordinary working people of Wales. As such, it was a demonstration, both to Robeson and to the authorities, that he still had an audience; that his enemies hadn't succeeded in silencing him completely.

After the tour, Beverley and I sat in the Grand Pavilion's little café, drinking tea and eating Welsh cakes. She told me about the conversation she'd had with Paul Jr, when he'd visited for the original Robeson exhibition. He'd been present in that studio while his father sang down the line to Porthcawl, and he told Beverley how much the concert meant to Paul. 'It was after years of isolation, and by then his spirit was really damaged. But Paul Jr said the connection really revived him — just to hear people talking, to know he wasn't alone.'

It was more than a psychological boost — the demonstrations of international support played a huge role in Paul's campaign for the restoration of his passport. When he was at last able to travel, Wales was one of the first places he visited. 'He came to National Eisteddfod, and there are wonderful photos of him sitting with [Welsh Labour politician] Nye Bevan and [Scottish socialist politician] Jennie Lee … just sitting in this audience, the only black face in a sea of white faces. They asked him what he'd like as a memory of it, and he said he'd like a Welsh hymnbook. Again, that meant a great deal because of our religious heritage: his request for Welsh hymns in the Welsh language.'

The concert had been important to Paul. But it was also, quite clearly, important to the Welsh.

Beverley had grown up in a musical household, and she'd always been interested in social justice. As a young woman, she'd known vaguely about Paul Robeson and his relationship with Wales, but not in any great detail. Yet her subsequent research about his career had given that history almost an epic feel. 'I knew it was true, I knew this man had really done all these things, but when I learned the details, it was like a film screening in my head. Of course, he's a historical character — he's gone, he's dead — but he suddenly became very present. To come back to these places, to know what happened ... it means a lot.'

A few days before I left Wales, I caught a lift with Beverley's friend Patrick Jones, from Pontypridd to Mountain Ash. He was a poet, and Beverley had asked him to run workshops in the local schools, helping the kids compose their own responses to the Robeson exhibition.

It was about fifteen minutes' drive between the two villages, and along the way we talked about the Welsh attitude to the mining past. I mentioned how Harry Ernest had been shaking his head about the state of choral music. Harry was a great aficionado of Welsh choirs, he'd explained. But the music came, of course, from the mines and the chapels. And now the mines were gone and the chapels were in steep decline, with many of the local churches struggling to keep their doors open. It was hard, I said, to avoid a sense of loss.

'Oh, there's definitely a lot of nostalgia,' Patrick said. 'I guess the harsh conditions forged a spirit of solidarity, of looking after each other. And people remember that.'

I could see why they would. What were the lines from the poet W.H. Davies? 'Such sorrow in the valley has,' he wrote in 'The Collier's Wife', 'made kindness grow like grass.'

The Pontypridd History Society maintained a little museum, a small collection of curiosities and artefacts pinned on walls and beneath the glass of dusty cabinets. There was an oil painting of a pigeon named Springfield Boy, annotated with his victories from 1932 (the bird had come second in Shrewsbury; third in Chester; second in Lancaster; and so on). There were portraits of eisteddfod winners: men with serious faces and generous moustaches, posed like victorious football teams. There was an array of miners' lamps, displaying an almost Darwinian evolution of the technology from candles to electric bulbs. There was a scale model of a colliery; there was a banner from the National Union of Mineworkers Cwm Llantwit Lodge.

A whole way of life had depended on coal. A whole way of life had been uprooted when the mines closed.

Patrick laughed. 'What they forget, though, is that things weren't actually so great.'

Outside the car, the hills passing by were iron red when the light hit them, and the green of the trees changed from chartreuse to viridian. But, of course, that was because the slag heaps had gone and the shafts had been filled in and the harsh scars gouged by the collieries rendered almost invisible.

Patrick dropped me off in the centre of Mountain Ash, near where a sign advertised the Mountain Ash Workman's Club and Institute. I stopped for a while at a statue honouring the legendary eighteenth-century runner Guto Nyth Brân, who'd been captured in bronze outpacing a weary hound. The streets in Mountain Ash were very similar to those in Pontypridd, lined with rows of little cottages, all adjacent to one another in long terraces. There was something comforting in their solidity: they were small, but they felt permanent and substantial, in a way that modern dwellings wouldn't, with each house embedded in the stone and in the community.

Mountain Ash was the site of another of Paul's famous interventions. At the pavilion here, he'd spoken and sung at a huge meeting in tribute to the thirty-three Welshmen who'd died in the Spanish Civil War. Most reports agreed that some five thousand people attended.

Now that I was in Mountain Ash and could see how tiny the village actually was, I realised how significant a crowd that must have been.

The pavilion, built in 1906 to host eisteddfods, had been demolished in 2012 — presumably because eisteddfods themselves were no longer so common.

There wasn't really much to look at. I paced up and down the street and then I started to walk back.

The return to Pontypridd took almost two hours. *Gyrrwch yn ofalus*, warned a sign. *Be attentive!* But the road snaking along the countryside was empty, and the skies cleared for a little while so that the rusted hills blazed orange in the sun, and I didn't feel in any particular hurry.

I was thinking of how Beverley had explained Paul's life to the children. She'd stressed his commitment to fairness, to making sure that no one was victimised. In the poems she'd shown me, the kids had picked up on the theme. They wrote about discrimination; they wrote about inequality; they wrote about bullying.

The project, the reclamation of Paul's story for a new generation, was an admirable one. But the conceptual difference between the language they used and the ideas that had gripped Paul in the 1930s was striking. For him, the labour movement had been a revelation because of the collectivity it represented. In Wales, in the pit villages and union lodges and little chapels, he'd found solidarity — a concept that thereafter had been central to him.

Today, though, Paul's importance could only be explained in individualised terms.

Maybe that was the explanation for the nostalgia Patrick and I had discussed. The coal industry was gone, and its disappearance had dissolved the bonds that had once textured impoverished mining communities. That wasn't merely a Welsh phenomenon, either — throughout the industrialised world, the decline of the labour movement meant that ideas of solidarity were increasingly difficult to articulate.

At the Mountain Ash meeting, Paul had explained that he'd been compelled to come. The Welshmen who'd travelled to Spain had been fighting for him, for black people throughout America, and for oppressed people everywhere.

The miners' leader Arthur Horner had also spoken. 'To die,' he'd said, 'is not remarkable or important, for all must die. The matter we have to concern ourselves with is: what did they die for ...'

For Horner, Spain had crystallised the great questions about what made a life worth living. Paul, I knew, had felt the same way.

What, exactly, had he found there?

6

WHAT FASCISM WAS
Barcelona and Madrid, Spain

In 1934, the Soviet film director Sergei Eisenstein, a huge admirer of Paul, invited the Robesons to Moscow. Paul and Essie were both enthusiastic travellers and already curious about the Soviet experiment, and they accepted with enthusiasm. But the journey was long, necessitating a change of trains in Germany, where the Robesons and their friend Marie Seton planned to rest for the night.

Paul had previously stayed in Berlin when touring *The Emperor Jones* and, back then, he'd felt entirely comfortable in the city. The German Left was legendarily strong; Berlin, famous for theatre and music. In the late 1920s, Hitler was little more than just another street-corner ranter, a faintly risible figure yelling about Jewish bankers and the Treaty of Versailles.

In 1934, he was in power. The Berlin the Robesons encountered proved entirely different from the place Paul remembered. Even the short walk from the station to the hotel felt tense, with brown-shirted stormtroopers glaring at Paul.

In the evening, a Jewish friend visited. When Paul and Essie inquired about the political situation, he spoke of a country gripped by fear. The Communist Party had been criminalised. Trade unions were illegal. Thugs were rounding up the Social Democrats — and rumours, too awful to believe, circulated everywhere about the camps in which dissidents were imprisoned.

His terror was raw and so infectious that Paul chose to eschew sightseeing, remaining in the hotel until they departed the next day. He was an obvious target on streets where violent racists now held sway.

In the morning, Paul and Marie waited on the platform for their train while Essie, ever the organiser, sorted their luggage with the stationmaster. The station was mostly empty … except for a few loitering stormtroopers. In Berlin, stormtroopers were everywhere.

Suddenly, Paul stiffened. 'Keep on talking as if you haven't noticed anything,' he hissed to Marie.

A German woman waiting for her train had observed the foreigners. Paul had heard her say something to the Nazis, who abruptly directed their attention to him. He knew enough German to understand what was said: they'd taken Marie for a local, an Aryan consorting with a black man. They drew closer.

'This is like Mississippi,' Paul whispered to Marie. 'It's how a lynching begins. If either of us moves or shows fear, they'll go further.'

With the luggage secured, Essie rejoined them. Though she'd avoided the earlier interaction, she noted the proximity of the soldiers and the menacing semi-circle they'd formed to separate the little group of foreigners from the other passengers. Violence appeared imminent. Paul was much, much bigger than any of the Germans, and he began silently calculating how many he might take down when the fight began.

Perhaps the stormtroopers understood. Perhaps they were reluctant to tackle such a huge man. Whatever the reason, when the train arrived, they still hadn't moved. Paul shepherded Essie and Marie on board and slammed the door behind him. As the engine pulled the carriage out of Berlin, he stared out the window in silence. Only when they'd crossed the border did he relax — and then he spoke wonderingly: 'I never understood what fascism was before.'

The incident sharpened his understanding of European politics in the age of Hitler and made his involvement in the Spanish Civil War almost inevitable.

In the mid-1930s, many Western politicians still admired Hitler and Mussolini — or, at least, refused to condemn them. The real menace, they said, was Bolshevism: the Italians fascists and the German Nazis might be boorish, histrionic, and brutal, but their rise saved their nations from revolution. Even those liberals who decried Hitler's anti-Semitism and violence often explained Nazism as a distinctly German phenomenon (and Mussolini's fascism as a distinctly Italian one), with no relevance to the democratic world.

Paul's engagement with the working-class movement in Wales and elsewhere already predisposed him to disagree. Across Britain, activists talked about the fascists destroying trade unions — and drew parallels with their own experiences of strikebreaking. But Paul's encounter in Berlin provided a demonstration of fascism as a particular instance of a broader phenomenon, a close cousin of the white supremacy prevailing in the United States. Nazism wasn't merely a hypothetical threat to black people, Paul realised. It was a lethal menace, its spectre implicit in every lynching.

National Socialism, he thought, represented Jim Crow taken to its extreme conclusion. That was why the suffering that African Americans experienced in their own country was not a justification to stay aloof from international politics, but rather a reason to oppose fascism everywhere.

And the key battleground was Spain.

I was staying in a little hostel in Carrer de Sant Pau, which meant that, to meet Alan Warren in Café Zurich, I walked fifteen minutes up Las Ramblas, Barcelona's most famous avenue.

It was on Las Ramblas that visitors to Spain during the civil war invariably took stock of how the revolution had reshaped the city. 'Everything seemed to be centred here,' wrote the poet and socialist Mary Low in 1936. 'Housefronts were alive with waving flags in a long avenue of dazzling red. Splashes of black or white cut through the colour from place to place. The air was filled with an intense din of loudspeakers ... We went from one group to the other and listened, too. It was nearly always people speaking of the revolution and the war ...'

Later that year, Eric Blair — or George Orwell — arrived in Barcelona. *Homage to Catalonia,* the book of his Spanish experiences, contains a very similar description. He writes of seeing every shop and café daubed with a proclamation explaining that the business, like all the private transport, had been collectivised. Up and down Las Ramblas, he wrote, the revolutionary songs played.

I struggled to imagine militant tunes drowning out the discordant music of commerce that dominated the avenue today. Las Ramblas, once the city's central thoroughfare, had been more or less ceded to tourism. The people streaming back and forth around me were backpackers; the din came from street vendors offering wallets and iPhone cases and religious keyrings.

The Australian writer Robert Dessaix describes cafés as the quintessence of travel, the places where, after a journey, 'you put yourself back together again, changed but still you'. At Café Zurich, on the edge of the Plaça de Catalunya, the tables outside were occupied by tourists engaged in that reassembly, a process fuelled by little cups of espresso. Inside was considerably quieter, with a decor more or less unchanged from the 1930s, except for the addition of a few high-tech cigarette machines.

Alan Warren was waiting upstairs. A British historian, he'd relocated to Barcelona, where he helped descendants of civil-war veterans retrace their relatives' experiences. His cropped hair and little moustache gave him the air of an old-fashioned army officer, I thought, as he rose to shake my hand.

He introduced me to Dani Caracola. A young man with a beard and ponytail, Dani told me he made his living as a teacher, but he might equally have been a social worker or a nurse: there was something gentle about him, a softness that suited a caring profession.

Yet Dani's passion was music. He played guitar, and later, when I listened to the CD he gave me, I liked the sweetness of his voice a great deal.

That album featured songs relating to the Spanish Civil War. By the end of the 1930s, Paul's repertoire included the Republican favourites 'Peat Bog Soldiers' and 'The Four Insurgent Generals', which he'd stamped indelibly with his extraordinary voice. Did Dani know his versions?

'Truthfully? The first time I heard of Paul Robeson was when Alan invited me to meet you.'

I'd become accustomed to a lack of recognition of the Robeson name. But this was not the same. In English-speaking countries, Paul's relative obscurity stemmed from McCarthyism. In Spain, it came from the veil the victorious fascists had cast over anything pertaining to the civil war.

'When we were taught about the war at school,' said Dani, 'they just put it at the end — one year at the end of contemporary history. They say, "Oh, sorry, we don't have enough time to teach this."'

In Germany and Italy, the curriculum covered fascism in detail, posing the war and its prelude as a problem for students to solve. How had such an evil doctrine arisen? To what extent had everyday people acquiesced to the dictatorship and its mandates, and why? In those countries, the past was recognised as imposing certain duties on living: a responsibility to avoid a repetition.

Spain was different. The regime that triumphed during the civil war did not fall in 1945. On the contrary, General Franco, the fascist leader, became a close US ally, providing Washington with military bases and other support during the Cold War. His administration survived until the 1970s — and even then, Spain underwent no systematic accounting with the past. Under the so-called *el pacto del olvido*, or Pact of Forgetting, politicians agreed not to discuss the war, on the basis that old divisions might tear the new society apart.

The Spanish Civil War, its participants, and its aftermath remained a strange blank, too recent to forget but too painful to consider. The Spanish national anthem still lacked official lyrics: the words written during the dictatorship had been scrapped, but no decision reached as to what might replace them.

In schools, Dani explained, students learned about the war as a sequence of dates. Spain went mad, they were told. Both sides had committed great evils; all the participants were to blame. With everyone guilty, no one needed to be held to account. 'But that,' he said, 'is not true.'

A chance discovery had transformed his understanding. 'My mother has a house in a village in Catalonia. In the attic, we found a pile of letters that my great-uncle, my grandfather's brother, sent back from the front. He died on the day of his eighteenth birthday. I didn't know anything about him, and nor did my mother. She never spoke with her parents about what had happened because after the fascist victory there was a lot of fear. Even years later, nobody would talk. But my grandparents had put all my great-uncle's stuff in the attic. So we found the drawings he'd done, his art, his schoolbooks: everything.'

The textbooks, in particular, were fascinating: a fragment of revolutionary hope, smuggled forward through time.

Formerly a great empire, Spain had entered the twentieth century as one of the most backward nations on the continent. The church and feudal landlords exercised extraordinary authority over the rural population; in the cities, workers lived in Dickensian slums. General Primo de Rivera seized power in a coup in 1923 to install a military dictatorship buttressed by King Alfonso XIII, the church, and the wealthy. But, with the onset of the Great Depression, the de Rivera regime came crashing down, and the elections of 1931 brought Republican progressives to office.

The new government's promotion of education and redistribution of land provoked a violent backlash from landowners and industrialists, and in the polarised mood anarchist and socialist groups swelled in number. A right-wing coalition regained power in 1933, determined to undo the Republic's achievements. As the Spanish Right adopted the language and strategies of fascism, the communists formed a Popular Front alliance with middle-class forces to win the 1936 election on a remarkably moderate platform. In response, right-wing military officers mutinied, promising to drown the Republic in blood.

In the urban centres, the parties of the Left took up arms, leaving the cities under the control of a radicalised working class. The generals dug in for a long campaign to retake Spain for its traditional owners.

The Spanish Civil War had begun.

In those years, the aches of the poor gave way to hope, a sense that everything was possible. Dani Caracola's textbooks documented that optimism.

The Republic founded an astonishing 27,000 schools in Barcelona between 1931 and 1939, facilities in which the curriculum was often shaped by anarchist and socialist theories about children and their rights.

As a teacher, Dani discussed the books hidden in his family's attic with professional admiration. 'It was all so very different from what we'd had under the dictatorship. They were in the vanguard of education. They cared a lot about how to educate people. They tried new methods. They innovated.'

For the Nationalists, however, both education and innovation were anathema. In the areas they occupied, schoolteachers were generally shot — as were trade unionists, lawyers, intellectuals, and others corrupted by modernity. Reading the wrong newspaper, mentioning Charles Darwin, failing to attend Mass: the slightest inkling of liberalism could get you killed. The repression only intensified when the Republicans were finally defeated, with Franco, the *caudillo* (or total leader) of the Nationalists, systematically rooting out the supporters — and the memory — of the revolution.

The Caracola family papers, the experimental textbooks of an idealistic curriculum, hinted at the new horizons opened up by the Republic. But they also documented the appalling misery endured on its behalf. For why had Dani's great-uncle died so terribly young?

By 1938, the war was so obviously being lost that the desperate Republicans began drafting teenagers — a policy immediately dubbed 'baby bottle conscription' (*quinta del biberón*). The ill-trained recruits who marched off to fight the Battle of the Ebro — essentially, the Republic's last stand, and the war's longest engagement — were little more than children.

The letters that Dani's great-uncle sent home weren't particularly political. 'Mainly, he was trying not to worry his family. He tells them that his shoes were broken, but he has found some leather and made some new ones. He says, *I am still alive; we're eating very well.* He tells them things like this.'

I saw Alan Warren grimace at Dani's summary. Afterwards, he explained to me that in fact the troops wouldn't have been eating well; that, by the time of the Ebro, the Republic's soldiers were chronically under-supplied, not only lacking food but also cruelly short of weapons and ammunition; that, in essence, the boy was lying to ease the anxieties of his mother and father. He was a child soldier conscripted to near certain death — and as he waited for battle, he did what he could to comfort a family he'd never see again.

In the wake of his discovery of the attic trove, Dani became curious not only about his family's story but also about the war more generally. He marked the seventy-fifth anniversary of his great-uncle's death with a blog post telling the story. And his interest grew from there. 'I started to get more involved and more interested. I never had read so much. I met many people. It was a feeling that I had to do something, it was urgent, there was no more excuses. It all relates to today. The same kind of people as then are still in government.'

His research left him more convinced than ever that disinterring the past mattered. 'For the first concert I did, I invited many friends. One of the first people I invited was a teacher. She was forty-five. She'd been teaching for many years, teaching children. And yet at the end of the concert, she came and said to me, "I didn't know anything about this — anything!" That's typical in Spain.'

I'd come here to recover what the Spanish Republic had signified to Paul. When Alan and I left the café, I was thinking of Dani, imagining him playing those old Republican songs to an audience hearing them for the first time. My task seemed suddenly daunting, since even in Spain, the revolution's meaning had been lost.

In 1937, Paul was holidaying in the Soviet Union when he received a plea to support an anti-fascist fundraiser in London's Royal Albert Hall. By then, much of the British intelligentsia was backing the Spanish Republic's struggle, so that the event was endorsed not only by the labour movement but also by writers, artists, and musicians: W.H. Auden, Cecil Day-Lewis, Stephen Spender, Rebecca West, H.G. Wells, Virginia Woolf, and many, many others.

Everyone recognised why Spain mattered. Franco's fascists relied on Hitler and Mussolini for supplies and modern equipment. While the Soviet Union aided (to some extent) the Republic, the neutrality of Western powers signified, for progressives, flagrant appeasement. After all, the Nazi support for the Nationalists represented more than mere ideological affinity: Spain possessed resources crucial for German re-armament, and the fight against the Republic allowed Hitler to perfect new weapons and new tactics. The war was thus an obvious precursor to something much worse.

For that reason, it also offered a last chance to halt fascism's advance. Much to the surprise of the Spanish generals, popular resistance had pushed back the coup in Barcelona and Madrid, forcing the Nationalist armies to regroup in the provinces. And when Dolores Ibárruri, the Republic's famous 'La Pasionaria' ('the Passionflower'), shouted, 'No pasarán!' ('They shall not pass!'), she was understood as urging a stand against fascism not just on behalf of the Spanish but also for everyone threatened by Hitler and Mussolini and all the imitative fascist movements across Europe.

The most dramatic response came in the shape of the International Brigades. In 1936, the Comintern, the Moscow-based leadership of the communist movement, proposed an anti-fascist volunteer army. Eventually, more than 40,000 people enlisted in the Brigades: soldiers drawn from some fifty nations, in the most diverse army in history. The vast majority were ordinary workers — usually, but not always, communists.

For progressives, the Spanish Civil War represented almost a generational test: a chance to fight not for the 'old lie' of 1914 but for democracy, freedom, and fraternity. As the Irish poet Louis MacNeice explained, Spain was where 'our blunt ideals would find their whetstone'.

That was Paul's sense, too. His discovery of the working class rekindled his optimism after his illusions in respectable Britain had been shattered. But Spain, where revolution and reaction contested openly, raised the stakes higher. In Spain, the battle had been joined; in Spain, Europe's fate would be settled.

Here was a cause worthy of Paul's mighty talents.

For the Albert Hall rally, he had at first intended to record in a Moscow studio and broadcast the message to London via radio. But Nazi Germany threatened to jam the transmission, while the Albert Hall management expressed a disinclination to receive communications from Red Russia. That joint opposition — so redolent of the tacit alliance between fascism and liberal democracy — infuriated him. He made the recording anyway, conscious of the huge audience the airwaves could reach — and then caught a special flight back to England. 'Nothing,' he said later, 'was going to stop me from sending or giving my message to the British public on the subject of Spain.'

That evening, the stage was studded with celebrities. For the British artist William Townsend, sitting in the audience, there was no question as to who left the biggest impression. Robeson, he said, 'was the great man of the evening ... his personality eclipsed all others as his speech overwhelmed theirs'.

By then, Paul's formal study of oratory had been honed by years of theatrical and concert stages. When he spoke, people listened. 'Fascism,' he told the massive crowd, 'fights to destroy the culture which society has created; created through pain and suffering, through desperate toil, but with unconquerable will and lofty vision.'

The argument possessed particular force because of the man making it. Paul's people knew about desperate toil, yes, and they knew about pain and suffering. If anyone had the right to scoff at the civilising pretensions of European culture, it was the son of a slave, a man denied basic rights in the most advanced of democracies. Yet here was Paul urging a defence of those achievements, not so much for what they were but for what they might become.

'Every artist, every scientist, every writer must decide now where he stands. He has no alternative. There is no standing above the conflict on Olympian heights. There are no impartial observers ... The battlefront is everywhere.'

It was another of the moments that Paul produced so regularly, an occasion that the men and women in attendance remembered for the rest of their lives. His speech, delivered with characteristic sincerity, embodied what they took to be at stake in Spain: all that was good and decent and honest pitched against all that was barbaric and cruel and backward.

The applause went on and on and on.

From then, Spain obsessed Paul. He remained as popular as ever as a singer and an actor, but he regularly interrupted his commercial tours to lend his talents and reputation to meetings and rallies and benefit concerts. He sang at the Third Spanish Concert at the Scala Theatre and at another event on behalf of the International Brigades; he delivered a radio broadcast appealing to his audience to support the Republic.

Most memorably, he gave the climactic address at a second monster Albert Hall meeting, a gathering so huge that attendees spilled out of the venue and overflowed into the Hammersmith Town Hall. The attendance showed how much Spain had come to mean to ordinary people as well as to sections of the Labour leadership, for even though British citizens were supposedly banned from intervening in Spanish affairs, Clem Attlee, the opposition leader, appeared on the stage.

'I have been criticised for going to Spain,' Attlee said, 'but I care nothing for the criticism of the other side. No one need be ashamed for standing for those ideals of freedom, democracy and justice for which our forefathers fought.'

When Paul stood at the podium, he sang the slave songs for which he was known, and the crowd's sense of the impoverished Spanish people shaking off their yoke gave the old words about liberation a new relevance.

He concluded his performance with 'Ol' Man River', already his signature tune. But, for the first time, he sang his amended lyrics. The version from *Show Boat* — the rendition with which the audience was familiar — began like this.

> *There's an ol' man called de Mississippi*
> *Dat's de ol man dat I'd like to be*
> *What does he care if de world's got troubles?*
> *What does he care if de land ain't free?*

At the Spanish rally, Paul changed the second line to 'I don't like to be'. He *wouldn't* like to be indifferent to the world's troubles, he announced — and everyone grasped that the tiny alteration meant a condemnation of the British government and its policy of neutrality.

The next lyrical change — '*I must keep fightin'* / *until I'm dying*' — brought the house down.

By the end of 1937, Paul was indelibly associated with the Spanish cause. He was speaking wherever he was asked. He was raising money; he was giving quotes to the press. Yet it wasn't enough.

He must, he decided, go to Spain himself.

Alan walked me down to the Majestic Hotel, where the Robesons stayed their first night in Barcelona. As we crossed the Plaça de Catalunya, he gestured at one of the buildings. 'The Communist Party headquarters.'

In 1936, the Hotel Colón had stood on that spot, draped with huge red banners and giant pictures of Lenin and Stalin. Patriarchal Spain traditionally excluded women from public life, but in the early stages of the uprising many had enlisted in the anti-fascist militias. On the roof of the hotel, a German photographer had snapped one of the most famous images of the war: seventeen-year-old militia member Marina Ginestà with a rifle on her shoulder. The little smile with which she stared back at him captured the confidence of those days, the sense of endless possibilities unfolding.

The building there now housed an Apple store. You couldn't see, I mused as we walked on, anything of what this streetscape had once meant.

The fountains had been dry during the war, I knew, but other than that the square had looked very similar: the same sculptures and buildings and open spaces. Thousands had rallied in the Plaça de Catalunya during the anti-austerity protests of 2011, but the monumental architecture and the throng of tourists spoke more of stability than of transformation.

When Paul had raised the trip to Spain, Essie hadn't liked the idea one bit. Their differing attitudes exemplified their contrasting personalities: Paul increasingly sympathetic to radical ideas; Essie still wedded to respectability. 'I am essentially a practical person,' she wrote later, 'and I thought: Paul is doing some very good work for Spain, here in England ... Why need he go into the war area, into danger, perhaps risk his life, his voice?'

Yet, characteristically, once she realised Paul was determined, Essie threw herself into making the visit a success.

They arrived in Barcelona on 23 January 1938, accompanied by the journalist and novelist Charlotte Haldane. Haldane had been working with the International Brigades, and the movement in Britain had assigned her to the Robesons as a guide and translator. She'd brought with her thousands of cigarettes and a huge quantity of chocolate to give to British volunteers: she knew, far better than her charges, the scarcity prevailing in Spain.

Alan and I found the Majestic a few blocks further down the Passeig de Gràcia, another of the city's grand avenues. The building loomed over the corner, a hulking seven stories of arches and columns and balconies. The Republicans had requisitioned the hotel and used it to house foreign journalists. Ernest Hemingway had stayed in the Majestic with his lover, the journalist Martha Gellhorn, who was reporting from Spain for *Collier's Weekly*. Gellhorn later remembered the scarcity of soap and how the proprietors refitted the beds each day with filthy (though neatly ironed) sheets.

Alvah Bessie, the American scriptwriter eventually imprisoned as one of the Hollywood Ten, had sat through air raids in the Majestic's huge dining room, expecting at any minute the glass dome above him to come crashing down on his head. But he'd also returned to Spain in the late 1960s and been shocked at the renovations to the hotel. The façade was the same, he'd written sadly, but inside the building was almost unrecognisable.

We found the interior was just as Bessie described: all gold and cream, the fittings an obvious and ugly supplement to the old building's grandeur.

Alan stared, somewhat doubtfully, about the lobby. 'I wonder if they have any information about its history.'

He approached the front desk for a long dialogue with the smartly dressed woman on duty. They spoke in Catalan, of course, but even so I could tell she was baffled by the inquiry. The leaflet that she eventually produced explained a great deal about the spa treatments on offer. But it contained almost no references to the past.

Were we anywhere else, the connection with Hemingway would have been ostentatiously commemorated. But, as Alan said, this was Spain, where, under Franco, the Nobel Prize–winning novelist had been known primarily as a sympathiser with the hated Reds.

When Paul had come to the Majestic, he caused a sensation. Immediately recognisable, he was besieged by reporters and well-wishers. Why had he come? What were his plans? What did he hope to achieve?

He explained as best he could to the crowds, reiterating his conviction about the global significance of Spain's fate and the importance of international solidarity in preventing a fascist victory.

As soon as he finished speaking, the Robesons were rushed on a tour of the sites bombed the morning they'd arrived. They saw the empty shells of apartments, ruined schools, and damaged hospitals: the everyday facilities of ordinary people reduced to bricks and rubble. In the evening, they were warned to sleep with their clothes packed, ready to evacuate the building if the planes returned in the night.

I had seen enough. Alan and I left the Majestic and walked back to his car.

'This will you give some idea,' he said as he started up the engine.

We drove for ten minutes or so on the Carrer de Padilla, along a route that began to incline sharply as we made our way up to the Turó de la Rovira, a hilltop looking down on the city.

In the hard years after the war, squatters had made homes on the mountain. When we left the car and walked, we passed remnants of the rude dwellings pulled together by the city's poor and desperate — a shantytown high above Barcelona.

But Alan wanted to show me a different archaeology: the entrenchments built during the 1930s, back when the Turó had been central to Barcelona's air defences.

From March 1937 until the fascist victory, Barcelona was bombed more than two hundred times, by Italian planes and, to a lesser extent, by the German Condor Legion. The aerial attacks on Republican towns shocked the world, not just because of the numbers they killed but also because of the manner in which they rained death on the innocent.

The Great War had already revealed how industrialisation had changed violence, with advances in weaponry stripping any lingering romance from armed conflict. But air raids on Spanish civilians still constituted a qualitative escalation. Hence Picasso's *Guernica* depicted a Nazi bombing through a wrenching visual dislocation, the artist using his canvas to show how, in the era of modern barbarism, nothing could appear the same.

The slaughter in Guernica, like the devastation of Barcelona, relied upon the most advanced technology. Fascist violence didn't originate from backwardness; on the contrary, modern wonders such as the aeroplane could co-exist with — and even facilitate — inhuman cruelty.

The political implications were obvious. You might, perhaps, attribute a lynching in Mississippi to the poverty and ignorance of the locals, but you couldn't offer a similar explanation for the pilots trialling new weaponry on the bodies of Spanish children.

At the very highest point of the hill, Alan showed me several circular concrete slabs, bounded by waist-high defensive walls. In the middle of each was a smaller circle of earth where a heavy weapon had once rested.

Harlem poet Langston Hughes had been in Barcelona, reporting on the war for *The Afro American*. He arrived a few months before the Robesons, and he, too, witnessed fascist air raids. 'The anti-aircraft guns bark into space,' he'd written in 1937. 'The searchlights make wounds / On the night's dark face.'

Standing on the very place where the guns Hughes had heard once barked, I thought over those lines. His racialised image of the Barcelona evening — 'the night's dark face' — was not accidental. From the very beginning of the war, African-American newspapers had editorialised in favour of the Republic. Religious and other organisations in Harlem lent their names to protests and rallies for Spain; musicians of the calibre of Fats Waller, Count Basie, and Cab Calloway played benefits for Spanish relief. Fascist Italy's assault on Ethiopia — an attack by a white European nation on an independent African monarchy — had generated outrage throughout the black world. Mussolini's support for Franco made the Spanish struggle seem a continuation of the same fight. That's why Hughes was there — and that's why Paul had come, too.

'Have you seen enough?'

I nodded.

'Come on, then. We have a long way to go.'

The next day, we drove from Barcelona to the resort town of Benicàssim, following, more or less, the route taken by the Robesons.

Before the war, Benicàssim had been a playground for the privileged. Along the edges of the beach, wealthy Spanish clans had built themselves modern French-style holiday villas. With the coming of revolution, Benicàssim became a hospital base for the International Brigades.

The Robesons had been given every assistance on their journey by a Republican government who knew the publicity value of their presence. They were provided with a huge Buick, driven by a uniformed chauffeur called Pepe, who'd recently escaped from a Moroccan prison. The officer guiding them, a certain Fernando Castillo, had five brothers in the fighting. The war felt very close.

The Robesons' progress into Benicàssim — 'driving past orange and tangerine groves with trees whose leaves are a rich shining green color', wrote Essie, '[and] then palms, red earth and gleaming white villas on the sea front' — slowed as the roads became clogged with wounded troops, each individual a testament to the varied ways that modern weapons could cripple and maim. The Brigades, poorly trained, ill-equipped, and generally sent to the most dangerous fronts, suffered appalling casualties. Something like a quarter of the volunteers died; many, many more were injured.

Remarkably, when the car came to a standstill, the first person to greet the Robesons was an African-American volunteer. He gaped at Paul with utter astonishment.

Paul and Essie found themselves in the midst of men from England, Canada, and the United States. They all knew who Paul was — one Canadian even boasted of hearing Robeson sing in Toronto's Massey

Hall. Paul was soon swapping anecdotes and jokes, distributing cigarettes, and listening to the soldiers' stories.

But the black volunteers — 'Negro soldiers from Chicago and other cities', as Essie put it — moved Paul the most.

About eighty African-Americans fought Spain. By opposing fascism, they saw themselves as contributing to Ethiopia's cause. But they were also, they thought, fighting for racial justice in the United States. 'Fascists is Jim Crow peoples, honey,' wrote Langston Hughes in 'Dear Folks at Home', 'And here we shoot 'em down.'

The possibility of striking back, of shooting down the murderous racists to whom you had to nod and smile in America, likely felt a kind of liberation in and of itself — especially since black men within Brigades recruited from all over the world experienced an interracial solidarity they'd rarely encountered before.

'I felt like a human being, like a man,' remembered the volunteer Crawford Morgan. 'I was treated like all the rest of the people were treated, and when you have been in the world for quite a long time and have been treated worse than people treat their dogs, it is quite a nice feeling.'

Hemingway was already a celebrity when he came to Spain. But on one occasion, he made a joke out of his temporary poverty using, as he put it, 'the wrong word for negro'. In the United States, Hemingway's racially insensitive quip would have generally got a laugh from white listeners. In Spain, an American volunteer responded by giving Hemingway what the writer ruefully described as 'a package ... in the teeth'.

We pulled into Benicàssim in the early afternoon. The tangerine groves were still growing along the roadside; the beach was still speckled with both villas and palms. The town, though, had grown substantially, hosting a population of 20,000 rather than the 1,200 who'd lived there during the war. It was once again a tourist resort, catering to overseas travellers through events such as the Festival Internacional de Benicàssim, its annual music festival.

A tiled walkway ran along the water, and the neatly trimmed lawns by the palm trees lent the place an air of almost Californian prosperity. The sand was bleached by the light; the sky was a perfect blue, faintly brushed by white cloud.

'Here for a little we pause,' wrote the English novelist Sylvia Townsend Warner, in the poem she composed in the town during the war. We walked along the strand that she'd described, where once she'd watched the wounded ('the risen-from-the-dead') hobbling along in their bleached pyjamas and rope-soled sandals.

Alan had arranged for us to meet the local historian Guillem Casañ, a short man in his early fifties, whose completely shaven head might have seemed intimidating were he not so immediately and evidently generous.

Guillem's family lived in Benicàssim. But, like Dani Caracola, Guillem had learned next to nothing about the war. 'I was born in 1961, and my generation, we were not much informed. In school, the education was very superficial. In the books, the Franco regime and its supporters were heroes; the others were criminals. In the Seventies and the Eighties, when I started asking about it, the older generation were not happy to talk.'

Studying English literature at university, he'd stumbled on Warner's poem 'Benicasim' (the misspelling is in the original). He'd read her description of the villas 'in a row like perched macaws' — and then the translator's notes explaining that the English soldiers had stayed in 'Villa Ralph Fox', named after the British novelist killed in the Battle of Lopera. His curiosity stirred, Guillem had begun to research the Brigade's stay in the town.

He walked us down to the Via Verda path, a charming little track that seemed almost purpose-built for tourists. You could hire a bike; you could ride from Benicàssim to nearby Oropesa, a pleasant five-kilometre journey along the scenic coast.

Guillem pointed down the path. 'This was the train line. This was how they brought the wounded in.'

Before our eyes, the past slowly re-emerged. The tracks had been uprooted and replaced with asphalt, but the gentle curve of the Via Verda route was exactly that of a railway. Nearby, the outlines of a vanished station were visible, the shape of the platform unmistakable when you'd been alerted to it.

'They came in convoys. And as the war went on, the convoys became bigger.'

We were just behind the five-storey Hotel Voramar, a yellow building looming over the beach. The hotel — renamed General Miaja by the Republicans — had been the main hospital of the International Brigades, the centre of a massive medical complex extending throughout the town. Paul had sung here, touring the wards and chatting with the staff and the patients.

Guillem gestured at a driveway, disappearing into what seemed like the hotel's garage. 'That was —' He frowned. 'I don't know how to say in English ... where they first brought the injured.'

'The triage centre,' said Alan.

'Yes, triage. The injured came here first and they were assessed. In the evenings, this was the Henri Barbusse theatre. For performances and so on.'

The duality epitomised the Brigades: the men had volunteered to face brutal violence, but they were motivated by a distinctly high-brow idealism. In the morning, they trolleyed in casualties from the Battle of Teruel. Then, the blood mopped away, those still able to walk applauded amateur theatre in a tricked-out garage named after a great French novelist.

Paul performed again and again in Benicàssim: to the healthy men seeking recreation; to the wounded, supported by crutches and wheelchairs; to the critically injured, propping themselves up as best they could in their beds. He couldn't have helped but contrast these performances to his concerts for London high society. Here, he sang unaccompanied, usually without even a proper stage, and sometimes in the open air. But in Benicàssim, even more than in Wales, Paul's songs meant something other than a momentary diversion.

And it wasn't merely the volunteers who Paul affected.

In the evening, we met Guillem's father, Domingo. He was very old, his fierce moustache almost completely grey. He sat, upright and dignified, next to his wife in the garden of the Casañ family hotel, his cane balanced across his knees.

Guillem watched his father carefully (he'd told us he was worried about the old man's memory), translating his words and sometimes adding a gloss. 'My father says, back then he was living in his grandmother's house.'

In 1938, Domingo was about ten. He lived a few kilometres from the beach. In the evenings, the soldiers sufficiently recovered from their wounds to walk would make their way into town. 'In the morning, the unmarried girls would do their housework; in the evening, they would meet in front of their houses and knit. The wounded Internationals would make friends with them.'

Domingo's grandmother's house was one of the places where young men shadowed by death would congregate to talk with women, who, in the aftermath of battle, seemed unbearably attractive. A relative owned a piano; some of the Internationals liked to play it. As they flirted with the local girls, the men noticed Domingo: a boy sitting reading by the gate. An officer from the Brigade struck up a conversation.

We have a big library down at the Club Azaña, he said. Perhaps you would like to borrow some of the books?

The men of the International Brigades were some of the most literary soldiers in history. It wasn't surprising that they'd compiled an impressive library, nor that their array of texts enraptured a bookish Spanish boy in an isolated seaside town, so much so that Domingo began visiting them regularly.

One evening, Domingo came down to the villa and found it set up for an event, with chairs laid out so that the wounded men could sit. He was the only child present — the kindly soldiers urged him up the front. And then, he told us, a tall black man appeared and began to sing.

'It was,' said Guillem, somewhat superfluously but with an air of great drama, 'Paul Robeson.'

Alan and I looked at each other. He'd become as enthusiastic about tracking Paul's Spanish travels as I was.

'Did he remember what songs Robeson sang? Can he recall what he said?'

Guillem consulted the old man.

'He says he does not know. Most of the songs were in English. But the music seemed to him to be very … what is the word? Profound? Very profound, he says.'

I wasn't sure whether 'profound' referred to Paul's low notes (listeners often described the almost physical sensation produced by his voice) or whether Domingo was describing the sublimity of the experience. Either meaning seemed fitting.

'He says that when the man started singing, it was sunlight, and when he finished, it was dark.'

Domingo nodded vehemently and spoke again, gesturing with his hands to indicate the passage of the sun.

'Yes, he says, from sunlight until dark.'

In Essie's Spanish diary, she described the passion Paul's Benicàssim performances stirred, how the soldiers crowded him with wild enthusiasm. The consequences for Domingo Casañ were equally significant.

Warner's poem culminated in a meditation on the fragility of the oasis constructed here in a Spain wracked by war. '[N]arrow is this place,' she wrote, 'narrow is this space / of garlanded sun and leisure and colour, of return / to life and release from living.'

And so it had proved.

Benicàssim fell to the fascists in 1939. The institutions created by the Republicans were systematically demolished, the halls of culture and the hospitals returned to the rich, and the villas became holiday homes once more. Republican supporters were imprisoned or shot.

The building where Domingo heard Paul was known at the time as the Club Azaña, after the last president of the Republic, Manuel Azaña. Now, though, it traded as Villa del Mar, a rechristening typical for its conscious depoliticisation.

The sea was eternal; the republic was transitory, a historical anomaly best forgotten.

Domingo survived the war and the repression that followed, and then, in due course, he established his own bookshop. Did his experiences in 1938 — his delight in the Republican library — motivate his career?

Guillem considered. 'He liked reading already. But, yes, that made an impression on him. I think so. Definitely.'

He explained more. While Domingo's mother came from a Republican family, his father was a Rightist, briefly imprisoned by the Republicans. Domingo himself was not particularly left-wing. But under Francoist censorship, bookselling was a fraught occupation, especially since the shop catered to a new generation, increasingly resentful of the dictatorship's restrictions about politics, sex, and religion.

'You understand?' Guillem asked. 'My father sold forbidden books. Books that were published in Argentina — political books. First floor was general books. Second floor was where the other books were, the books he wasn't allowed to sell. The customer might ask for a forbidden book. If my father didn't know the person, he would say, "I don't have it." If he knew the person, he would sell it. At the time, political parties were banned and meetings were banned. He hosted some cultural meetings. But, at them, people would somehow end up talking about politics. You begin by talking about literature; at the end you were talking about politics.'

Domingo had come to the authorities' attention for selling, of all things, a book of poetry. 'By Pablo Neruda. The Chilean writer. You know him?' Guillem asked.

I nodded.

'Well, my father says he had put Neruda's book on the first floor by mistake and someone denounced him. He says the regime probably knew about his bookshop, but once he was denounced, they had to do something. So he had to pay a big fine.'

Domingo beamed at me, clearly enjoying both the attention and the recollection.

It wasn't a heroic story, perhaps. There were others who'd resisted the dictatorship in more dramatic ways and paid a dearer price for their actions. But as we drank beer and ate cakes and talked into the night, the anecdote stayed with me, growing in power.

The men of the International Brigades possessed a burning faith in ideas and the books that conveyed them. Something of their conviction — an ember of their passion — had passed to the child who'd heard Paul sing, sufficiently so that, after the volunteers had been dispersed, he'd stood up against the censors and their police.

Today, in a town changed almost beyond recognition, I could still feel a faint warmth from a fire lit so very long ago. I was surprised by how much it meant to me.

In the morning, Alan and I continued our journey, driving along the route the Robesons had taken.

In 1938, Charlotte Haldane had complained that after Barcelona, they passed 'the only ugly landscape I found in Spain … As the large Buick purred along the excellent roads, all around us the flat plain extended with a monotony reminiscent of the less attractive parts of Holland.'

I'd never been to Holland and, to me, the fields were unexpectedly Australian, the yellow emptiness you'd see on any excursion through country Victoria. Aileen Palmer, the young Australian who served as a nurse for the Brigades, said something similar, writing in her letters that certain views made her 'much more homesick than usual'.

We drove into Albacete, looking for the hotel where the Robesons had been housed: the 'so-called Grand Hotel', as Essie had sniffed.

From her scorn, I'd expected it to be modest, even cramped. But the building was massive and massively ornate, its façade a peculiar mix of architectural styles, culminating in the baroque turrets above its fifth floor. The exterior seemed largely unchanged but, as in Barcelona, extensive renovations meant the lobby presented the kind of bland comfort associated with any international hotel.

The Robesons had arrived, I knew, in the wake of an air raid. That was why we walked over to the Plaza Altozano, the park opposite that contained the underground shelter into which the occupants of the hotel had climbed whenever the bombers came.

The bunker had been preserved as a museum, one of the few memorials to the war in all of Albacete. The entrance was now a tourist bureau. But the woman staffing the little booth shook her head when Alan addressed her. 'She says that it's closed for renovation,' he translated for me.

A progressive local government had restored the old bunker as a 'Interpretive Centre of Peace', a diplomatic way of acknowledging the city's divided past without necessarily attributing any responsibility. But, by its nature, a museum based in a bomb shelter raised the question of who'd been bombing whom — and those questions remained uncomfortable even today.

When a right-wing administration came to power, the facility had been shut, ostensibly to be refurbished.

'It's politics,' Alan said. 'It's the same everywhere in Spain.'

I could see the steps leading deep underground. But the woman was adamant. No, it was closed. No, she did not know when it would open. No, we could not go in, not even for a brief look.

We drank some coffee and drove on to Tarazona de la Mancha, the Robesons' next destination.

It was a small town, where the houses were crowded together and the streets were narrow stone constructions, obviously laid before the age of the automobile. In the middle of the day, the alleys and lanes were silent and still. The traditional siesta was still observed here, uneroded by the imperatives of modern commerce increasingly felt in Barcelona and Madrid.

We slept, too, resting in the old-fashioned hostel where we'd booked rooms. A few hours later, we emerged and walked down to the Plaza Mayor, where the children kicked a football around the cobblestones and the ancient men sat and smoked outside the little bar grandiloquently entitled Gran Casino. It was all oddly familiar.

Alan had shown me a few minutes of black-and-white footage filmed in the town: the Brigaders marching, those smiling young men swinging their arms as they paraded. The plaza — a fountain inside a cobbled square, bounded by white buildings with distinctive brown balconies — remained largely the same. We walked past the houses where Brigaders had been billeted, the building the officers had commandeered, and the bullring outside which Paul had sung.

As we ate pork and drank red wine in one of the taverns, I felt closer to the Spain that Paul must have encountered than in anywhere else we'd stayed.

Tarazona had been the training camp for the Internationals. When the Buick arrived, many of the soldiers stationed there flatly refused to believe that Paul was among them. They were only kilometres from the enemy, and Paul Robeson was a Hollywood superstar: a man you encountered on the screen, not in a war zone. 'You don't get people like that every day of the week,' said the Brigader Tommy Adler, 'running into a war to see how things are going.'

By that time, the reality of the conflict had become clear, even to the most idealistic of the Internationals.

When the American volunteers had first arrived, they'd lacked sufficient ammunition to practise-fire their guns, most of which were ancient and unreliable. Bob Merriman, an economist from California, had been tasked with training them, largely because of his brief experience as a reserve officer at the University of Nevada.

The Abraham Lincoln Brigade had been sent into battle for the first time in the Jarama Valley and had been cut to pieces by the better-armed fascists. Again and again, the volunteers took casualties; again and again, they returned to the fight, overcoming, at least for a while, material weakness with political commitment.

Paul watched the Internationals parade and then listened as their commander addressed them. They were told they'd be heading into battle the next day — and they cheered in response.

The meeting was in the massive church in the plaza, a building expropriated (or 'secularised', as Charlotte Haldane put it) by the Republic. The morning after our dinner in the Plaza Mayor, Alan and I visited the church, arriving immediately after the service. There were a few elderly women praying quietly in the dimness, but other than that the huge space was empty.

There were, however, ghosts everywhere.

On one of the walls, Alan pointed to the faint lettering '*prensa*', a sign that had marked the location of the Brigades' press office.

'Saw lots of Negro comrades,' Essie wrote in her diary, 'From Oklahoma, Baltimore, St Louis.'

Even today, Tarazona was extraordinarily distant from America: not just geographically but also culturally and politically. Yet all those years ago, young African-American men had come here to fight for a principle, knowing that they'd quite probably die in the process.

For an instant, the faded word reached out to me through the distance separating their time from ours.

This had happened. It had really, truly happened.

'They shot the priest,' Alan whispered, as we moved to stand near the altar. 'The anarchists. In 1936, some anarchists came from outside the town and took him away.'

The anti-clericalism of the Left had led to atrocities throughout Spain, as well as pushing believers to support the Nationalists. But in a place such as Tarazona, you could understand what nurtured that hatred.

Even today, the place was evidently poor. Yet all around us in this vast church were spectacular icons and gilt-edged saints, a reminder of the tremendous wealth of the Catholic authorities, who exerted all of their influence to preserve the status quo.

It was here that Charlotte Haldane had addressed the men: perhaps two thousand of them. She assured them that their struggle mattered to people back home. She invoked the solidarity rallies, the mass meetings, the funds raised; she distributed the cigarettes and chocolate that she carried.

Then it was Paul's turn.

He, too, talked of the international significance of Spain, about what fascism meant for the oppressed everywhere. In another context, with a different speaker, the words might have sounded trite. But, again, Paul's gravitas came not merely from his oratorical power but also from who he was and what he represented.

In his memoirs, the black volunteer James Yates recalled travelling to Guadalajara in an old Russian truck alongside a Brigadier from Germany. In broken English and fractured Spanish, the other man explained that he'd come to fight fascism because his relatives were detained in a Nazi camp. Yates sympathised immediately — his own family in Mississippi, he said, were also imprisoned, in a sense: hemmed in by 'whites only' signs and hooded lynchers.

The German then produced a picture — an image of him shaking hands with Paul Robeson. Yates remembered the strange warmth he felt when the photo came out. In his mangled Spanish, he tried to explain to his new comrade how, to him, 'there was no other man or woman who represented freedom for mankind more than did Paul Robeson [...with] his endless struggle for the rights of the Black people'. But he wasn't sure if the German understood. '*Comprende?*' he said.

'*Si,*' said his companion. '*Si.*'

Paul Robeson, both men believed, epitomised everything for which they were struggling — and it was that widely shared perception that made his speech in Tarazona so moving.

Naturally, Paul sang, too. A German volunteer had been deputised to provide musical accompaniment on the only piano available, an instrument woefully out of tune. It didn't matter. Paul stood on the platform for hours, crooning until his throat was hoarse, as the soldiers yelled out their favourites. They called for all the tunes they knew, staples such as 'Water Boy', 'Ol' Man River', 'A Lonesome Road', and 'Song of the Fatherland' — as Essie put it, 'the men stomped and applauded each song, and continued to shout requests'.

In Wrexham in Wales, Paul had declared folk to be 'the truly great music of the world', pledging himself to learn new languages so as to communicate across cultures. The rough concert in Tarazona represented a stunning vindication of that perspective. He could make himself comprehensible to working men from scores of different nations; he could sing to them songs that expressed specific traditions, and thus, when aggregated, invoked the internationalism that the fight in Spain embodied.

The men understood that many of them would die in battle. During the performance, Haldane was watching the Brigade's commissar, Eric de Witt Parker, as he stood by the side of the stage. When Paul sang 'Sometimes I Feel Like a Motherless Child', with its mournful chorus, she realised Parker's face was 'the colour of beetroot with the effort to repress the rising tears'.

He would be killed soon afterward.

'I doubt if they really care who wins.'

That was Essie's comment in her diary about the reporters crowding around Paul at his final press conference before they left Spain.

The Robesons had continued on into Madrid, driving without lights to elude the fascist artillery shelling the road.

In Madrid, the enemy was, quite literally, at the gates. The Nationalist lines were so close that, during one of Paul's performances in the city, loudspeakers had been erected to carry his song so it might discomfort those in the fascist trenches.

'We hear artillery and machine-gun fire,' wrote Essie during their stay here, 'but, by now, like real Madrid people, we are used to it.'

They left Spain the way they came, first making their way back to Barcelona. It was there, when Paul again talked with journalists at the Majestic, that Essie voiced her bitterness about the press — an expression of how moved she'd been by their experiences.

At the beginning of their journey, Charlotte Haldane, who liked Essie tremendously, assessed her as considerably more conservative than her husband. But Spain changed Essie.

In Madrid, the Robesons had attended a performance of Cervantes' *Siege of Numantia*, a play in which the people of ancient Spain commit mass suicide rather than submit to Roman occupation. At the conclusion of the uncomfortably topical drama, the actors sang and danced a tribute to Paul until, eventually, he rose and serenaded them in return.

There, Essie had remarked on the peculiarity of enjoying sophisticated theatre in a place where annihilating bombs might fall at any time. Death was all around them: it was the likely fate of many of those they'd met, unless, somehow, the world took action. Hence her anger at the journalistic cynicism, the seeming indifference to what was happening to the people and the country. Essie was not militant by temperament, but after their journey she identified wholly with the Spanish cause.

As for Paul, he maintained for the rest of his life that Spain had fundamentally altered him.

For Paul, it was more evolution than metamorphosis. He'd been raised as an anti-racist even before his encounters with the labour movement convinced him of the possibility of racial unity. But everywhere in Spain, people told him of Oliver Law, the black volunteer promoted to battalion commander after the chaos and slaughter of the Jarama Valley. When the Abraham Lincoln Brigade attacked Mosquito Ridge during the Brunete offensive in July 1937, Law led his men from the front, leaping over the trenches to his death in a charge he must have known was suicidal.

Paul had been nursed on stories of black men fighting Confederates during the American Civil War. He'd lived in the neighbourhood through which the triumphant Hellfighters had marched after returning from France. This, though, was different. Law was the first-ever African-American officer to command white soldiers in battle, and he'd done so in the name of an international people's army.

'We came to wipe out the fascists,' Law had told a reporter shortly after his arrival in the country. 'Some of us must die doing that job. But we'll do it here in Spain, maybe stopping fascism in the United States too, without a great battle there.'

In a way, Law's was a story foreshadowed in the writings of the Harlem Renaissance. 'Like men we'll face the murderous, cowardly pack,' promised the poet Claude McKay in 1919. 'Pressed to the wall, dying, but fighting back!' Law had done precisely that, not as an act of individual self-sacrifice but as part of an enormous movement, encompassing people of all colours and nations.

For Paul, Spain opened up new horizons, both in politics and in art.

He'd already been supplementing commercial film and concert work with smaller, radical performances. In 1935, he played Toussaint Louverture, the great Haitian revolutionary, in a script written by the West Indian polymath C.L.R. James. In 1937, he starred in Unity Theatre's *Plant in the Sun*, a script about an interracial sit-down strike. But he left Barcelona desperate to make more art that was explicitly political. In particular, he wanted to tell Law's story, to bring to the screen, as he said, 'the heroic atmosphere I have breathed in Spain'.

That never happened. Nevertheless, back in London, Paul continued, in a way, to breath that Spanish air. Several of his intimates noted that he seemed almost a new man. The despondency resulting from the end of his affair with Yolande was gone, replaced by a consuming desire to defeat fascism.

'I often think Paul never had a personal life except when he went to sleep,' said Lawrence Brown, loyally accompanying Paul on a gruelling schedule of benefits and fundraisers. 'Paul couldn't say no to anyone who asked his help.'

But if the compulsion emerged from the hope Paul had witnessed, it also reflected its fragility — his awareness, almost as soon as he arrived back in England, that the Republicans were going to lose.

It was in Corbera d'Ebre that I understood what that meant.

Alan guided me to the town: the place in which the collapse of Paul's dream could be seen carved into brick and mortar.

There were two villages at Corbera d'Ebre, the older of them a bleak ruin perched above the functional buildings of the newer. We walked the higher reaches, amid the remnants of the devastation wrought by constant battle during the dying months of the war. Around us, the houses were skeletons, their brick walls crumbling, their wooden beams snapped and shredded. The church retained sufficient integrity that I could identify individual wounds gouged into the concrete, each a specific tale of violence. The chunk torn from the tower meant a shell screaming over the horizon; the patterned holes in the nearby wall signified the *rat-a-tat-tat* of incoming machine-gun fire.

'Just here,' Alan said, gesturing at a field fringed by olive trees. At one end stood a crumbling wall of stacked stones. 'That's where they were shot.'

The brief optimism engendered by the Republican successes at the end of 1937 had faded as the Nationalists' military superiority reasserted itself. On 22 February 1938, the fascists recaptured Teruel. A few weeks later, they launched an offensive in Aragon, their tanks, aircraft, and artillery a precursor to the blitzkrieg Hitler would unleash against Poland.

By March 1938, the fascists were advancing inexorably towards victory. Alvah Bessie, rushed to the front with the last group of recruits reinforcing the Lincolns, remembered the stony faces of the peasants he passed.

He knew what they were thinking: 'Franco is coming; Franco is coming.'

When he joined the Brigaders, he found them equally grim. 'They had week-old beards,' Bessie wrote. '[T]hey were filthy and lousy; they stank; their clothes were in rags; they had no rifles, no blankets, no ammunition, no mess kits, no pack sacks. They had nothing but the rags in which they were dressed and the filth in which they were covered.'

Exhausted, massively outnumbered, and completely outgunned, the Lincolns could do little but retreat and retreat, taking casualties all the time. After a firefight near the town of Gandesa, they sheltered in the higher ground, expecting at any moment to be slaughtered.

Bob Merriman, the Lincolns' highest-ranking officer, rallied his men for a desperate night-time escape from their encirclement. But Corbera had already fallen to the Nationals — and so, in the darkness, the Internationals stumbled right into a fascist camp.

Survivors said later that, amid the chaos and the terror, they'd heard the voices of the Nationalist sentries: shouts of '*Rojos! Rojos!*' ('Reds! Reds!') and then '*Manos arriba!*' ('Hands up!'). Some recalled shots being fired. The Brigaders scattered — and Bob Merriman, the Lincolns' great inspiration, disappeared into history.

There'd been much speculation, mostly inconclusive, in the subsequent years about his fate. Alan, though, thought he'd pieced together Merriman's last hours. It was a horrible story.

He told me that Nels Madsen, a Canadian International imprisoned at Corbera, remembered a group of Brigaders escorted into the town as captives. One of them looked like Merriman.

The fascists killed high-ranking prisoners — especially foreigners — as a matter of routine. 'Madsen says they were later shot,' Alan said. 'There are accounts from Nationalists, too, that mention a tall soldier wounded in the leg.' That, most likely, was Merriman.

Alan pointed to the tumbledown wall by the olives. 'One officer says the tall soldier started arguing with the firing squad to give the others a chance to escape. But of course none of them did.'

I shuddered. Unlike the shattered houses, the field carried no obvious scars from bullets or bombs. Nonetheless, the scenario felt terribly immediate in a place largely unchanged since 1938. I could imagine — almost see — the terrified, exhausted men dragged by their captors into the open to be shot.

'We know that Internationals are buried here — we have a witness who says he saw the graves being dug. But we can't get permission to excavate and find out for sure.'

It wasn't merely that the captured Lincolns lost: it was that they'd lost so totally and utterly, casually annihilated by the fascists and consigned to obscurity in a scrubby yellow field kilometres from anywhere. They'd been murdered and then, shortly afterward, the cause for which they'd given their lives had been shattered, with the disintegration of the Republic wiping out even the memory of their sacrifice.

We walked in silence back through the wrecked village.

That night, we ate pork and beans in the front bar of the Can Rius in the town of La Fatarella. Alan had friends there, local men. He was joking and sharing photos with them during the meal.

I was exhausted and didn't pay much attention to the conversation, which was, in any case, mostly in Catalan.

Suddenly, Alan nudged my shoulder. 'Come on. I think you'll want to see this.'

I looked up and saw that the others were already leaving. We got up, too, and followed them across the road, where a garage door attached to a nearby house was open.

Inside the little carport was an arsenal. Or, more exactly, a museum, a private collection of bombs, grenades, pistols, rifles, daggers, and all manner of other military accoutrements. The owner had constructed a little split-level platform to give himself more space, and on both platforms the walls were racked with ordinance.

'This is all material he's found on the battlefields,' Alan announced.

In July 1938, the Republic launched a last great offensive across the river Ebro, a final attempt to repel the fascists. The intensity of the Battle of the Ebro meant that for decades afterwards, locals complained their crops tasted of metal. Even now, the fields still disgorged rusty remnants. Helmets, pocket watches, badges, glasses, binoculars: all of the material, obvious and not, with which men made war on other men.

In that private collection in a La Fatarella garage, I could see exactly why the battle — and the conflict as a whole — ended the way it did. The largest of the bombs came almost to my waist. '*Italiano*,' said someone, and gave the casing an affectionate clout.

With support from Mussolini and Hitler, the Nationalists had more weapons, and the Nationalists had better weapons, and the Republic simply possessed no counter.

I couldn't help another shudder, both because the cache provided such a striking glimpse of the military superiority that had rained down on the Republicans and because we were clustered around a monstrous unexploded bomb that someone was casually thumping.

The next day, I glimpsed how such a collection might be amassed. We stopped the car at the edge of a scrubby olive field and then proceeded on foot to a crumbling construction of old stone, which served the local farmer as a storage shed.

I bent to fit inside the entrance and waited until my eyes adjusted to the filtered light.

Rubbish was strewn everywhere: straw and string and bits of plastic. But there were also bombs — lots and lots of them. Lafitte grenades — crude explosives used by both sides — spilled out of a mouldy cardboard box. I saw, scattered on the ground, bullet casings, mortar rounds, and a massive artillery shell — a thing maybe 30 centimetres long.

These weren't the polished trophies displayed in La Fatarella. They were tarnished and broken and losing their shape. Did that make them more or less likely to detonate? I didn't know, but I assumed the former.

Alan explained how the farmer used the hut to dump the wartime debris uncovered as he went about his daily routine. Every now and then, the government sent someone to dispose of everything the earth had gradually expelled.

Alan handed me a piece of metal casing, the outside of a grenade. 'A souvenir.'

I dropped it into my bag while he pushed the rubbish around with his boot, identifying bits and pieces of shrapnel and ammunition.

During his last visit, he said, there'd been far more to see. He'd been showing some travellers the shed and its contents when their dog loped through the door with a bone proudly in its mouth. They'd all laughed — and then they realised the animal was carrying part of a human arm.

We came upon a body, too, later that day, when we walked along the remnants of a Republican defensive position. The trenches over which the soldiers had battled had lost their shape and become less distinct over the passing decades, so that many were now little more than ditches in the clay. At the edge of one field, Alan pointed to the ground. The yellow-white bone fragments he indicated were the same colour as the rocks and tree roots beside them, and I would not have noticed them without his direction. The femur, though, was unmistakably human.

Someone had died here, almost certainly a Republican soldier. In all probability, the bulk of the body lay beneath the nearby embankment, from where disarticulated fragments had gradually washed into the field.

Alan gathered together the scraps of the dead soldier and built a small cairn of stones above them. It was precious little dignity, but it was better than none at all.

'In Spain,' wrote the poet Federico García Lorca, 'the dead are more alive than the dead of any other country in the world.'

Certainly, the bones of the Spanish Civil War spoke very loudly about the conflict and its aftermath. Madrid fell in March 1939, and the fascists declared victory shortly thereafter. In the years that followed, any association with the defeated cause became lethally dangerous. Attempts to recover a loved one's corpse from the fields in which the Nationalists had annihilated their enemies exposed a family to immediate risk.

Not surprisingly, many chose not to investigate the fate of their fathers and brothers and sons — and so thousands of bodies remained spread across the old battlegrounds.

By contrast, the commemoration of the fascist dead began at once.

I left Spain via Madrid, and while I was in that city, I made the long trip out to the Valle de los Caídos (the Valley of the Fallen), the grand memorial Franco started building in 1940, almost as soon as the guns fell silent.

My bus stopped first at the mountain village near the royal monastery of El Escorial, about an hour from Madrid. The huge complex dated from the sixteenth century. Both a Catholic retreat and a monument to the royal family, it combined two of Spain's traditional sources of power in overwhelming renaissance architecture.

The Valle de los Caídos was twenty minutes further on, deep in the Cuelgamuros Valley. We came to a sudden stop near the visitors' centre. Outside the bus loomed a large grey cross, its sheer enormity almost an act of aggression, designed to send visitors reeling in awe.

The other passengers and I walked down to where a vast granite plaza stretched out under the shadow of the mountains. The basilica was constructed around gigantic arches, each resembling an entrance through which, at any moment, some great hero might stride. The design glorified size and strength and power, rendering the merely human insubstantial by comparison. Even the Christ sculpted on the basilica's top was muscled like a boxer.

In Madrid, I'd spent hours tramping through the city streets, looking for traces of the war. The central Gran Via had once been known as 'Death Avenue' because of the Nationalist artillery attacks that rained down on the street. The Telefónica building there had been a particular target, and I found a plaque near the elevators commemorating the communication workers who'd given their lives to keep Madrid in contact with the rest of Europe. By the Parque de la Montaña, I looked at the stylised sculpture of soldiers acknowledging the Nationalist troops killed when revolutionaries stormed the (now demolished) Montana barracks. At the university, where bullet holes still pockmarked the medicine building, a monument repeated La Pasionaria's tribute to the International Brigade: 'You are history, you are legend.' But it was much, much smaller than Franco's Arco de la Victoria, which stretched across the road running into the city near the edge of the campus.

In Madrid, I couldn't discern any single narrative about a war that was barely acknowledged. The Valle de los Caídos, by contrast, was entirely unambiguous: it was an unabashed celebration of fascism.

That was why modern Spain didn't know what to do with it. Once the centre of great national celebrations, the Valle de los Caídos was now an embarrassment: too obviously totalitarian for assimilation into the democratic order. But any attempt to demolish or reform the place was equally problematic, since the basilica — with its thousands of dead — remained talismanic to many on the Right.

The consequences of the stalemate could be seen in the square, an expanse sufficient for an entire army to drill. There were weeds growing up through the cracks in the stone, and I took a certain satisfaction in their diminution of the architecture's power. Fascist aesthetics demanded precision, crisp lines and sharp demarcations — and here nature was slowly blurring those boundaries.

The place had fallen on hard times. But that didn't make it any less sinister. If the Valle de los Caídos was designed to commemorate, it was also a claim on the future, an effort by Franco to immortalise fascism. Paul spent much of his life fearing, with good reason, that Franco and his heirs would succeed, that the values expressed by this monument would triumph. That was, at least in part, why he pledged himself to a different social order.

But that came later.

I walked to the entrance. A sign demanded 'silence in this sacred place' while I lined up in the queue, where visitors waited to pass through a metal detector. It was only as the guard hoisted my satchel onto the conveyer belt that I realised I was still carrying the casing from the Lafitte grenade that Alan had given me. I didn't have time ,to react, but simply stood in horror while he scanned my bag. Valle de los Caídos was still revered by Spain's far Right, with elderly Francoists and young neofascists regularly making pilgrimages of veneration. Now I was about to be caught entering their holy site with the remnants of a Republican bomb.

But the satchel passed through the detector, and the bored guard waved me through. I was relieved, but also oddly disappointed. Part of me had imagined a dramatic confrontation in which I might have vented the anger I'd been harbouring since Corbera d'Ebre, through a public denunciation of Franco and his heirs.

Of course, I also knew that any such outburst at an underpaid guard performing his job would have been meaningless — and besides, I was temperamentally unsuited to such a confrontation. I composed myself, muttered my thanks, and proceeded inside.

The basilica extended hundreds of metres deep into the mountain stone. The gruelling labour necessary for that construction had been performed, at least in part, by former Republican soldiers working off the huge prison terms they received after the defeat. Some — no one seemed quite sure how many — of the slave labourers died in the process.

The iconography inside, stone angels with swords guarding the wars, was unapologetically militarist — a celebration of victory, not a commemoration of loss. As one plaque explained, it was a place 'caídos por dios y Espana' ('For those who fell for God and for Spain'). Alongside the bones of thousands of Nationalists, the basilica contained bodies excavated from Concud village in Teruel, where, after the fascist triumph, hundreds of men, women, and children were shot and thrown into a pit known as Los Pozos de Caudé. Years later, the government partially dug out the grave. Without consultation with the relatives, the remains were laid in the Valle de los Caídos, so that they rested alongside the marble tributes honouring their murderers.

The Valle de los Caídos explained a great deal, it seemed to me, about Paul's political affiliations with communism in the 1940s and 1950s.

It was easy, from our vantage, to imagine fascism a historical anomaly, an evil but ephemeral phenomenon crushed by democracy. But this mausoleum was completed in 1959. It was, in other words, an expression of a normalised dictatorship: the product of a fascist regime that had already survived two decades.

When Paul left Barcelona, it was with a sick dread at the looming defeat that with every day became more likely, a catastrophe that presaged a fascist order spreading inexorably throughout the world. That was why, during the Second World War, he devoted himself to the Allied cause, doing whatever he could to help the American government win what he considered an anti-fascist crusade. But the Cold War that began immediately afterwards revived the awful fears he'd felt in Spain.

In 1959, the year that the Valle de los Caídos opened, General Eisenhower had travelled to Madrid to celebrate Washington's new military alliance with Franco. Oliver Law and Bob Merriman and their comrades lay in unmarked and untended graves. They'd given their lives not only to defeat Spanish fascism but also to prevent a similar regime arising in America. Yet here were US generals raising their glasses to their Spanish counterparts while the *caudillo* — the assassin of the Republican hopes — looked on in approval.

I reached the centre of the complex, where the body of Franco rested, lain out like a medieval saint. When the dictator died in 1975, he was, as per his wishes, interred in the basilica, at a ceremony attended by the Chilean tyrant Pinochet, King Hussein of Jordan, and the US vice president Nelson Rockefeller. I stood by his tomb for a moment, thinking of the nameless bones we'd unearthed, and then I turned and walked into the mountain air.

PART THREE
REVELATIONS

7

YOU CANNOT IMAGINE WHAT THAT MEANS
Moscow, Russia

I arrived at the beautiful Art Nouveau building late one winter afternoon. The long flight had delivered me to Moscow in a state of scratchy-eyed exhaustion, and then I'd walked out of Domodedovo airport into a snowstorm, for which the warm fug of the plane had been no preparation.

At Mokhovaya Street, an elderly porter in frockcoat and top hat swung open the hotel door with tremendous ceremony, and yet somehow his deference still signalled a faint disapproval at the foolishly under-dressed foreigner. I registered, vaguely, the splendour of the lobby — the marble columns sculpted into marble youths; the thick carpet, intricately patterned in scarlet; the chandeliers and the mirrors. But all that really mattered to me was the heat.

I had booked into the famous Hotel National, even though a single night's lodging there substantially depleted my accommodation budget. But despite my exhaustion, I was much too wired to sleep and so, after dumping my bags in my room, I ventured back out into the storm.

This time, the doorman's slight elevation of his eyebrow was a response to a surfeit rather than a deficit of clothing, for I'd layered almost all the garments I'd brought in an unflattering bulge beneath my jacket. It scarcely helped. Outside in the street, the Russian winter clawed at me again, nipping at my fingers and toes.

Still, Red Square was only five hundred metres away, and I could see the turrets of the Kremlin, just across the road. Paul had stayed in the National many times, and Paul had walked the path I was now taking, stepping over to the symbolic heart of Soviet power.

The defeat in Spain made a broader war inevitable, as Paul had predicted. In 1939, with that conflict looming, he and Essie and Pauli sailed back to America, determined to spend the duration of the Second World War in their native land.

That year, he recorded 'Ballad for Americans'. Its lyrics celebrated the multitude of American ethnicities and faiths; they lauded 'old Abe Lincoln' as a man who 'hated oppression', and asserted that 'man in white skin can never be free while his black brother is in slavery'. The song presented the United States as an unfinished project, a democracy that should and could extend its foundational principles to those historically marginalised by power.

Over the next decade, Paul enjoyed the greatest acclaim of his career. In 1943, *Time* magazine dubbed him 'probably the most famous living Negro'. In 1944, when Paul turned forty-six, his birthday was marked with a huge celebration in New York. Twelve thousand people sought to attend; four thousand were turned away. The guests included Duke Ellington, Joe Louis, and Richard Wright, and almost every other African-American celebrity of note. Babe Ruth, the baseball legend, toasted Paul; so too did the African independence fighter Kwame Nkrumah, the singer Cab Calloway, and the variety host Ed Sullivan.

The breadth of affection might have seemed improbable, given Paul's increasingly public radicalism. But the war had created a massive new audience for his politics.

Paul had returned from the Spanish carnage a fervent anti-fascist, committed to an international Popular Front: a global movement uniting democrats and radicals against Hitler, Mussolini, and their allies. That was how he understood the Second World War (at least, after 1941). The fight against Hitlerism was, he said, a People's War, a new incarnation of the cause embraced by Oliver Law and his comrades in Spain. It would extend democracy at home, it would end colonialism abroad, and it would abolish racism everywhere.

Conservative America did not, perhaps, like such rhetoric. Certainly, mainstream politicians were more circumspect with their words and promises. But with the country struggling against both Germany and Japan, Paul's long opposition to fascism provided him with more political capital than men who'd either sympathised with or been indifferent to the dictators and their regimes. Paul's ideas were now aligned with the mainstream — or, more exactly, the mainstream was aligned with him.

Even his strident support for the Soviet Union became, for a time, an asset rather than a liability. For the moment, the USSR was a key wartime ally, with the Red Army keeping Hitler's troops occupied on the Eastern Front. As the United States channelled billions of dollars in aid to the Soviets, President Roosevelt explained to his countrymen: 'We are going to get along with [Stalin] and the Russian people — very well indeed.' Hollywood duly consulted with the government's Office of War Information in the production of a string of pro-Soviet movies, while *Life* magazine issued a special USSR edition (packaged with an avuncular cover portrait of Joe Stalin), in which readers learned that the Russians were 'one hell of a people', who 'look like Americans, dress like Americans and think like Americans'. Paul's passion for Soviet Russia suddenly seemed patriotic rather than subversive — so much so that President Roosevelt enlisted him to advertise US war bonds.

After ten minutes of slipping across cobbles gleaming with ice and moonlight, I reached Red Square. The cold felt somehow metallic, an assault on my extremities that began from the inside rather than the out. But I wiped the snow from my eyes and peered around. Lenin's tomb looked much as I expected, an ugly cider-coloured ziggurat squatting morosely next to the Kremlin's fortified walls. But I hadn't anticipated the wheezing merry-go-round flashing its lights in the parade ground where the Soviet army had once marched past Stalin and his generals — and I certainly wasn't prepared for the Cathedral of Vasily the Blessed.

Though I'd seen pictures, somehow I'd still imagined the basilica in Western terms, as a Russian variant of the dour Anglican churches to which I was accustomed. But the snow fell faster and heavier and the cacophony from the hurdy-gurdy reverberated and the preposterous towers seemed to jump out of the night sky in psychedelic green and blue and apricot.

That was my first experience of Moscow: the city as a kind of slow-onset hallucination.

Yes, I was exhausted and frozen and ready to drop. All the same, there was something in that moment, a perception that remained with me throughout my stay. In some ways, Moscow presented as merely another modern European capital, equipped with the usual array of historical, architectural, and cultural attractions. Yet the city's Russianness — a tradition defined, after all, as much against as with Western Europe — asserted itself unpredictably, confounding the expectations of the English-speaking visitor.

What had that meant for Westerners such as Paul, coming to the Soviet Union in the 1930s? What had it been like to simultaneously confront a radically different culture and a radically different social system? How, as an outsider, did you distinguish between the two? It would be easy to mistake the specifically Russian for the specifically communist. It would be easy, I realised, to go disastrously wrong.

'I hesitated to come. I listened to what everybody had to say, but I didn't think this would be any different for me from any other place. But — maybe you'll understand — I feel like a human being for the first time since I grew up. Here I am not a Negro but a human being.'

Paul's first outburst of enthusiasm for the Soviet Union occurred in the National, in a conversation with the film director Sergei Eisenstein, on whose invitation he and Essie and Marie Seton had voyaged to Moscow in 1934.

In the morning, when I was at least somewhat restored, I was better able to appreciate the National. The hotel had been built at the very beginning of the twentieth century to serve aristocrats, politicians, and other dignitaries, blending modernist and Renaissance elements in an architectural celebration of Russian opulence. Damaged by gunfire during the revolution and then expropriated by the Bolsheviks, the National had briefly provided accommodation for Lenin and Trotsky, before becoming home to the first Soviet government.

In the early 1930s, Stalin decided to encourage foreign visitors, through the state-run Intourist travel bureau. When the Robesons arrived, the National had just been re-opened as a luxury hotel. As honoured guests, they'd been provided with an extensive suite looking over Red Square, complete with a grand piano. Their bath was made of marble, an overawed Essie recorded, and a huge white bearskin rug stretched across their floor.

My room, the cheapest available, was significantly smaller: a serviceable but unspectacular billet, with no piano and no bearskin. Such was commerce, I told myself: you got what you paid for. But in the lobby, the corridors, and the dining hall, the extravagance in which Essie had luxuriated was still very much in evidence. All the lightshades were tassled and brocaded, all the marble was gilded, and the ornate chairs were so delicate and overstuffed that I found myself reluctant to ever sit.

On this, his first visit to Moscow, Paul was treated as an honoured guest — almost a head of state — by a regime conscious of the political importance of impressing him. This pattern would continue on all subsequent trips.

It would be easy, then, to see his enthusiasm for the Soviet Union as the drearily familiar tale of a gullible celebrity flattered by the attentions of a dictatorship. Yet that wasn't the whole story.

Yes, the Robesons were taken on the customary tour of factories, schools, and hospitals, and yes, they were assiduously duchessed by the Soviet elite. But if Paul was impressed, it was also because Moscow in

1934 was genuinely impressive.

He had arrived in the midst of the so-called 'Three Good Years', when the effects of industrialisation were becoming apparent, and the worst manifestations of the Terror were yet to come. By then Paul knew something of working-class life in Britain: he'd seen the bleak squalor of the Welsh mining towns; he understood intimately how millions of lives had been blighted by the Great Depression. He couldn't help but notice that Moscow, by contrast, was bounding forward, its economy apparently defying the worldwide slump.

From his window, he'd remarked to Essie on the scaffolding erected where the new underground metro system was being built.

On my first morning in Moscow, I went straight to Teatralnaya, the station whose construction Paul had witnessed. I let the escalators glide me under the ground and into a startlingly grand hallway, where the columns were lit with crystal lamps, and chandeliers hung from the ceiling.

The elegance reflected the sensibilities of the 1930s, yet the design remained futuristic rather than old-fashioned. The facility was intended as a palace of the people, an architectural anticipation of the world to come and an effusive statement about the value accorded to Soviet citizens and their daily commute.

The Moscow metro astounded me, far more so than the luxury in the National. The old stations were gorgeous, and, on every mundane journey I took in the city, I marvelled anew at the care lavished by those long-dead designers on a public utility, particularly when I contrasted the system with the general shoddiness of the privatised rail networks of the twenty-first century. The Moscow stations were spectacular now — and they must have been all the more so then, in a city dragging itself out of the starvation of the Russian Civil War.

That was why among young Muscovites, in particular, there was genuine enthusiasm in the 1930s for the Stalin regime and its grandiose plans. 'We were born to make fairytales come true,' proclaimed a popular song — and the belief in transformation, in the conscious remaking of the old order, lent credibility to the other claims Paul was hearing.

The leaders of the Soviet Union said they opposed racial prejudice. That didn't seem so extraordinary today — but in 1934, of course, discrimination was state policy throughout the United States, even as the Russians were lavishing hospitality on the Robesons, a pair of visitors who both happened to be black.

Besides, Paul quickly developed an intense friendship with Eisenstein, the great filmmaker and pioneering film theorist, who explained the Soviet attitudes further. The two men bonded partly over the movie about Haitian revolutionary Toussaint Louverture they planned to shoot, and partly over their ideas about national minorities and the relationship between different cultures.

Though Paul didn't know it, Eisenstein had already fallen from Stalin's favour (a situation that meant the Toussaint project would never be realised). But the director genuinely believed in what he saw as the USSR's efforts to overcome racial and national oppression. Paul accompanied him to the state-funded Jewish Theatre, where a major Yiddish production of *King Lear* was rehearsing. The comparison was irresistible: Paul had struggled mightily to secure the opportunity to play Othello, the one Shakespearean role marked as non-white; in Moscow, Lear could be a Yiddish-speaking Jew.

One day on their trip, he was walking with Essie and Marie through the snow in Pushkin Square when they encountered a group of children. A girl spied Paul — so much bigger and darker than anyone else nearby — coming towards her, and she screamed. But it was a cry of delight, not of terror. She ran over and hugged Paul's knees. When he picked her up, her playmates came running, too, until Paul was almost buried beneath a mound of children, all squirming to touch this fascinating stranger.

The encounter was, in a sense, utterly trivial. But it stunned Paul. In Moscow, white children could greet a dark-skinned stranger with unfeigned happiness. He put the girl down and said goodbye in Russian, and then he turned to the women. 'They have never been told to fear black men,' he said, with something like wonder.

Paul had long known that racism could be fought — William had taught him that. But in Soviet Russia, he thought he'd found practical evidence that it could be defeated. Suddenly, a society without discrimination by colour was not a mere fantasy; it was, he concluded, the everyday experience in a communist city.

That conviction sustained him for the rest of his political life. And in the 1940s, in particular, he was in a position to put his principles into action. Accordingly, throughout the war, he used his new stature as a weapon against Jim Crow, in interventions prefiguring some of the more famous protests of the civil-rights era.

Early in one concert in Kansas City, Missouri, in 1942, Paul stopped performing and addressed the crowd. He'd suddenly realised, he told them, that his listeners had been allocated segregated seats, contrary to the explicit promises made to him.

He would continue with the show, he said, because he didn't want to disappoint his African-American fans. But he would be singing under protest.

The apology Paul received from the booking agent illustrated his newfound political currency, with a local African-American editor approvingly declaring that his militant stance had 'spurred the Negro citizens here to wage a campaign against discrimination in our tax-supported buildings'.

Again and again, Paul insisted that the destruction of fascism meant freedom for the people of India and the Caribbean; that after the war, Africa would not return to colonial subservience. America needed to accept, he declared, that the downfall of Hitler would herald massive social change, with the oppressed everywhere demanding their liberation.

He believed that so fervently because he thought he'd seen how liberation might look. That was the import of his discussion with Eisenstein, that day in the National.

'Before I came, I could hardly believe that such a thing could be,' Paul had said. 'Here, for the first time in my life, I walk in full human dignity. You cannot imagine what that means to me, as a Negro.'

'Some people call me the Russian Oprah Winfrey,' Yelena Khanga told me in one of our early telephone conversations.

The implications of that hadn't really sunk in until, on my second day in Moscow, I headed down to meet her at an expensive inner-city restaurant.

Yelena was a Russian-born journalist and talkshow host. Slim and chic in elegant furs, she possessed the effortless charm of someone accustomed to public life. In the late 1990s, she'd hosted a television program on which sex had been discussed frankly and honestly. Her show broke taboos in a still-puritanical society, famously providing the first opportunity for gay Russians to talk about their lives on television.

Clearly, people remembered this — for, at the LavkaLavka restaurant, the proprietor greeted her with tremendous deference, making a show of fussily escorting us to our seats. Then, while we were studying the menu, a middle-aged man at the next table turned and addressed her. I couldn't understand the Russian, but I sensed that he spoke with great formality, since at the end of the exchange he gave a bow before returning to his meal.

'Are you famous?' I asked her.

She considered the question, which I'd intended half as a joke.

'Yes. Yes, I am.'

Russia was a macho and very white society, and she was a black woman. That was, in fact, why I'd wanted to meet. Yelena was descended from an African-American man who'd chosen to live in communist Russia: a member of the small but influential community of black expats whose decisions influenced Paul greatly.

On his first trip to Moscow, Paul had been greeted by a surprising number of familiar faces. Essie's brothers, Frank and John Goode, were both making good money in Russia: John, driving busses in Moscow;

Frank, performing in touring circuses. Alongside them, Paul found William Patterson, his friend from Harlem. In the years since then, Patterson had become more and more radical, eventually becoming a Communist Party stalwart and moving to the USSR. Like the Goodes, Patterson assured Paul of Russia's freedom from colour prejudice.

At the time, Yelena's grandfather, a man called Oliver Golden, had agreed.

Later in the 1930s, Paul had been performing in the Soviet Union when a baby in the audience began to cry. He walked over and took the infant from its mother. Cradling it in his huge arms, he sang in English, 'Sleep, baby, sleep.'

That child was Lily Golden, Yelena's mother, who thereafter was known as 'baby'. She passed the nickname on to her daughter. 'People still call me "baby",' Yelena said, 'and that came from Paul Robeson.'

A waitress arrived, and Yelena ordered us sparkling water and vodka.

Her grandfather, she explained, was born in Mississippi. Like Paul, Oliver Golden was the son of a slave. He was radicalised after realising that the only white men who would shake hands with him as an equal were communists, and had then travelled to Uzbekistan with a group of 'Negro specialists'. Theirs was supposed to be a temporary visit, a brief trip to provide technical expertise for the Soviet cotton industry, but for Oliver it became a permanent relocation.

Bertha, Yelena's grandmother, was a Polish Jew. She and Oliver had fallen in love in Harlem. A relationship between a black man and a white woman was difficult enough even in bohemian New York. But in the South, the only place a cotton specialist might expect work, a mixed-race baby could get Oliver lynched. How could they return to America?

Plus, there was Lily to think about. 'They were scared that as a black female she wouldn't be able to get an education in the United States,' Yelena said. 'Which was true. Instead, my mother went to a good high school, and then the Moscow State University. She could sing, she became the tennis champion of Uzbekistan: she had opportunities she'd never have been given in the United States.'

I nodded.

I'd found a 1953 article in which Paul explained his ongoing faith in the Soviet Union with an anecdote about the time he and Essie had spent with 'an old friend of mine, Mr Golden' in 1937. He discussed returning in 1949 to see Lily 'now grown and in the university ... a proud Soviet citizen'.

The Golden story exemplified for Paul the promise of the USSR: a triumphant narrative of social advancement in a single mixed-race family.

Of course, the story wasn't true. But it wasn't false, either — or, at least, not entirely.

'Were you ever a believer in the Soviet system?' I asked Yelena.

'Oh, no!' She sounded almost shocked to be asked. 'Never!'

She'd always been acutely conscious of the failings of the regime; she felt no nostalgia at all, she said, for communism's passing. Nevertheless, she acknowledged her good fortune. She'd been raised in privilege, attended a fine school and a prestigious university. Her career was a string of successes; she'd made a happy marriage and today lived in one of Moscow's wealthiest suburbs.

And, by and large, she'd escaped racism — or at least the institutional racism that her grandparents knew in America.

The official rhetoric of the Soviet period dismissed colour prejudice as a remnant of the capitalist past. But in reality, racism had flourished under Stalin, particularly against Jews and particularly after the Second World War. Still, those of African descent weren't a traditional target, simply because there weren't very many of them. In the 1930s, the few black faces in Moscow belonged to foreigners — and foreigners were mostly understood as exotic, wealthy, and interesting (hence that little girl's enthusiasm for Paul).

Even later, being black in Soviet Russia meant facing ignorance as much as oppression, Yelena told me. As a child, she rarely met others who looked like her, and when she visited the countryside, older people asked her — out of naivety rather than malice — whether her colour would rub off on the sheets.

'I thought I was ugly. I thought that no one would ever date me, that I would never have children. I will not say that was racism — I had lots of friends, I had a beautiful childhood. But still, you can be traumatised if you don't see anyone who looks like you.'

We talked, then, about the complexities of racism, about how oppression could give rise to a culture that mitigated the effects of bigotry.

She'd always known of her African-American heritage. She'd listened to black music growing up; she'd studied American literature. But, during perestroika, she'd finally travelled to the United States — and it was there she'd realised how Russian she was.

She explained that she went on a date with an African-American man while in New York. The restaurant they visited was full. When the proprietor offered them a table at the back near the bathroom, Yelena couldn't grasp why her companion took offence. But for him, the restaurateur's 'solution' was patently racist, a suggestion that would never have been presented to a white patron.

'You're not black,' he'd snapped at her. 'You don't understand the things that black people see, that they feel with their guts.'

In a sense, she acknowledged, what he said was true. She'd been protected from the institutional bigotry of America, and so her experience of blackness was quite different.

That was why she could respect the choice that her grandfather and Paul Robeson had made, and their appreciation of the advantages that Russia offered, even though she didn't share their socialist convictions.

Oliver Golden died in 1940 when his kidneys, damaged years earlier by a policeman's truncheon during a protest in his New York days, finally gave out. For the remainder of her days, Bertha presided over Moscow's African-American community, a small and ageing cohort still politically wedded to the Soviet Union even as they ached with nostalgia for the culture they'd left behind. She remained a loyal communist to the end of her days, for reasons that were entirely explicable. Had she and Oliver returned to America in the 1930s, the couple faced a very real risk of violence. In Moscow, at least, they'd made a life. In Moscow, they'd been together.

Yelena recalled Bertha as a very old woman unable to rise from her chair to greet visitors. 'She couldn't get up, but she'd say to me, "Go to them [the visitors] and tell them I made the right decision to come here." She'd say, "It didn't work out as we hoped, but the idea, the idea was right."'

That idea, the great vision of equality and freedom, sustained Paul, too.

With some reluctance, I left the National and relocated to a less luxurious but more affordable billet in an apartment just to the south of the Moskva River. There, I was renting a room from Elena, a pleasant woman in her early thirties, who explained, on my first evening in her home, that she'd abandoned a successful career in publishing and now taught classes in the callisthenics developed by the twentieth-century mystic G.I. Gurdjieff. I knew something of the Gurdjieff Movements from studying the New Zealand writer Katherine Mansfield, a devotee of the cult in the 1920s. But Elena was a kind and attentive host, and, if I found her enthusiasm for Gurdjieff quite baffling, she clearly felt the same about my interest in Paul Robeson (whose name meant nothing to her), although she was polite enough never to say so.

As soon as I could, I caught the train to Tverskaya and then walked down Staropimenovskiy Street, looking for Moscow High School No. 175. It was in a fashionable inner-city location surrounded by chic apartments that reminded me, rather unexpectedly, of the Harlem brownstones.

In the 1930s, the building was School No. 25, the most famous educational institution in Soviet Russia. I could see that it had since been extended, with the addition of two extra floors. But other than that, it was the same school in which, in 1936, Pauli was enrolled among the offspring of the Communist elite — including two of Stalin's children.

Paul and Essie had deliberated about their son's future, mulling over the same issues that preoccupied Yelena's grandparents when they thought about Lily and her prospects. The Robesons didn't want Pauli stunted by the racism that had scarred their generation. Already, the boy had been racially abused in the United States and then snubbed by white children in England, whose nurse instructed them not to play with him. Essie had taken Pauli with her on a long expedition through Africa in 1936, a trip intended, at least in part, to expose the boy to different facets of black life. Then, when she joined Paul in Moscow (where he'd been performing), they resolved to educate Pauli there. Again, Ma Goode would tend to him, allowing him to attend classes in the school where I now stood.

School No. 25 was a model institution, designed to give its students the very best education Russia could offer. In that respect, it was comparable to a prestigious private institution in the United States — except that in the United States such a school wouldn't have welcomed a black pupil.

The news of Pauli studying alongside Vasily Stalin, the dictator's youngest son, circulated internationally, publicised by supporters and detractors alike as an illustration of Paul Robeson's preference for Soviet mores. Paul didn't care: in School No. 25, his boy would walk past the life-size portraits of Lenin and Stalin in the vestibule; in School No. 25, he would be taught about the equality of the races.

In actuality, Pauli didn't stay in Moscow for very long. When the looming war threatened to isolate the Soviet Union from the West, Paul conveyed his son to England so the family could travel together to the United States.

But in a way, the school mattered less as a reality than an idea. In Paul's mind, School No. 25 represented, like the nation whose values it trumpeted, an oasis of tolerance that, by its mere existence, reproached the capitalist order and offered a template for what the West might still become.

That was particularly important, since, in the next years, everything that Paul had learned over his journeying coalesced into a conviction that mighty changes were not only possible but also imminent. The

USSR provided what he thought was a working model: a flourishing society in which black people were honoured. If poor and backward Russia could be reorganised to dignify labour and promote racial and social equality, what could be done with the phenomenal resources of the United States?

In this period, the era of Paul's greatest fame, he and Essie settled, upon their return to America, into a pattern that seemed to suit them both. They often lived apart (she preferred the family home in Connecticut; he tended to stay in New York) but they remained an acknowledged partnership, bonded by their now teenage son and a shared commitment to progressive ideals.

In 1938, Paul had explained his politics to a journalist by outlining how, even within Hollywood — an industry centred on stars — ordinary people still possessed real power, if only they'd realise it. He spoke of being on set when the director had ushered in a major financial backer to assess the film's progress, and of his astonishment that production had simply stopped. '[T]he electricians had decided,' he said, 'it was time to go and eat, and they put out the lights and went off and ate. That's my moral to your readers.'

Upon his return to the United States, Paul was earning vast sums of money, but was just as generously subsidising and patronising an array of organisations and causes. In 1937, he'd helped found the International Committee on African Affairs (later known as the Council on African Affairs) to link black Americans with the anti-colonial movements in Africa. In 1940, he signed up (alongside Richard Wright and Alain Locke) to the new Negro Playwrights Company, an attempt to replicate within the United States the radical theatre he'd known in London. In 1941, he supported the campaign by the United Automobile Workers Union to organise against the Ford Motor Company; he sang and spoke for the convention of the National Maritime Union.

In 1942, he played a sharecropper in his last Hollywood film, *Tales of Manhattan*. Again, he was appalled by what ended up on screen: he'd hoped to dignify the lives of the rural poor, but instead the movie portrayed his character as a simple-minded rustic. He endorsed the pickets outside the film's screenings and announced his retirement from Hollywood.

But throughout the war years, he was bolstered by the tremendous mobilisation of men and material necessitated by the conflict, something that, to him, demonstrated the capabilities of ordinary Americans, even as it made a moral case for a new post-war order in which their interests would be paramount.

In 1943, Paul reprised *Othello* on the Broadway stage. If his London performance had hinged on the line 'Speak of me as I am,' the wartime version emphasised a different aspect of the same soliloquy.

'I have done the state some service, and they know't,' Robeson's Othello growled, moments before sacrificing himself.

Inevitably the audience imagined not only the African-American recruits heading overseas, but also all the young men drawn — as soldiers invariably are — from the lower ranks of American society. If the poor and the outcast and the oppressed did the state some service, exactly what might they expect in return?

The circumstances surrounding the Broadway *Othello* production hinted at an answer. When Paul had launched his acting career in New York all those years ago, his presence next to a white woman led to bomb threats. Now, he was openly challenging American race codes, portraying a mighty black general in the bedchamber of his white wife.

When *Othello* toured, Paul insisted on the integration of audiences in all the theatres in which it played. His contract even stipulated that, at the first hint of segregation, Paul would walk from the stage and bring down the curtain.

Uta Hagen, the Desdemona of that production (and Paul's sometime lover), remembered performing in Detroit and looking out into the venue at the horrified whites discovering themselves allocated seats next to elegantly dressed blacks. The onstage action, she said, affected the audience much less than the drama playing out in the stalls.

Everything was changing; anything seemed possible.

At Paul's gala birthday celebration in 1944, the playwright Marc Connelly lauded the guest of honour as the representative of 'a highly desirable tomorrow, which, by some lucky accident, we are privileged to appreciate today'. His words demonstrated how the meaning of Paul Robeson had changed in light of the expectations swelling as victory over Germany drew closer. Paul was, the toast implied, a living prefiguration of what the twentieth century would deliver.

Here was a man born in the humblest of settings — that little wooden church in Witherspoon Street — who talked with presidents and scientists and aristocrats. He'd taken folk songs to the concert hall; he'd brought Shakespeare to the factory worker. He'd struggled for equality for his people even as he showed, with his own achievements, what racial equality might enable. Paul's greatness, in the midst of the people's war he championed, was now collective, even democratic. With the banishment of poverty and prejudice — and wasn't that what victory would deliver? — everyone would have opportunity to develop. Black or white, rich or poor, from the global North or the global South: all might become a Paul Robeson, a multifaceted human being equally at home on the lecture podium, the concert stage, or the athletics field.

Standing outside the gates at School No. 25, I decided that I might have been in any prosperous American or European city. The mothers wore smart furs; the cars into which they ushered their carefully bundled offspring were modern and stylish. It was hard to imagine Paul watching his son complete lessons here, in a room adorned with banners celebrating the building of socialism.

By the end of the Second World War, Paul — and a growing number of others — believed that the values in which he'd tried to educate his child were about to be realised in his native America.

He could not have been more wrong.

———

The Exhibition of Achievements of National Economy, or Vystavka Dostizheniy Narodnogo Khozyaystva (VDNKh), offered, it seemed to me, a chance to see Russia as it had been — or, more exactly, as Paul had imagined it.

The permanent amusement park was a massive aggregation of stone pavilions and display buildings, opened in 1939 to showcase collectivisation, before being substantially renovated in 1953. The VDNKh was where the USSR displayed itself to its citizens and to visiting foreigners. It was the Soviet imaginary, spread out over 237 hectares.

Most of the park's facilities had survived the regime's fall, probably because such a quintessentially communist space couldn't easily be repurposed. The area was instead renamed the All-Russian Exhibition Centre and allowed to fall into disrepair, with its crumbling architecture presiding, rather anomalously, over ad-hoc open-air markets, family picnics, and the occasional show or exposition. More recently, as nostalgia for the USSR revived, the old name had been restored and the old structures renovated, making the place almost a theme park for a vanished time.

The disintegration of the Soviet Union had been so comprehensive as to retrospectively define Russian communism as, above anything else, an economic failure, a regime of shortages and stagnation and perpetual inefficiencies. But when I emerged from the VDNKh station, I found myself outside the cosmonautics museum, where the Monument to the Conquerors of Space curved high into the air, with the rocket at the sculpture's peak supported by a long titanium exhaust trail. It was a soaring reminder of how different the USSR's image had once been.

For decades, the fear of Western strategists was not that the Russian system would fail, but that it would succeed. The Soviet economy steadily expanded at a rate greater than that of most capitalist states, as the Soviet Union amassed a remarkable array of technical and scientific achievements.

By contrast, when the war ended, Paul saw an America reverting to its worst self, as the African-American soldiers returning from Europe and the Pacific confronted, just like their fathers in 1918, a concerted campaign of racial terror.

Between June 1945 and September 1946, fifty-six black people were murdered, in an outbreak of lynch law deployed to restore the pre-war social order. During one grim day in Georgia, four African-Americans — Roger Malcom, Dorothy Malcom, George Dorsey, and Mae Murray Dorsey — were gunned down outside the town of Monroe, at Moore's Ford bridge, in a reprisal for the injury of a white man.

After the Moore's Ford atrocity, Paul telegrammed the new president, Harry S. Truman, demanding the government 'apprehend and punish the perpetrators of this shocking crime and to halt the rising tide of lynch law'. With his friend and mentor W.E.B. Du Bois, Paul endorsed a rally in Washington, D.C., to launch 'an American crusade against lynching'. Three thousand delegates met at the Lincoln memorial; Paul led a smaller group to the White House, where he was ushered into a meeting with the President.

The encounter did not go well.

When the guns fell quiet, the wartime harmony gave way to violent discord, with the vision of the America-that-might-be crashing into the reality of the America-that-still-was. An upsurge of industrial combativeness was in progress, as unionists who'd accepted the imperative of military production insisted on their share of the peace.

'We will not go back to the old days,' proclaimed a placard during the general strike in Connecticut.

That was Paul's attitude, too.

When Truman acknowledged the absence of any government plan to forestall the murder spree, Paul pointed to the alacrity of Washington's intervention to break the recent rail dispute. Why hadn't the prevention of lynching been an equal priority?

It was not good enough, he told Truman. The temper of black people was changing. African Americans had once again fought for their country — and unless they were provided with protection, they might cause 'a national emergency that called for federal intervention'.

The President's face reddened. He got to his feet. 'That sounds like a threat.'

Paul rose, too. He was forty-eight years old but he was still huge — nearly twenty centimetres taller than Truman.

The secret-service men by the President's side moved forward as if expecting a physical confrontation.

'I meant no offence to the presidency,' Paul said, calmly and evenly. 'I was merely conveying the mood of the Negro people, who constitute ten per cent of the US population.'

The meeting came to an abrupt end. Outside, a journalist asked Paul if he thought that African Americans should adopt a stance of Christian non-violence. In the face of the brutality directed at them, shouldn't they turn the other cheek and forgive their oppressors?

The answer he expected was obvious.

But Paul said slowly, 'If a lyncher hit me on one cheek, I'd tear his head off before he hit me on the other one.'

The entrance to the park was marked by a gigantic propylaea supported by six great pillars and surmounted by a huge sculpted worker and a huge sculpted peasant. They jointly brandished a bundle of grain like triumphant athletes sharing a trophy.

The cold had kept away most visitors, and the emptiness of the central alley made the space seem more expansive, with the scale itself an illustration of the Soviet productive capacities the facility had been intended to laud. Alongside me, the lampposts emerging from the snow in rows were modelled after individual strands of wheat, collectively implying the bountiful harvest of a communist economy.

In the distance, I saw a huge stone Lenin. This was not the shrunken doll I'd encountered in the Red Square mausoleum, but a colossus in a long coat, glaring down at me with sardonic disapproval. As I came closer, the details of the gigantic central pavilion behind the statue emerged: an edifice of more classical columns larded with every conceivable emblem of the communist state — red stars, hammers and sickles, sheaves of wheat, brawny workers staring triumphantly at the sky, and so on.

That building, like most of what I was seeing, dated from the mid-1950s. But the Soviet power it celebrated was already apparent in the immediate aftermath of the Second World War, as Washington ceased hailing the USSR as America's anti-fascist partner and reclassified it as a dangerous rival.

In March 1946, Winston Churchill announced that an Iron Curtain had descended on Europe. Bulgaria and Albania had both become communist states. The Soviets were consolidating in East Germany. Romania, Poland, and Hungary would adopt the Soviet system in 1947, as would Czechoslovakia in 1948. The Chinese revolution followed in 1949.

The emerging order entirely unsettled the foundation upon which Paul's wartime popularity had rested. In 1943, progressives could enthuse over Soviet achievements and still proclaim their patriotism — the Russians were key allies, after all. But in the post-war climate, Communist Party members became associated not only with a radical domestic agenda but also with a hostile state. An accusation of communist sympathies thus implied disloyalty — and possibly treason and espionage.

Paul discovered that almost at once. In 1947, an actor called Adolphe Menjou (who'd once starred in Charlie Chaplin's silent drama *A Woman of Paris*) appeared at the US House Hearings Regarding the Communist Infiltration of the Motion Picture Industry. In response to a question from a young Richard Nixon, Menjou explained how he unmasked communists. 'I think,' he said, 'attending any meetings at which Mr Paul Robeson appeared, and applauding, or listening to his Communist songs in America — I would be ashamed to be seen in an audience doing a thing of that kind.'

Paul had never formally joined the Communist Party. But since the late 1930s, he'd accepted most of its ideas, and loyally followed its doctrinal twists and turns. He'd become close to leading communist activists in the United States, and he publicly defended the party's right to exist as the government began a campaign against it.

For a while, his fame and personal popularity allowed him to shake the Red-baiters. He continued to speak and perform, and huge crowds continued to hear him. He sold out concerts in Symphony Hall in Boston, and Lewisohn Stadium in New York; he polled highly in a Gallup Poll selecting the public's 'ten favourite people'.

But in 1948, the FBI, which had been quietly monitoring Paul for years, approached venue owners, warning them not to allow Robeson to sing his 'communist songs'. If a planned tour went ahead, they were told, the proprietors would be judged Red sympathisers themselves.

The same operation was conducted in all the art forms in which Paul excelled.

All at once, Paul could no longer record music, and the radio would not play his songs. Cinemas would not screen his movies. The film industry had already recognised that Paul was too dangerous; major theatres soon arrived at the same conclusion. The mere rumour that an opera company was thinking about casting him led to cries for a boycott.

With remarkable speed, Paul's career within the country of his birth came to an end.

He did not realise, at first, quite what was happening to him, partly because his overseas popularity shielded him for a while. Indeed, his initial response to the domestic blacklist was a new European tour, which became, as one observer noted, 'something like a triumphal procession'.

The enthusiasm of concert-goers in Britain and elsewhere probably convinced Paul that he could tough out the hostility in the United States. Certainly, when he spoke at an international peace conference in Paris, on 20 April 1949, he did not compromise. Instead, in his address, he linked the African-American struggle against Judge Lynch and Jim Crow with the cause of the USSR. Why, he asked, would black people oppose Russia, one of the few nations that explicitly rejected racism?

'We shall not make war on the Soviet Union,' he said. 'We shall support peace and friendship among all nations, with Soviet Russia and the People's Republics.'

Again, though, he'd misjudged how much the environment had changed. He had given similar speeches in the past without particular reaction. But the mood now was different, and the US press insinuated that Robeson had stood up in a crowd of foreign radicals and voiced a kind of treason. Even the African-American papers denounced him: 'Nuts to Mr Robeson' read the headline in *The Chicago Defender*, while the *New York Amsterdam News* assured its readers that '[Black] Leaders Disagree with Robeson'. The respected civil-rights activist Channing Tobias attacked Paul for choosing a foreign country in which to 'declare his disloyalty to his native land'; Paul's friend Mary McLeod Bethune distanced herself from what she called his 'presumption' in speaking for the African-American community.

Paul returned home to mounting hostility.

The outbreak of the Korean War in 1950 set US troops battling against communist soldiers backed by both China and Russia. When journalists asked about the deployment of nuclear weapons in the Korean peninsula, President Truman pointedly refused to rule out their use.

For Paul, the violence in Korea further justified his comments in Paris. Why shouldn't the long-suffering peasants of that nation embrace the Soviet system that seemed to be so successfully feeding the hungry? Why would African Americans, most of whom couldn't vote or find a decent job or live where they chose, take up arms to prevent the self-determination of others? 'I have said it before and say it again,' he told an anti-war rally in New York, 'that the place for the Negro people to fight for their freedom is here at home.'

It was only when the journalist Robert C. Ruark published a widely syndicated article calling for Robeson's internment that Paul truly grasped the peril he faced. He realised that he needed to leave, to head back to Europe.

London had sheltered him once. It could do so again. In Britain, he could sing — and, just as importantly, he could speak.

But he'd waited too long, and now escape was no longer possible. When Paul applied for a passport, the state department simply refused to grant him the document. His movement abroad was, it said, 'contrary to the best interests of the United States'.

Without a passport, he was effectively imprisoned, locked inside a nation that considered him a traitor and a threat.

I spent the day meandering around the VDNKh's strange expanses, pausing every now and then to contemplate another ornate edifice or monument to a Soviet hero.

Each pavilion celebrated a unique endeavour, usually signalled in the architecture itself. Some were associated with specific regions. Pavilion 18, for instance, showcased the former Byelorussian Soviet Socialist Republic, with the pillars garlanded with the region's typical produce, and a rooftop sculpture honouring the local collective farmers. But just as often, the pavilions represented particular industries. At Pavilion 47, I admired the two handsome porkers displayed in relief on the doors, and then realised the building had been intended as a celebration of Soviet pig production. Just as at 44, I found motifs of bunnies frolicking across the walls in a tribute to the successes of communist rabbit-rearers.

After encountering the rocket sculpture, I'd expected the VDNKh to emphasise Soviet technology. I located buildings dedicated to chemical, oil, gas, and atomic energy, as well as a model of a Buran-class spaceship. But the celebrations were just as frequently of far more bucolic pursuits: poultry and tobacco, for instance; beekeeping and seeds.

The more I walked, the starker the gulf seemed between these agricultural accomplishments and the scattering of fashionable young Muscovites hurrying by on their way to the giant ice-rink — an urbanised generation more adept at *Farmville* than farming.

But, of course, it would have been different for Paul.

During my American trip, I'd travelled to Monroe, Georgia, to the site of the nation's last mass lynching: that terrible event at Moore's Ford bridge.

At the Cotton Cafe, a pleasant little coffee shop, I'd sat down with an African-American man named Norman Garrett and a woman called Sharon Swanepoel, a journalist on the local paper who'd written about the town's past. She was a white South African, and that ethnicity brought with it a particular experience of racial reconciliation and the politics of memory.

'When we met,' she'd said, pointing at Garrett, 'Norman told me he could tell that I was not from here because a white woman would not normally talk to a black man. It was strange: in South Africa, with all its history, we didn't have that.'

At least a dozen people were involved in the murders of 1946 — a huge number in such a small community. It was whispered locally that the lynching had been arranged by some of the town's most reputable citizens; that some of the streets in Monroe still carried the names of killers.

Garrett explained how the older generation of the black population shied away from the subject. 'Even now, when I'm talking to my parents, you cannot get them to discuss what happened. It was a deterrent ... trying to keep you scared. And it succeeded, I can tell you that.'

Later, I'd driven about fifteen minutes along the highway from the town and turned off at Locklin Road, to the site of the murders. The bridge was a recent construction, but the field where the four people had been murdered looked, probably, much as it would have back in the 1940s: a green hill sloping down from the roadside and into scrubby forest. Once I stepped out of the hire car, I heard no sound other than the occasional bird cry, even though Athens, a substantial college town, was only a forty-five-minute drive away.

In 1946, it would have been even lonelier, even more isolated.

All four of the victims were sharecroppers, like most African Americans near the town. That meant they picked cotton for white landowners in an almost feudal arrangement, a system of grinding economic dependence that underpinned Georgia's racial inequalities.

Yes, I could understand why the idea of collective farming mattered to Paul.

I could also see how the campaign to isolate Paul as a communist built upon the experience Garrett had described: that long American tradition of deterring 'uppity blacks' with violence and the threat of violence.

In 1949, when Paul returned from Europe, he'd been scheduled to sing for the Civil Rights Congress at a park near the town of Peekskill, just out of New York. But, in the new conservative atmosphere, the Peekskill *Evening Star* denounced the event, calling Paul 'an avowed disciple of Soviet Russia' and insinuating that if locals tolerated the performance they'd be approving communism.

Predictably, the concert was attacked by a right-wing mob and, predictably, the mob's patriotism cloaked an old-fashioned bigotry. A cross burned on a nearby hill while the vigilantes searching for Paul chanted, 'Lynch the fucking niggers!'

In his subsequent press conference, Paul decried a 'preview of American stormtroopers in action'. It was precisely what he'd feared after Spain: KKKism blending with modern anti-communism into a star-spangled variety of fascism.

His second concert attracted twenty thousand Robeson supporters — and eight thousand right-wing protesters. The thugs warned, 'You'll get in but you won't get out!' — and then attacked the convoy of cars heading back to New York.

On my trip to Peekskill, I'd walked the only road leading to the green fields where the performance had been staged. I could see, even decades later, how terrifying driving along the narrow path must have been, with angry white men pulling black individuals from cars.

But it wasn't just racists turning against Paul in those years. After the Paris speech, he'd been approached by his old Harlem friend Walter White. White, a NAACP activist, explained he'd come on behalf of the Secretary of

State, and, by implication, the President. The authorities, he said, wanted to bargain. If Paul signed a private pledge refraining from political activity for at least a year, there would be no objection to him resuming performances. He could have his career back — so long as he kept quiet.

Paul refused, politely but firmly.

A few years earlier, there was an almost unstoppable momentum to social progress in America, with reform a cause to which most intelligent and well-meaning people adhered. Suddenly, though, everything had changed, so that even liberalism required considerable courage. In the Cold War, progress no longer seemed at all inevitable. In the Cold War, supporting a group on the Attorney General's List of Subversive Organizations could ruin your life.

The playwright Lillian Hellman dubbed the period 'scoundrel time', not merely because demagogues such as Senator Joseph McCarthy built careers out of hunting Reds, but because the fear of contagion from those under suspicion fostered a culture of denunciation and betrayal, conformity and cowardice. African-American leaders, in particular, came under immense pressure. They all knew that if they didn't attack Paul Robeson, they would receive the same treatment he did.

At a meeting of the House Un-American Activities Committee, Jackie Robinson, the first African-American baseball player to break into the major leagues, was induced to condemn Paul's Paris statement as 'very silly'. A few years later, White himself published an article entitled 'The Strange Case of Paul Robeson', in which he described his former friend as 'a bewildered man, to be more pitied than damned'. The NAACP derided Paul as a puppet of Moscow; the boxer Sugar Ray Robinson labelled him a communist propagandist.

With the support of W.E.B. Du Bois, Paul tried to fight back by launching his own magazine, *Freedom*, through which he hoped to speak directly to ordinary blacks. But, unable to sing or act, he wasn't earning enough to sustain a necessarily loss-making publication — and, inevitably, *Freedom* faltered and folded.

In January 1952, Paul was scheduled to perform for mine and mill workers in Vancouver, a trip made possible under Canadian law that allowed Americans to visit without passports. But at the border, a US official ordered Paul from his car. The state department had forbidden his journey, he was told, on the basis of wartime legislation restricting activities contrary to American interests.

As Paul said, the refusal essentially put him under domestic arrest without any charges being laid. He responded by singing to the unionists by telephone (an anticipation of the strategy he'd later use to reach audiences in Britain and Wales).

In May, a special concert was organised for forty thousand people in the Peace Arch Park straddling the boundary between Washington State (America) and Canada (British Columbia). Paul sang atop the back of a flatbed truck, with the deep notes of 'Ol' Man River' rolling unimpeded across the border.

For four years, these so-called Peace Arch concerts became annual protests and a symbolic defiance of the restrictions on Paul.

'I want everybody,' he said at the second event, 'in the range of my voice to hear, official or otherwise, that there is no force on earth that will make me go backward one-thousandth part [of] one little inch.'

Yet, for all his defiance, Paul would have been aware that each year's concert drew a smaller crowd than the one before.

What kept him going in those grim years?

I'd hoped that the VDNKh would provide a kind of answer, not so much intellectually as emotionally. The revamped exhibition had opened just after the USSR had bestowed the International Stalin Prize for Strengthening Peace Among Peoples on Paul, an award that signified how closely the Soviet authorities believed his ideals mirrored theirs.

Everywhere I walked in the park, I could see the iconography of Stalinism and I kept wondering if I'd feel even a hint of what such symbols had conveyed for Paul. The instances of Soviet design I'd seen from the decades immediately following the revolution still possessed a definite power, with the exuberant confidence of the metro a clear example. But the architecture in the VDNKh felt much more obviously phoney, a collection of visual clichés, as if the builders had a quota to fulfil. The place was, I reflected, like a speech by an orator who no longer believed his own words and compensated for his cynicism with increasingly florid rhetoric.

At the park's centre, I stood at the huge and gaudy Friendship of the Peoples Fountain, where sixteen gold women — each in the national costume of a different Soviet republic — cavorted with the wheat I had now come to expect as inevitable, water jetting high around them. The thing was truly hideous, a piece of unabashed Stalinist kitsch. It was hard to work out what was worse: the sentimentalised femininity of the maidens, the clichéd depictions of regional cultures, or the blinged-out excess of the gold gloss in which the sculptures were slathered.

Again, though, mine was a response from a different time.

I reminded myself of the novelist Richard Wright's early infatuation with the Soviet Union, an admiration spurred by accounts of Moscow's policy towards its national minorities. He'd read of specialists preserving and celebrating the various local cultures, and then compared their efforts to those of his own country. 'How different this was,' he said, 'from the way in which Negroes were sneered at in America.'

Similarly, in 1937 the Robesons had shared a holiday with Yelena's grandparents, in which Paul had been stunned by the support given to the Uzbeks ('a rather dark Mongolian people of Southern Asia') so they could celebrate their distinctive culture. For him, the fountain would likely have represented a Soviet commitment to the self-determination of the oppressed, a commitment that contrasted starkly with America's role as the imperial power supplanting the declining British Empire.

For where Paul had imagined the fight against fascism growing inexorably into a struggle against colonisation, the reverse had taken place, with Washington identifying the anti-colonial movements as stalking horses for communism, to be treated with suspicion and hostility.

I understood that the tenacity with which Paul clung to his views reflected everything he'd learned in his travels. By resisting the Red-baiters, he was fighting for his own people: African Americans denied their most basic rights at a time when any agitation against Jim Crow was smeared as 'communism'. He was maintaining solidarity with the labour movement he'd come to appreciate in Wales, the anti-imperialists he'd met in London, and the anti-fascists who'd given their lives to Spain. All of that was embodied in his refusal to disavow the Soviet Union, the land where, for the first time in his life, he'd walked in full human dignity.

By the early 1950s, Pauli was a young man, married and living in New York. He convinced his father to establish the Othello Recording Company so at least he'd have one musical outlet. 'When we attempted to market the albums,' Pauli recalled decades later, 'no commercial distributor would handle them, no stores would display them, nor would any radio station play them. The boycott of Paul Robeson was airtight.'

In 1953, only a fortnight after Julius and Ethel Rosenberg were electrocuted as communist spies, Essie was called before McCarthy's Senate Investigating Committee. Ostensibly, the summons pertained to her 1945 book *African Journey*, passages of which had been judged un-American. But everyone knew she was also there as Paul's wife.

Did she belong, they asked her, to an organisation dedicated to overthrowing the American government by force and violence?

'I don't know anybody that is dedicated to overthrowing the government by force and violence,' Essie replied. 'The only force and violence I know is what I have experienced and seen in this country, and it has not been by communists.'

The committee's pointed questioning of Essie, and the defiance of her response, drew the Robesons closer, as their shared persecution compounded their shared suffering. Both were facing serious medical conditions, with Paul receiving treatment for prostate degeneration and Essie undergoing a double mastectomy after a breast-cancer diagnosis. For the first time in years, they began living together, presenting a united front against the hostile world.

What hurt Paul the most wasn't the attack from conservatives, or his disavowal by African-American leaders. It was his new isolation from the African-American struggle that was slowly re-emerging.

At the end of 1955, Rosa Parks remained in her seat when a white passenger commanded her to stand. Naturally, Paul voiced his support for Parks and for Martin Luther King Jr and the new civil-rights activists engaged in the Montgomery bus boycott and other actions so reminiscent of the protests he'd pioneered in the 1940s. But his dogged commitment to his political views separated him from the very cause in which he believed the most. He could offer little more than a rhetorical endorsement of the Montgomery campaign, for anything else would embarrass a leadership desperate to avoid the taint of communism. Besides, he'd been excluded from public life for so long that he could no longer exert the same degree of influence on a generation of younger African-Americans who'd never heard him perform or seen his movies.

When Yolande Jackson had broken off with him in 1933, the disintegration of what he thought he'd forged in London had sent Paul into a deep depression. Now, as he became conscious of his separation from the African-American struggle, he experienced something similar: periods of mania alternating with debilitating lassitude. He developed a fascination with folk music's deployment of the pentatonic scale, the universality of which, he thought, established fundamental links between widely separated peoples. Some days he'd argue the point obsessively, buttonholing acquaintances about musicology with a strange fervour. Other days, he'd remain in bed from morning to night.

But the Red-baiters still had not forgotten him.

When, in 1956, he received a summons before a committee investigating the use of passports 'in the furtherance of the objectives of the Communist conspiracy', Essie, his friends, and his doctor urged him to plead ill health.

For weeks, he'd been almost entirely inactive and unresponsive. All those around him judged him in no state to undergo the ordeal, an interrogation in which every answer would be parsed and analysed and used against him.

Paul disagreed. He had been threatened the entirety of his life. He'd never backed down. He wouldn't start now.

The session began on the morning of 12 June, in a room crowded with journalists and photographers. HUAC hearings made for irresistible theatre, particularly with a star of Paul's calibre facing the inquisitors. Besides, everyone knew the broader implications of the encounter. Francis E. Walter, HUAC's chairman, was a crusader for immigration restriction. A link between lax passport allocation and communist subversion would provide him with invaluable material for future demagoguery.

Almost as soon as Paul appeared, Richard Arens, the HUAC staff director and a former aide to Senator McCarthy, cut to the chase. 'Are you,' he asked, 'now a member of the Communist Party?'

Paul could have simply said no. Even at that late stage, had he disassociated himself publicly from the party, and laughed away his past commitments as youthful enthusiasm, HUAC would likely have left him alone.

Three years earlier, Langston Hughes had made that choice. Hughes had travelled to Spain and Russia, had celebrated communism, and had written poetry about revolution. But he'd come before HUAC as a friendly witness, praising the American justice system and thanking the investigators for their 'courtesy and friendliness'. As a result, Hughes emerged with his career intact.

Paul embraced a different fate.

'What do you mean by the Communist Party?' he asked. 'As far as I know, it is a legal party, like the Republican Party and the Democratic

Party. Do you mean a party of people who have sacrificed for my people, and for all Americans and workers, that they can live in dignity? Do you mean that party?'

Paul hadn't acted on stage since 1945, eleven years earlier. This was a performance, too, a role every bit as gruelling as Othello — and with a lot more at stake. But, despite his recent illness, he displayed no sign of nervousness.

As a footballer, Paul played, as per his father's instructions, entirely within the rules, using that scrupulous legality as protection when he landed the occasional (perfectly legitimate) blow against his white opponents. The method served him now. He answered the questions put to him with clipped courtesy — and he waited for a chance to strike.

'Are you,' pressed Arens, 'now a member of the Communist Party?'

'Would you like to come to the ballot box when I vote and take out the ballot and see?'

The session was interrupted as Walter directed the press photographers to take their pictures. He craved as much publicity as possible; he knew that images would help his cause.

'Do you want me to pose for it good?' snapped Paul. 'Do you want me to smile?'

Gordon H. Scherer, the most senior Republican panellist, protested about Robeson's manner. The HUAC investigation, he said, was not a laughing matter.

'It is a laughing matter to me,' Paul answered. 'This is really complete nonsense.'

Then Paul did something that the panel liked even less: he began to ask his own questions. When Walter spoke, Robeson insisted that the chairman introduce himself. Who was he? Where did he come from? Who, exactly, did he represent?

Almost certainly, Paul already knew the answers. Walter was famously racist, an overt white supremacist. A thin-lipped Democrat from Pennsylvania, he was a director with the Pioneer Fund, an organisation that promoted eugenics in the United States. He was also one of the architects of the Immigration and Nationality Act of 1952, which allowed the United States to restrict entry to migrants based upon racial quotas and political affiliations.

After Walter announced his name, Paul said: 'You are the author of all of the bills that are going to keep all kinds of decent people out of the country.'

'No,' Walter snarled back, 'only your kind.'

Walter was heading an all-white panel interrogating a black man. The implications of the phrase 'your kind' escaped few listeners. Even so, Paul spelled them out for the journalists in attendance. 'Colored people like myself, from the West Indies and all kinds. And just the Teutonic Anglo-Saxon stock that you would let come in.'

'We are trying to make it easier to get rid of your kind, too.'

'You do not want any colored people to come in?'

Walter refused to take the bait any further. 'Proceed!'

'I am being tried,' Paul continued, 'for fighting for the rights of my people, who are still second-class citizens in this country … You want to shut up every Negro who has the courage to stand up and fight for the rights of his people … And that is why I am here today.'

The verbal fencing resumed, until the committee returned, as they had always intended, to Paul's attitude to the Soviet Union. It fell to Scherer to put the query so characteristic of the era. If, he asked Paul, you think so very highly of Russia, then why don't you go and live there? You criticise the United States: why don't you leave?

The question engendered one of the most ringing answers given to interrogators throughout the duration of scoundrel time.

'Because my father was a slave,' Paul said, 'and my people died to build this country, and I am going to stay here, and have a part of it just like you. And no fascist-minded people will drive me from it. Is that clear?'

Those three sentences, delivered with the stentorian elocution Paul had learned from William, a slave-born preacher, brought the moral weight of the African-American struggle crashing down upon the session. What did HUAC's denunciations of the 'communist threat' mean to the millions of people denied decent jobs or education or houses merely because of their colour? How dare these wealthy white men lecture the children of the Middle Passage about freedom and justice!

It was the accusers who ended the conversation. 'I've endured all of this that I can,' muttered Walter, as he moved to adjourn.

The white press agreed with Walter: Paul, they reported, had been insolent and contemptuous. But the African-American papers took a different view. 'Mr Robeson is Right', declared the headline at the *Afro-American*, endorsing Paul's contention that HUAC should investigate white bigots rather than black anti-racists, while the *Sun Reporter* suggested that he was voicing what all African Americans really thought about race relations.

With the civil-rights campaign spreading, a new mood was making itself felt in America, even as the international effort to restore Paul's passport (those meetings in London and Wales) was gathering strength.

Not long after, Paul was permitted to sing in Canada, and he resumed touring within the United States.

On 16 June 1958, the Supreme Court decided, in a 5–4 split, that the secretary of state could not deny a passport on the basis of a citizen's political beliefs. A little over a week later, the state department announced that Paul could have his passport again.

As quickly as possible, the Robesons prepared to leave.

The long ordeal was over, they thought. They would go to England, just as they had in the past. They would regroup and rebuild. Everything, at last, was going to be all right.

8

CROSSED WITH BARBED WIRE
Moscow and Perm, Russia

'Here there is no law. If they really think that you should be in prison, you will be in prison in five minutes. They do not want to start real mass repressions simply because the state is so weak. But they do want to create an atmosphere of fear, where people think, *Don't go to demonstrations, don't go to protests, or you will find yourself in the zone of danger.*'

Ilya Budraitskis was stocky and balding, and spoke with a sardonic humour so dry that it often took minutes for me to register the sarcasm. He was a political activist, heavily involved in the anti-Putin movement that began after the flawed elections of 2011 and continued until the repressions of the following year. We were sitting in a restaurant near where I was staying, with the clatter of Eastern European techno threatening to drown out the conversation.

'Cynicism is the main basis for this state,' he continued, raising his voice over the music. 'They say, yes, maybe we are corrupt. Maybe we use violence. Maybe we are unjust. But the choice is to have a country or not — and corruption and violence are all part of Russian history.'

The waitress came over then and, seeing my incomprehension, Ilya ordered for both of us: a sort of borscht, along with some kind of regional spirits.

I wanted to know more about the assessment that Paul, like so many of the African-American visitors of the 1930s, had formed about the absence of racism in the Soviet Union.

Like Yelena, Ilya laughed at the idea. 'No, of course it was not true. Blacks were not a real part of the composition of the Soviet Union, so prejudice against them was not significant. But there were lots of national conflicts and problems. Yet it was a society in which all these things were very hidden, where the main narrative was the brotherhood of all Soviet nations.'

The last Soviet generation's turn from the official rhetoric of internationalism to overt nationalism and ethnic cleansing was also rooted in the politics of the communist era, Ilya told me. The fall of the regime brought a wave of immigration, mostly from the Soviet Central Asian republics. The people now cleaning Moscow streets were not ethnic Russians but immigrants living without documents and openly targeted by police, far-Right gangs, and ordinary Muscovite racists.

Anti-black violence had boomed in the 1990s and 2000s, in the midst of the disintegration of Soviet society and the catastrophic plunge of living standards. The neo-Nazi groups emerging in that time imported the racial categories favoured by English and German skinheads. They shouted for 'white power'; they casually bashed anyone with dark skin.

Since then, Ilya said, the neo-fascists had declined, mostly because the state identified them as potential rivals and then crushed them without mercy. The hundred thousand or so people of African descent living in Moscow were still not safe, but they weren't being murdered at the same rate as in the recent past.

Instead, an everyday racism was mobilised by the government and its compliant media.

'It's a pity that you can't read Russian, because if you read the mass media here, you'd see a big campaign being run about the Muslim refugees in Germany.' He adopted the voice of a newsreader. '"Germans have lost their will; they've forgotten their fathers and grandfathers, and that's why they're offering their women to the black terrorist Muslim rapists who rape them everyday."'

I must have looked sceptical, because he continued: 'It's on TV —
exactly as I told you. It's coming right from the top: this argument about
the terrible tolerance that is killing the identity of the Christian state in
Europe. That is different from Russia because Russia successfully saved
its spirituality and its Christian soul, which, unfortunately, was lost in
the European Union because of their tolerances and liberalism. It's not
the rhetoric of some crazy far-Right group. It's in big newspapers, it's on
TV — and it has a resonance. If you ask people what they think about
Germans, they say, "Oh, poor Germans: the Germans are being raped
everyday by black Muslim terrorists."'

The waitress brought us with little glasses of an evil-looking fluid.

I took a cautious sip and choked.

'Go like this,' said Ilya, and downed his. 'It's spicy ... very traditional.'

Ilya returned to the conversation. You could only understand the
current situation, he said, by thinking about the collapse of the Soviet
Union and the resulting privatisation of the economy. 'The Nineties are
a real trauma that is still alive in Russian society. That is the moment of
birth for this regime. But like every regime, it tries to hide its origins.
And it does so through a rhetoric of power and continuity, a mix of all
the reactionary elements of Stalinism and of pre-revolutionary Russia.'

That evening we talked, well into the night, about the extraordinary
difficulties in trying to present progressive arguments in a country where
the ideas of the Left and the Right were so deeply entwined.

A few days later, Ilya contacted me again through Facebook. There
was a historical exhibition in Moscow organised by the government and
the Russian Orthodox Church. He was planning a visit — would I like
to come? 'You might find it interesting.'

I was not surprised to learn the exhibit was in the VDNKh.

This time, though, I wasn't meandering as a tourist. Instead, we
made our way directly to Pavilion 57, which, in the late Soviet period,
had celebrated consumer goods, but had since been repurposed precisely
for big exhibitions.

And this exhibition was very big indeed. The huge glass windows near the entrance carried enormous images of tsars and aristocrats and generals in their extravagant uniforms, alongside the title 'Russia — My Story'.

Inside, the hall was crowded, full of young people transfixed by the interactive maps and the looping films and the other high-tech visualisations. In some parts, the rooms were so crammed that we had to wait before we could see anything at all.

The displays were mostly in Russian, but Ilya translated for me, taking particular pleasure in the more reactionary passages, which he read with dry disdain. 'Russia — My Story' traced seven hundred years of history, but did so to distill, over and over again, a small number of simple themes, spelled out in panels illustrated with portraits of nationalist historians, church leaders, and (surprisingly often) Putin himself. Russia, the text explained, was defined by martial prowess and a certain kind of spirituality; Russia flourished when its people embraced Orthodoxy, state power, and decisive leadership.

The narrative was unselfconsciously mystical, a tale in which faith and prayer could be relied upon to deliver Russia in its hours of need.

'Here it is explaining about the Russian soul.'

We were standing beside a depiction of a chieftain of the ancient Rus: a fierce, scowling fellow garbed in fur and clutching a huge sword.

'It says that we Russians are a very special people and we have a soul that is quite unique.'

'Unique? How?'

Ilya clapped me on the shoulder. 'Ah, unfortunately, you would not understand. You are not Russian.'

I laughed.

The heroes on display were saints, warriors, tsars, and other political and military strongmen. The villains (handily depicted on panels labelled 'Enemies of Russia') were dissidents, Western Europeans, and Ukrainian nationalists.

'See,' said Ilya. We were looking at an exhibit about the Decembrists, the liberal army officers who protested against the ascension of Tsar Nicholas I. 'The Decembrists were bastards. They were trying to destroy Russia.'

Again, his delivery was utterly deadpan.

I'd known that the Russian church was profoundly reactionary. But I hadn't realised the depth of its attachment to the tsarist autocracy. I was even more surprised still by Putin's prominence — a picture of him appeared in almost every room — in an exhibition that explained the Russian Revolution as a conspiracy organised by Freemasons and other enemies of the motherland. Wasn't Putin's rhetoric full of nostalgia for the Soviet era? Why was a former KGB officer celebrating the aristocracy that the Bolsheviks had overthrown?

'The ideology of Putinism is power,' Ilya said, as we walked back into the cold. 'It's both Stalinist and anti-Stalinist; Orthodox and Soviet. Everything is combined, and no part totally rejected.'

Putin didn't, he said, like the revolutionary aspect of Bolshevism, for obvious reasons. He was, however, quite happy to celebrate Stalin's role in the Second World War, even as he decried the repression of the Great Terror. It was all right to pick and choose in that way, as long as you venerated Russian history as a narrative of the state, which culminated in the present regime. 'The continuity from Nicholas II to Stalin: they're part of one great Russian tradition. That's the line.'

Ilya clapped me on the shoulder again. 'Enough. Now let's go and get a drink.'

The Sovietsky Hotel on Leningradsky Prospect was, in many ways, similar to the Hotel National, in that it was ostentatiously grand and had once been used by the Soviet government to house important foreigners. Indira Gandhi stayed there once; so, too, did Margaret Thatcher and King Juan Carlos I of Spain.

The difference was that, while the National predated the revolution, the Sovietsky was an artefact of High Stalinism — the fervent period after 1945 when the regime had seen off all internal threats. The hotel was designed by the dictator's own son, who'd built a special apartment for himself in the building.

I walked there from Elena's apartment, and the length of the journey revealed something, I thought, about the place's evolution. You didn't normally find a luxury hotel on the side of a highway, far from any obvious tourist attractions. But the Sovietsky had been constructed around the old Yar restaurant, a Moscow institution since the 1820s. Tolstoy, Turgenev, and Rasputin had prized the Yar's gypsy cuisine; Pushkin reminisced about its cold veal truffles (which were presumably less revolting than they sounded).

In a way, the Sovietsky represented an earlier version of the process Ilya had outlined. If Putin had assimilated Stalin into a narrative of national power, the Stalinist authorities had done the same with their predecessors, incorporating a famous eatery from tsarist times into a prestigious hotel of the communist era. The inconvenience of the address didn't matter, since the people for whom the place had been intended generally travelled in official limousines.

Certainly, that was the case with Paul.

On the morning of 27 March 1961, Paul's Russian guide arrived to collect him from the Sovietsky. He was in Moscow alone, on a brief visit before a scheduled appearance at the Scottish Miners' Gala in Edinburgh.

There was no response when the woman knocked on his door. Fearing Paul might be ill, she let herself in.

The room was empty.

She tried the bathroom. It was locked. When she prised the door open, she found Paul semiconscious on the floor, bleeding from both wrists.

He had tried to kill himself.

While the horrified guide applied first aid, Paul mumbled something. He was barely coherent, but she could make out a few words.

I am unworthy, he was saying. I am unworthy.

Paul's suicide attempt seemed so shocking because, on the surface, the years after the restoration of his passport had been everything for which he might have hoped.

When he and Essie arrived in London in 1958, they'd resumed more or less where they'd left off. Paul featured in a series of television programs; when he sang in the Albert Hall, critics marvelled at how superb his voice still sounded for a man approaching his sixth decade. He published his memoir *Here I Stand* and, although white reviewers in the United States largely ignored it, the book was discussed extensively in the African-American press and throughout Europe.

Part autobiography and part manifesto, *Here I Stand* introduced Paul's views with a sensitive account of his childhood in Princeton, in which William Robeson's travails became an interpretative frame for his son's Cold War struggles. The structure implied that William's rise and fall and rise again presaged Paul's own fate, just as Paul's struggles anticipated what the new generation of activists were facing. The book ended in Arkansas, and Paul's tribute to the first African-American students attending classes at Little Rock Central High School. 'You are our children,' he wrote, 'but the peoples of the whole world rightly claim you, too. They have seen your faces, and the faces of those who hate you, and they are on *your* side.'

They were also, it seemed, on Paul's side — much more so than in the past.

In defiance of his critics, Paul flew to Russia for a month in 1958, in a visit that included a personal meeting with Khrushchev. But the gesture, a deliberate slap in the face to enemies at home, did not dampen the public enthusiasm for his subsequent tour of the British Isles. He even presented a recital at London's St Paul's Cathedral, where he read from the pulpit, an unprecedented honour for any layman — and especially for one as calumniated against as Paul.

Then, in 1959, Paul returned to *Othello*, in a season for the centenary of the Stratford Festival. By this time, he'd made the role so thoroughly his own that, in the discussions of his casting, race was barely mentioned — though some critics quietly wondered if, thirty years after his London triumph, Robeson could still do the Moor justice.

His first Othello had emphasised physical menace — that big cat prowling the stage. Then, in the wartime production of 1943, he'd portrayed the Moor as a soldier, a man doing his duty for a state that did not recognise his true worth. Now, Paul's third Othello was a veteran, an ageing general, scarred but still standing after decades of combat.

If the ovations he received recognised the still-abundant charisma of Robeson the actor, they also paid tribute to Robeson the man. 'I am overwhelmed by the reception I have been given tonight,' Paul said, taking his bow on the first night. 'It is the greatest moment of my life.'

He seemed vindicated, even triumphant. In 1954, the US Senate had condemned Joe McCarthy, the spiritual leader of that decade's Red-baiting. McCarthy had died, disgraced and alcoholic, three years later — while suddenly Paul's career was resurgent.

At the end of the Stratford season, there were more tours across Britain and the continent, and then a lengthy trip to New Zealand and Australia. By 1961, Paul was discussing retirement from the concert stage — but before him still stretched a full schedule of interesting and fulfilling events; even, perhaps, the possibility of a return to the United States.

So why did he open his veins in the Sovietsky?

Essie, who rushed to Moscow to tend to her husband, knew more than anyone about the pressures Paul had been under and the psychic toll they'd taken from him.

Even during happier times, being Paul Robeson was never easy. The most talented child of a demanding father, Paul was expected, from a very early age, to succeed. He'd been made aware of the importance of achievement, not just to the parent he loved deeply but also to the community in which he lived and his admirers throughout the nation. He'd absorbed the impossible etiquette required for a black prodigy, understanding that, even as he made his race proud, he needed to placate the white people around him with displays of humility.

His extraordinary abilities allowed him, most of the time, to make his accomplishments look effortless, simply a manifestation of his inherent dignity.

But, of course, they weren't.

Essie knew that Paul often found public performances utterly terrifying. He would be undone by nerves up until the moment he stepped on stage — and only then, with the faces staring up at him, would he somehow put himself together again. The anxiety did not recede with success; on the contrary, the more he was praised, the more he feared failing to meet expectations.

He'd nearly withdrawn from his first Othello; he endured a similar anguish before the Stratford production — and only his consciousness that others were depending on him induced him to continue. '[H]e was sure he would forget his lines,' Essie wrote. 'He did once, and it terrified him. But he always expected to. He suffered agonies with that Othello, from April to November, when it finished. Often he would stay in bed all day, with fear.'

The public Paul was calm and measured. But the persona required constant effort. He'd learned, for instance, never to show anger, no matter the provocation. Yet during their tour of Australasia, Essie had been dismayed at the tremendous rage she sensed simmering within him.

Ostensibly, he'd remained an oak. But inside, he was more fragile than almost anyone knew.

The Soviet doctors who treated Paul diagnosed 'depressive paranoid psychosis' with an organic basis, an assessment with which Essie concurred. They gave him tranquillisers; they prescribed him rest.

Pauli, who arrived soon after, was much less sanguine. He attributed his father's condition to a chemical intervention by the American state. The FBI were, at the time, waging a campaign to drive Martin Luther King to suicide, and Pauli wondered if there might be a similar operation directed at his father, a scheme involving drugs or chemicals or other skulduggery.

He could never prove his suspicions. But his investigation drew out more details of what had happened that night in the Sovietsky.

A boisterous party had, it seemed, been thrown in the Robeson suite, with the revelry so loud that other guests had complained. No one knew who the attendees were or where they'd come from.

Though Paul refused to discuss his suicide attempt, he did let slip that he'd been approached repeatedly by Russians imploring him for assistance. Some sought to free relatives from the gulags. Others simply wanted to escape the Soviet Union. 'Please,' they begged him, 'for the love of God, help me to emigrate from here.'

It was impossible, I knew, to recover Paul's state of mind. Anything said now about his motivations in 1961 was entirely speculative.

Nevertheless, what we did know was horribly evocative.

When Paul recovered slightly, Essie brought him back to London — and he relapsed into suicidal depression almost at once. She returned with him to Moscow, where he remained in a state of near catatonia. After three months of treatment, he seemed better, and the Robesons flew once more to Britain.

Again, Paul worsened — and this time, Essie decided to take him to a local psychiatric hospital.

On the way, their car passed (by sheer coincidence) the Soviet embassy, a proximity that frightened Paul immensely. Thinking they were entering the embassy grounds, he cowered in his seat, muttering, 'You don't know what you're doing; you don't know what you're doing.'

Because Paul Robeson was Paul Robeson, his personal problems were innately political. In the 1930s, his depression after Yolande's rejection reflected not only his heartbreak but also his sickening recognition of his true status in the eyes of respectable London. He re-emerged from that despond when he encountered the labour movement, just as his confrontation with his Cold War tormentors pulled him back from the breakdown in the 1950s.

But what would sustain him in 1961?

Even without an encounter with distraught relatives of political prisoners, the inspiration Paul had once found in the Soviet Union must have been increasingly difficult to recapture.

The Sovietsky Hotel, when I finally reached it, was much more Soviet in feel than the National, with its name emblazoned in communist scarlet, and the allegorical figures on the roof (who looked to me part Greek goddesses, part Russian commissars) posed next to an ornate sickle. Paradoxically, it also seemed considerably older, simply because of how much the Stalinist classicism had dated.

The inside was still luxurious: red carpets, marble stairs, polished wood panelling. But, if it was a grand statement, that statement was articulated in a different time, and in accordance with the communist aesthetic in which the place was frozen. The Sovietsky was not shabby, per se, but I found myself thinking of Miss Havisham, waiting in a once-fashionable veil for a wedding that would never come.

I asked at the front desk about the Stalin Suite, the rooms in which Vasily Stalin had lived. I was a writer, I said. I just wanted to glimpse the place. Would that be possible?

The woman on duty didn't speak much English and, when she started tapping at her keyboard, I realised that she'd taken me as wanting to stay in the suite, something that would utterly bankrupt me. I backed away, muttering my apologies.

It didn't really matter. I'd seen the photos of the rooms, furnished in the gaudy luxury that children of dictators always seemed to favour — the usual tasteless excess piled upon excess.

Besides, Vasily didn't remain there for long.

By virtue of his patrimony, the young Stalin had become a powerful figure in the Soviet military: the commander of the Air Force of the Moscow Military District. But in 1953, two months after his father's death, Vasily was arrested by Russia's new rulers and sentenced to eight years in prison.

Then, in 1956, Khrushchev delivered the famous speech in which he denounced the mass deportations and killings conducted by Stalin. The implications for communists and the fellow travellers of communism were shattering. Here was the leader of the international socialist movement acknowledging that the accusations hurled at the Soviet Union were true; that, rather than building a workers' paradise, Stalin had presided over suffering on an almost Dantean scale, with unimaginable atrocities inflicted on millions.

Paul had been briefed on the Khrushchev speech through his Communist Party contacts, even before the transcript appeared in *The New York Times*, and he'd discussed the revelations with his son. In that conversation, Paul repeated what was then the party line. The speech should not discomfort progressives in the United States, he told Pauli, since the internal situation in the Soviet Union was something for Russians to resolve.

But it was one thing to shrug off abstract crimes from an apartment in New York. It was surely quite another for Paul to encounter distraught and frantic people begging to escape the place in which his political hopes had been invested.

I didn't know what had triggered Paul's collapse. But, in the fading splendour of the Sovietsky, I found myself imagining that day in 1961.

It would have been easy, I thought, for Paul to feel that everything that had sustained him was falling apart. It would have been easy to think that all the sacrifices had been for nothing — and that, worse still, he'd become complicit in something very wrong.

'All archives are still closed. It is not so simple to identify where people were arrested, where people were killed, mass graves, and so on. Sometimes we come across new documents and then we find a new prison in Moscow.'

In the offices of Memorial, a Russian history and civil-rights society, Alexandra Polivanova was explaining her work. She talked like any youthful historian: impassioned and yet slightly pedantic, brushing the hair from her face as she discussed the difficulties with sources.

But there was a decidedly non-academic edge to the conversation, a horror that came from this history's peculiar double status. On the one hand, the atrocities she researched were unpunished and mostly forgotten; on the other, they remained integral to Russian politics today.

Memorial was dedicated to chronicling and publicising the repression of the Soviet past. The obvious referent for Alexandra's work was the Holocaust. For instance, Memorial's project 'Last Address' placed little plaques on the houses from which Stalin's victims had been snatched, in an echo of the *Stolpersteine* commemorations of Nazism's victims.

But, much more than their German counterparts, Memorial confronted a state that was equivocal about its work. 'They don't have an ideological position at all,' Alexandra said. 'They only have a pragmatic attitude to survive and conserve their power. When they need the church, they cultivate the church; when they need Stalin, they talk about Stalin as a great manager and general. Then, when they feel that that could be too much for an international audience, they say something about democratic values.' She made a face. 'Blah, blah, blah.'

The Russian schools now taught a patriotic curriculum, in which the Great Terror took a backseat to Soviet heroism in the Second World War. As a result, the hostility to Memorial didn't come exclusively from the top. 'Often, ordinary people are totally indifferent to what we do,' Alexandra told me. 'But sometimes they are very aggressive: calling us American agents, accusing us of receiving foreign money.'

Alexandra explained that she'd been denounced in Facebook debates for manufacturing atrocities, accused of blackening Russia's reputation with made-up stories about Stalin's alleged misdeeds. When that happened, she sometimes typed her interlocutor's name into her databases. They were sufficiently extensive that she could often reveal information that a person with their surname — possibly even a relative — had disappeared into the Stalinist murder machine.

In Moscow, she said, mass graves lay throughout the city. 'Some of them are very easy to identify. We have documents. But it's not simple in Moscow to start archaeological research. We can say that we know where they are, but we cannot prove it.'

Alexandra was also working on a project called 'The Topography of the Terror', another concept borrowed from Berlin. Essentially, she was compiling a directory of Moscow, marking where Stalin's victims were detained, where they were executed, and where they were buried.

I'd used her map the day before.

On Varsonofevskii Lane, just off Bolshaya Lubyanka Street, I had stood outside a cream stone wall opposite the Zefir Beauty Salon, looking at an entrance blocked by an iron gate.

This had been the transportation hub of the Narodnyi Komissariat Vnutrennikh Del (NKVD), Stalin's secret police. The building had been equipped with special chambers for executions and a morgue for disposing of bodies. The 'shooting garage', some called it: a place where between ten thousand and fifteen thousand people had been killed.

A block further down Bolshaya Lubyanka, near the intersection with Kuznetsky Most, I stopped at the site of the NKVD's former reception and information desk. The building was brutal and geometric, and you entered through a metal grille, much like the door of an old-fashioned elevator. That was where they'd queued, I realised. The anguished relatives of the disappeared had stood just there, lining up for clues as to their loved ones' fates.

Then, of course, I came to the Lubyanka Building.

I had not expected it to be so striking. The Lubyanka resembled a giant wedding cake, its upper floor an incongruous yellow and striped with an almost Renaissance styling. A clock was mounted in its façade, beneath the little dome on its roof, which was still decorated with a hammer and sickle.

This was the headquarters of Stalin's NKVD, later known as the KGB. It was the centre of Soviet repression, the place where the arrested were first conveyed. Wags called it the tallest building in the city: you could see Siberia from its basement, they said, in a cruel reference to the proximity of deportation. The accused in Stalin's show trials had been tortured here; many of the ensuing executions had been conducted in its underground death cells.

I'd known about the repression, of course. I'd read Solzhenitsyn and Victor Serge and Maria Joffe and Anna Akhmatova and the other chroniclers of the Terror. But until I'd walked Alexandra's map, I'd never grasped its geography, its centrality to the metropolis and thus to the ordinary life of the city. The Lubyanka, for instance, stood across the road from Children's World, a Moscow institution since the 1950s. On one side, a toy emporium; on the other, a torture chamber.

In a sense, Alexandra's 'Topography of the Terror' was a kind of metonym for the Stalinist repression, since the spiderweb of bureaus and offices and execution grounds in Moscow was merely a microcosm of the immense nationwide infrastructure of the gulags.

I asked her why, given that millions upon millions of Russians had passed through the camps, so little remained of that archipelago of misery. Many institutions of Hitler's genocide still stood — indeed, they'd often been transformed into places of pilgrimage. But where were the physical traces of the Russian ordeal? There'd been so many camps — why weren't they sites of veneration, too?

Part of the answer was politics.

In Lubyanka Square, Memorial had erected a monument to the forty thousand people shot in Moscow. It was built from stone quarried from near the Solovki prison camp.

But the effect was negated (or at least I thought so) by the flag flying from the Lubyanka's roof — a flag bearing the emblem of the Russian Federation, which was still using the building to house Putin's Federal Security Service (Federal'naya Sluzhba Bezopasnosti Rossiyskoy Federatsii, or FSB).

You couldn't imagine modern police in Germany working from a former Gestapo base. Russia, though, was different.

'There is an absolute continuity between the security services then and now,' Alexandra said. 'The Cheka, the NKVD, the KGB, now. They still have calendars with all the chiefs of the past: Yagoda, Beria, and the rest. The men responsible for the Great Terror. They have portraits of the Cheka founder Felix Dzerzhinsky in every room. If you are arrested and interrogated, you will always see Dzerzhinsky.'

A similar dynamic determined the fate of the old gulag sites. She explained that, while untold Russians had suffered in the camps, vast numbers had worked there, too. The guards, the bureaucrats, the commissars: they survived when the inmates didn't, and many had subsequently built political careers for themselves. In Germany, the Nazi perpetrators (or, at least, many of them) had been stripped of authority after the war. In Russia, the communist elite had stayed in power, transitioning smoothly from state-run enterprises to the corporations of free-market capitalism. For such people, the places in which the old regime committed its crimes were uncomfortable reminders of their own origins.

'In 1956, most of the gulag camps were closed,' Alexandra told me. 'But there was no de-Stalinisation, nothing like the de-Nazification in Germany. The camps were just left. During the Fifties, Sixties, Seventies, Eighties, no one worried about what happened to them.'

The buildings were cheaply constructed from poor-quality materials in harsh environments, and once abandoned, they often disintegrated, collapsing into their constitutive elements.

But there was one notable exception to the process by which the camps ceased to exist: Perm-36.

That facility (more formally, Camp WS-389/36) had remained operational until 1988 on the edge of Siberia, about a hundred kilometres from the city of Perm. As a result, when activists and academics associated with Memorial began assembling a gulag museum, they'd had, in Perm-36 Maximum Security Camp, an almost complete facility with which to work.

Nonetheless, the political problems remained the same. When the Perm museum opened in 1994, it quickly attracted state harassment, with the government fining its administrators for accepting money from overseas donors.

Then, in 2015, Perm-36 was reclaimed by the state.

Many thought the museum would close. Instead, it was re-opened, with a ceremony at which the Perm Oblast Culture Minister Igor Gladnev spoke. According to newspaper reports, his remarks mostly addressed Russia's need for patriotism.

It should be remembered, he had explained, that WS-389/36 played a heroic role in the defeat of the Nazis. 'Glory to the heroes. Glory to those who fought, who laid down their lives in the name of our great victory and the preservation of our country.'

He didn't sound as if he was commemorating the victims. He sounded as if he was celebrating the perpetrators.

As far as I'd been able to ascertain, the museum remained operational, at least in some capacity. 'That's right, isn't it?' I asked Alexandra. 'I mean, I can still go there?'

'Yes,' she said. 'Yes, you can still go there.'

The train left from Moscow's Yaroslavskaya station on an overnight journey, more than a thousand kilometres along the Trans-Siberian Railway.

I didn't sleep much that evening. The carriage was jammed with travellers assembling elaborate meals on their knees and passing mugs of tea and alcohol and shouting boisterously to their neighbours. But no one spoke more than snatches of English and so, after a while, I excused myself and retreated to the top bunk.

We were rattling through snowscapes, and the window was icy to the touch. Yet the cramped space quickly became overheated with a funk of odours. I was drowsy, but the mattress was too small for me to stretch out properly, which meant I spent a long time flexing my cramped legs.

When we reached Perm early the next morning, I clambered blearily out of the carriage and into a very different city.

Until 1957, Perm had been called Molotov, after the Stalin-era foreign minister, whose son had also attended school with Pauli. In those days, it was a centre for aircraft manufacturing — a closed city, accessible only with special documentation. Perhaps as a result, the modern Perm felt far more Soviet than inner Moscow, with the skyline dominated by the architecture of Stalin and Khrushchev. I walked past row upon row of boxy apartment towers, most of them slightly dilapidated. A huge Lenin monument still decorated Lenin Street; the administration building retained all the totalitarian stylings of the High Stalinist era.

My hotel was on Monastyrskaya Street, near the iced-over Kama River. Like the Sovietsky, it harked back to the communist period, but far more prosaically, with its distinctly 1970s décor culminating, rather oddly, in a full-size bowling alley located near the dining room.

Mikhail Krasnov was waiting in the lobby. I'd been discussing the trip with him on the internet, but this was the first time we'd met. He was a vigorous man in late middle age: a former naval officer who'd settled in Perm and established his own travel business.

'I became a capitalist,' he grinned.

He'd brought with him an interpreter: a local historian called Nataly Pryachinaan. She spoke with the pleasant, careful intonation of a schoolteacher, telling me about Perm's many attractions — the woods, the wildlife, the art. Was I sure I wanted to go to the camp?

Yes, I said. I was sure.

We drove out of the city on a road flanked by fir trees. The car's dashboard reported an external temperature stuck at minus fifteen degrees. In the forests outside, the snow was deep and crisp and impossibly white. I looked into the woods as they flashed by and saw magic and fable, the setting of fairytales and folklore.

On the way, Nataly talked about growing up in the Soviet Union. Like most Russians I met, she was certain that life had been better before the USSR collapsed. 'We never talked about money, back then,' she said. 'We liked gathering and singing together. We had the same education and medical treatment. There were times when the shelves were empty, but it didn't last for long.'

'Growing up, did you have any sense that the camp was here?'

'No. It was a big secret. No one knew.'

There were whispers about the repression, she said, but it wasn't a subject they cared to discuss. Many of those taken in the worst of the Terror died, and those that survived didn't like to talk. 'It's better not to touch this thing, people said. Not to make a storm inside the house.'

We passed through the village of Kuchino, a little collection of houses nearly buried in snowdrifts, and then, almost unexpectedly, arrived at Perm-36.

You could not, I thought, mistake the purpose of the facility. Even beneath all the snow, a prison camp looked like a prison camp. Fences, wire, guard towers: they were the universal grammar of repression.

Perm-36 was made from heavy lumber lashed together in the ice. The external walls were unpainted; the buildings were industrially ugly and squat. The crudeness of the construction — the bare wood clearly assembled by unskilled labour — created a paradoxical aesthetic of impermanence. The camp reeked of indifference, I decided: a consciousness that what happened to the people incarcerated in the unforgiving cold of the West Siberian forests mattered not at all to anyone.

Mikhail stayed in the car when Nataly and I went out into the camp. I only understood why later.

The museum guide, a stocky man rugged up in a heavy coat, introduced himself as Sergei. He spoke only a few words of English but, when he learned I was Australian, he shaped up with his fists like a boxer. 'Kostya Tszyu!' he said, referring to the pugilist who'd moved from Russia to fight in Australia. 'Very good! Strong man!'

At the first heavy prison door, he signalled that I should hand over my phone. I thought perhaps images were prohibited. But that wasn't it.

Instead, he gestured that I should grip the bars. 'He wants to make a souvenir,' said Nataly.

I clutched at the doors like a desperate inmate while he snapped a series of photos and then handed the phone back.

It was not an interaction I could imagine occurring at Auschwitz. Commemoration of the Holocaust had been formalised and institutionalised, with the significance of the camps accepted by everyone. No similar consensus had been formed about the Soviet Terror, no agreement reached about what was being remembered or why, and as a result, staff and the visitors alike lacked the codified etiquette that governed behaviour at other memorials of atrocity.

When the tour began, Sergei fell into a practised routine, marching us to predetermined sites of interest where he delivered a rehearsed spiel for Nataly to translate. I couldn't detect any sign of the state influencing his presentation. In fact, he barely editorialised at all, instead presenting the camp's activities through strings of facts and dates.

From 1946 until 1953, he said, Perm-36 was a typical Stalinist gulag, one of hundreds across the nation. At 7.30 each morning, the prisoners would leave its gates and trudge for an hour and a half until they reached the forests. They worked felling trees with handsaws until six in the evening, when they marched an hour and a half back to their barracks. In the spring, they floated logs down the river to the city for processing, a desperately dangerous business made feasible only by the almost limitless supply of disposable people the camp received.

The display of the camp's tools — the crude blades and axes with which undernourished men, many of whom had never previously performed heavy, physically demanding work, were supposed to clear frozen timber — highlighted a distinctive aspect of the gulag system.

Despite the emphasis on labour, the camps were run at a tremendous loss by the Soviet state. They were a system of punishment rather than production, directed more at disciplining those who weren't incarcerated than those who were. The industrialisation Paul had admired in Moscow in the 1930s depended on a root-and-branch transformation of the Russian peasantry, an upheaval reinforced by almost unprecedented coercion. The camps were part of that. They were a warning, an implicit threat against most of the population and an awful penalty inflicted on a luckless minority.

After Stalin's death, Khrushchev ordered most of the gulags closed. But Perm-36 remained, repurposed as a facility for housing military prisoners, including KGB officers and former camp guards.

'It was the time,' Sergei said, 'when the people who repressed the people became themselves the prisoners.'

Then, from 1972 until its closure in 1988, the camp contained political detainees — those that Nataly called the 'human rights people'.

You could see the distinction between the three eras in the facilities that remained. We walked through the cold, bleak barracks, which were fitted out with bunk beds crowded in rows. The earliest of them were wood. They looked as if they'd been bashed together out of old packing crates, with each prisoner allocated some hessian by way of blanket. By contrast, the later beds were metal, an improvement that suggested at least some degree of reform.

Then we came to the isolation cells, which were tiny, with thick walls and huge doors — more like nineteenth-century dungeons than modern facilities.

'No sun, no clouds,' murmured Nataly. 'Nothing to make them happy, even for one minute.'

I knew exactly what she meant. The claustrophobic oppression vanished the moment we stepped outside, despite the surrounding wire and the towers with their free-fire zones. The snowdrifts banked by the path, and the azure sky lent the barracks and the ugly perimeter fence a kind of harsh beauty. Or perhaps that was merely the contrast with the cells.

I'd realised by now that Sergei wasn't an apologist for either the current or the Soviet regime. But I'd taken his initial informality — that clowning with the photos — as a lack of commitment to the museum and its mission. I'd assumed that he was simply a hired guide; that he'd embraced the task of showing visitors the facility just as he might have accepted any other job. Yet in the camp yard, he stopped, folded his arms across his broad chest, and addressed me with a great solemnity.

'He is saying that his family is Ukrainian,' Nataly explained. 'In 1944, they were moved.'

The Stalin Constitution had impressed Paul and other sympathetic Westerners with its formal guarantees of self-determination for ethnic minorities. In reality, of course, the dictatorship visited a terrible ruination upon those peoples whose aspirations clashed with Moscow's priorities. The forced collectivisation of the 1930s meant millions died of famine in the fertile lands of the Ukraine. Then, during the Second World War, the Soviet leaders, fearing Ukrainian collaboration with the Nazis, commanded mass deportations. As many as half a million people were resettled, marched at gunpoint out of the Polish Ukraine.

'He is saying that two uncles of his were shot. One of his uncles spent thirty years in the camps and lost his fingers and his eye. To the cold. Do you understand what I am saying?'

I nodded. Her translation made the words weightier, as if I was hearing something precious and heavy, a story laboriously transported across eras and cultures.

'He says ... how to put in English?' She thought for a moment. 'He says that all his life has been crossed, yes, crossed, with barbed wire.'

Sergei must have understood. He signalled his satisfaction and spoke again.

'He says that sometimes the people who never experienced political repression, they say there were not any political repressions. They defend Stalin. But those who had relatives who were under repression, they know what it meant. Some people want this place to close, they don't want the museum to exist. But Sergei says that people who are trying to forget about the repressions, they will approach the time when new repressions will come.

'He wants to know if you understand. Do you understand?'

I could barely speak.

We shook hands, and Nataly and I walked to the car in silence. The engine started, and we began the journey back to the city. She said to me gently, 'The first time I came here, I could not cease crying.'

Again, sleep eluded me on the train.

This time, it wasn't merely the cramped bunk keeping me awake all the way back to Moscow. Forewarned by the trip to Perm, I'd brought my own supplies of bread and sausage and soft drink, and so I spent the night in relative comfort, physically, at least.

But I couldn't stop my mind racing.

I was brooding, in particular, over what Mikhail had said on the return trip from Perm-36, a story that maybe explained why he didn't join us on the tour.

Nataly and I had been talking about Soviet repression, about how much people had known about the gulags, when Mikhail, from the driver's seat, began to speak.

His father, he said, had spent a decade in the gulag, after making a joke about Trotsky in the 1930s. He'd never spoken about his incarceration until, one night, he and Mikhail stayed up talking, and suddenly the whole ordeal had come pouring out — the cattle trains so cold that those by the doors froze to death; the bodies of dead prisoners stacked like logs in the snow; the casual violence of the guards, who had total control over inmates declared enemies of the revolution.

Then, after that single discussion, the old man refused to say anything more — and he never revisited the conversation, for the rest of his life.

I couldn't help but connect that interaction between a father and his son with William Robeson's stubborn refusal to discuss with Paul his enslavement. But the obvious comparison raised the issue posed by everything I'd seen at the museum: how could Paul, the child of a slave, a man who dedicated his life to battling oppression, have supported the system responsible for Perm-36?

The question had gnawed at me ever since I first read the Robeson story. And the shadow it cast felt particularly dark, because I knew how tragic the final chapter of Paul's story had been.

At the psychiatric institution at London, doctors subjected Paul to an intensive drug regime as well as more than fifty courses of electroconvulsive therapy.

Pauli was very critical of what the institution did to his father. But in the early 1960s, the science of mental health remained woefully crude. The treatment was probably not atypical for a depressive patient with suicidal ideation: Paul's chronic depression and delusional paranoia would have been understood as warranting intensive intervention.

And he did recover, at least up to a point, though he was never really the same afterward.

Even when the fog of delusion and paranoia lifted, the depression remained, at varying degrees of intensity, manifesting itself in a persistent feeling of unworthiness.

In 1963, Essie organised friends and supporters to deluge Paul with cards in celebration of his sixty-fifth birthday. She'd hoped that the messages would convey how much he was loved, would show how many people still cared for him even now that he could no longer perform and his public life was over.

But the mailbags produced a different effect. The more letters Paul read, the more distressed he became. He experienced their concern as a suffocating weight, a smothering set of expectations that he was unable to meet. He'd always been 'Big Paul', a figure both literally and metaphorically massive. Now, though, he was diminished and uncertain.

He told one friend that he'd failed his people; that, when it counted most, he'd been unable to manage the victory he'd always previously delivered; that he simply didn't know what to do.

Essie bundled him off to East Germany for more treatment. The photos of Paul that emerged from that visit were heartbreaking. In them, he looked both confused and, for the first time in his life, terribly frail.

While tending to Paul, the German doctors checked up on Essie's health — and their tests uncovered that her cancer had returned.

A few years earlier, Essie had investigated a return to America. But the state department refused to renew either Robesons' passport without a signed statement confirming they'd never belonged to the Communist Party.

Essie didn't hesitate. The HUAC days were over and, besides, she'd never held a party card anyway. She had no compunctions about signing a piece of paper.

But Paul flatly refused. As ill as he was, he was not going to budge from the stand he'd taken at HUAC.

In desperation, Essie appealed to senior American communists to convince him. They pleaded with Paul, arguing that he'd done his duty, that the political climate had changed, that there was no reason to hold out — and eventually he acquiesced, accepting their assurance that the struggle had moved on.

With both Robesons deeply sick, it was time, at last, to go home.

Paul's return in December 1963 made the front page of *The New York Times*. His condition had not been publicised, but the paper noted that he was 'much thinner and not his old vociferous self', a change it attributed to 'a reported circulatory problem'.

Over the next few years, Paul managed a few public interventions. He took briefly to the stage at an event honouring him on his sixty-seventh birthday, used as a fundraiser for the African-American political journal *Freedomways*. He spoke at a memorial to the communist leader Ben Davis in August 1964. He occasionally sang a song or two. But his appearances invariably exhausted him, and in 1965 there were more half-hearted suicide attempts.

Meanwhile, Essie — who, with her usual tenacity, had compiled a list of tasks she hoped to achieve in the time remaining to her — was becoming sicker and sicker. She died in December 1965, when Paul was in hospital receiving treatment for another manic episode.

He wasn't even able to attend her funeral.

The last decade of Paul's life was spent in the care of his sister Marian in Philadelphia. He had occasional good days, moments in which flashes of the old intellect, the famous charm, would be apparent. But often he would merely sit in silence, seeming entirely disinterested in the world around him.

His sister and his son did all that they could to preserve his privacy, with Pauli, in particular, handling the requests for public statements or appearances that still occasionally came.

In 1973, Pauli organised a large tribute to his father at Carnegie Hall — a star-studded event involving friends and admirers such as James Earl Jones, Sidney Poitier, Harry Belafonte, Coretta Scott King, Pete Seeger, Odetta, and many others.

Again, though, Paul could not be there.

'I'm just putting in time,' he told his son, during one of Pauli's regular visits, 'waiting to go. I would have checked myself out long ago, but for you, the grandchildren, the family, and the public. Anyway, if this is the way I'm to pay for my sins, so be it.'

That was in 1975. In January the next year, he succumbed to a stroke, aged seventy-seven.

On paper, that was a good age. Paul had lived longer than his father. But years alone don't tell the whole story.

When William Drew Robeson died in 1918, his passing came at the end of an era, before the Red Summer riots and the rise of the New Negro and the Harlem Renaissance. William lived to witness the successes of his son: his deathbed instruction about the oratory competition hinted at the old man's conviction that, through Paul, the goals of his own struggles were being realised.

In a sense, then, William died in his time, drawing his last breath in a context that made sense of his passing.

Could the same be said of Paul?

He'd never publicly altered his views on the Soviet Union. On the contrary, in the few times he spoke after his return, he insisted that his ideas remained unchanged, that he was still as committed to Soviet socialism as ever.

Yet by 1976, even on the Left, the vision of the USSR Paul had embraced in 1934 — that land free of prejudice and exploitation — had lost much of its lustre.

What, then, did the years of sacrifices mean?

EPILOGUE
The Graveyard of Fallen Heroes, Russia

It was my last day in Moscow. Once again, I'd run out of money; once again, I'd run out of time. I'd followed Paul for thousands of kilometres, across several oceans and three continents, and now I could go with him no further. Yet I wasn't quite ready to part. I'd reached an end, but not a conclusion.

I spent the final afternoon walking through the so-called 'Gravcyard of Fallen Heroes', the sculpture garden of the Muzeon park of arts. It seemed the right place to think about this country, and what it had once meant to Paul.

The garden emerged from the coup attempt in 1991, the desperate attempt by old-guard communists to preserve their regime. When the push faltered and failed, the outraged people of Moscow launched an attack of their own, against the Soviet sculptures that towered over their skyline.

The statue of Felix Dzerzhinsky outside the Lubyanka proved a particularly tempting target, an obvious symbol of communist repression. The mob tried to wrench it down with chains and an old truck, until the mayor, worried about the huge edifice toppling onto bystanders, organised firefighters to do the job properly. Later, a fire engine dumped the stone Dzerzhinsky down by the river, in a pile of discarded statues from all over Moscow.

That was how the park began: a higgledy-piggledy collection of socialist realist art, jumbled outside the Krymsky Val building simply because no one knew what else to do with tonnes of unwanted statuary. Since then, more monumental art had appeared in the grass. Some of the new work was political; some of it was not. But it came together in an extensive outdoor gallery — a wild, idiosyncratic supplement to the nearby Tretyakov Gallery.

I'd imagined the place as a celebration of freedom, a product of — and a memorial to — the popular revolt. That was why I'd half hoped it might shake the despondency that had settled on me since Perm. I'd been absorbed with Paul's final anguish; I wanted a reminder that sometimes justice prevailed.

But that wasn't quite what I found.

After a forty-minute walk alongside the Moskva River, I stood in the snow alongside a giant statue of Stalin. The dictator was carved from glossy, almost pink stone, spectacularly shattered where protesters had attacked his face with a hammer. The peculiar salmon surface of the ruined features somehow accentuated the defacement: totalitarian kitsch broken apart by a savage encounter with the real.

In 1933, the poet Osip Mandelstam compared Stalin's moustache to a cockroach. The 'Stalin Epigram' had cost Mandelstam his life — which was why the deliberate obliteration of the dictator's marble whiskers felt so satisfying.

Across from Stalin, the curators had posed a life-size representation of the dissident Andrei Sakharov, resting wearily on a bench. Nearby was a work entitled 'Victims of Totalitarian Regimes': a wire cage of severed stone heads, with their mournful faces gazing over at the tyrant in permanent reproach.

Nonetheless, the impact of the Stalin statue was, I thought, strangely diminished by its setting. The park was substantially bigger than I'd expected, so much so that, before I encountered the first of its many Lenins, I'd walked for fifteen minutes or so looking at the other works. It was as if I'd stumbled on a detachment of a frozen army, still standing at icy attention amid the snow and the skeletal winter trees. Classical figures in Grecian robes, whimsical representations of wild animals, spectral stone abstractions: all of them arrayed in the neat rows of a cemetery.

The further I wandered into the strange dreamscape, the more dissatisfied I became. The statues of Stalin, of Kalinin, of Sverdlov and the other leaders now rested alongside works of the Soviet avant garde and sculptures from the post-communist era. As a result, the so-called Fallen Heroes were no longer presented as the political wreckage of a failed regime, exposed to the elements in a kind of public shaming. Rather, they'd become examples of a particular artistic genre, contextualised within a broader history of Russian sculpture.

Which, in a way, made sense. That was what galleries did. But after the horrors in Perm, I'd come expecting the moral clarity of 1991, not the innate ambiguity of art. Suddenly, I didn't know what to feel.

Eventually I grew tired — of walking, of thinking, of everything. I slumped down on the bench next to Sakharov with my head in my hands, and I stared despondently at nothing.

Back in Sydney, almost two years earlier, I'd contrasted Paul's famous statement about Spain with the depoliticisation of the contemporary literary scene. 'I have made my choice,' he'd said. 'I had no alternative.'

At the time, I'd absorbed only the first sentence, and so taken the passage as an unambiguous proclamation of agency. Paul had, I thought, been proudly declaring not only his allegiance to the Spanish republic but also his freedom to make that commitment.

But since Perm, the lines felt more ambiguous. You could, I realised, hear an implied duress: Paul's insistence that he'd had 'no alternative'.

In Sydney, I'd been enamoured with Auden's great poem 'Spain', in which the civil war is discussed in very similar terms. Auden, too, describes 'a choice' — and then elaborates on what that choice entails. In the poem, he contrasts the gentle pleasures of peacetime (walks by the lake, bicycle races, poetry) with the imperatives of the struggle. Opting for Spain, he says, means sacrificing such commonplace joys. Spain means writing dull pamphlets instead of poems; it means attending everlasting meetings.

It also means 'the conscious acceptance of guilt in the necessary murder'.

Even now, the phrase shocked, with the word 'murder' breaking through our expectations of poetic idealism.

But Auden's lines were carefully chosen.

From very early in the Spanish revolution, the local communists and their Russian advisers set about purging militants to their left, arresting and even killing anarchists and anti-Stalinists. Non-communist Leftists were disrupting the struggle, they said. The dissidents were traitors, undermining the Republican cause, and thus their suppression was crucial to victory.

Everyone knew atrocities were taking place. The Republican crimes were on a far smaller scale than the murder sprees orchestrated by the fascists. But they were real, and they were brutal.

That was why Auden said supporting the Spanish cause meant accepting murder. Siding with the Republic, you took responsibility, he claimed, not merely for wartime violence but also for deaths that were morally wrong but strategically necessary. The struggle depended on Soviet assistance — and with that assistance came Stalinist control, under which the innocent would inevitably suffer.

Even at the time, George Orwell had declared Auden's argument morally and politically disastrous. Orwell fought in Spain; he'd seen how the Stalinists were demoralising revolutionaries and undermining the revolution. The repression was ethically abhorrent — but it was also allowing the fascists to win.

I had no doubt that Orwell was right. But I could still feel the power in Auden's final lines. 'The stars are dead,' he wrote,

The animals will not look.
We are left alone with our day, and the time is short, and

History to the defeated

May say Alas but cannot help nor pardon.

The words contained, I realised now, the key to Paul's fateful decisions.

For the privileged, politics could be a game, a contest between gentlemen, in which a loss was acknowledged with a rueful smile and a determination to do better next time. But for the oppressed, the consequences were different. For them, defeat meant a bullet and a shallow grave in the Spanish earth. Moral rectitude guaranteed nothing, other than, perhaps, the condescending sympathy of posterity.

Auden eventually renounced the line about murder — and then the entire poem. But, symptomatically, his change of heart corresponded with his abandonment of the radicalism of the 1930s.

Paul, by contrast, never recanted and never retreated.

'I am a radical,' he'd insisted in 1949, 'and I am going to stay one until my people get free to walk the earth.'

In that year, in the aftermath of his portentous Paris speech, Paul had performed in Moscow. During that visit, he'd endeavoured to meet with Itzik Feffer, a Yiddish poet familiar to the American Left from his wartime visits on behalf of the Soviet Jewish Anti-Fascist Committee.

But unbeknownst to Paul, Feffer was already incarcerated in the Lubyanka, swept up in Stalin's purge of 'cosmopolitans' — a campaign with a distinctly anti-Semitic tinge.

Not surprisingly, the Soviets did all they could to stall Paul's requests. Unfortunately, Feffer wasn't available today, they said. Perhaps tomorrow — or the day after that, or the next day following.

By then, Paul's Russian was fluent enough that he could read the headlines in the local press. He knew something disturbing was afoot and so he insisted on a meeting, even hinting that the success of his tour hinged upon seeing Feffer.

Eventually, his minders acquiesced. They dragged Feffer out of his cell. They made him wash. They changed his clothes and served him a decent meal, and then they marched him to the lobby of Paul's hotel, with instructions to return as soon as he was done.

Feffer arrived at Paul's room alone. The two men exchanged greetings, and then Feffer surreptitiously signalled that their conversation was being bugged.

'I am well,' he said in a loud voice, 'though I've been sick with pneumonia.'

Feffer pantomimed peering through the bars of a prison — and then drew a finger slowly across his throat.

While the two men made innocuous small talk, the poet communicated his real message by gestures and desperate scribbles. He told Paul that a mutual friend had been murdered on Stalin's orders; he explained that he expected the same fate.

The awful pantomime continued long enough for Feffer to implore Paul to reveal nothing publicly but instead to appeal to Stalin privately on his behalf. Then Feffer said farewell, steeled himself, and went down to rejoin his captors.

That evening, Paul sang at the Tchaikovsky Hall in a concert broadcast to millions across the Soviet Union. At the end of the scheduled performance, he announced a special dedication to Itzik Feffer — a good friend, he explained, a man with whom he had just been talking.

In Moscow at that time, the simple statement was a gesture of defiance. A declaration of friendship from the famous Paul Robeson would interfere with the efforts of the regime to declare Feffer a spy and a traitor.

The song Paul chose was more meaningful still. 'Zog Nit Keynmol' had been written for the heroes of the Warsaw ghetto, Jewish partisans who'd taken arms against the Nazi extermination squads.

Paul prefaced his performance by translating the original Yiddish into Russian.

Never say that you have reached the very end,
When leaden skies a bitter future may portend;
For sure the hour for which we yearn will yet arrive,
And our marching steps will thunder: 'we survive.'

In the midst of Stalin's anti-Semitic purge, the significance of a Jewish lyric urging courage and forbearance was evident to regime loyalists and oppositionists alike.

In the recorded version of the concert, Paul's remarks about Feffer were excised by Soviet censors. But the tape still captured the remarkable response from the crowd: tumultuous applause interspersed with violent booing.

That performance might have been a turning point for Paul, the moment in which he publicly rejected the barbarism of Stalin's Russia.

Unfortunately, it wasn't.

Almost at once, Paul returned to an America gripped by McCarthyism, a place where a mob, unleashed by the media and tacitly condoned by the authorities, could march on his Peekskill concert, shouting 'Lynch the commie', 'Kill the Jews', and 'Hitler should have finished the job'. He'd come to sing spirituals, and he faced a marauding group of protestors burning a cross and throwing rocks, jeering and yelling.

In the context of the Peekskill riots, a version of Auden's argument was particularly persuasive. If Paul spoke publicly about what he'd seen in Moscow, if he revealed the truth about Feffer, if he admitted the existence of an anti-Semitic campaign sanctioned and fostered by the Soviet regime, he would, he thought, be emboldening domestic reactionaries, anti-communists and racists, while discrediting the socialist vision inspiring those struggling for change.

As requested, Paul sent a private appeal to Stalin. Publicly, though, he remained silent about Feffer's imprisonment — and the poet was subsequently shot in the Lubyanka basement.

At the HUAC meeting in 1956, the investigators confronted Paul with Khrushchev's revelations.

When he'd visited the Soviet Union, said Counsel Richard Arens, had he asked to see the slave labour camps?

'You have been so greatly interested in slaves,' sneered Francis Walter. 'I should think you would want to see that.'

Paul provided the same answer he'd given his son. 'I am interested in the place I am,' he snapped, 'and in the country that can do something about it ... I will discuss Stalin when I may be among the Russian people some day, singing for them; I will discuss it there. It is their problem.'

Even in the 1930s, Paul heard rumours that the Soviets were arresting the innocent, although he likely didn't know the scale of the terror. But public criticism of the USSR would constitute, he believed, an unforgiveable capitulation. In Moscow, he'd first walked in full human dignity; in Moscow, he'd been persuaded racism could be abolished. If he acknowledged the Soviet atrocities, he'd besmirch the vision that had inspired him and all the people like him — the conviction that a better society was an immediate possibility.

Paul's decision — his 'necessary lie' — was, of course, utterly disastrous.

Throughout the 1950s, the organisations in the United States to which he had pinned his faith steadily declined, not only because of state harassment but also because their commitment to the USSR became more and more unpalatable to ordinary Americans. Khruschev's speech outlined Russian repression and directly attributed that repression to Stalin, a man whom the Soviets and their followers had lauded for decades as a genius and a statesman. Then, in 1956, Khrushchev ordered troops to smash the Hungarian Revolution, a popular insurgency against the Stalinist regime. In the ensuing intervention, thousands of people died.

In the long run, the refusal to acknowledge the crimes of the USSR fostered precisely the outcome Paul intended to prevent: an erosion of the American Left's moral authority and influence.

Still, even as I knew Paul was wrong, I could understand the calculation he'd made, the tracks along which his mind had run.

Discussing 'Spain', Orwell had denounced what he called 'Auden's brand of amoralism'. It was, he said, a posture, a cynicism only available to dilettantes and poseurs: 'a kind of playing with fire by people who don't even know that fire is hot'.

Whether or not that assessment was fair to Auden, it wasn't fair to Paul.

As a black man born in the United States, Paul Robeson recognised how hot the flames could be — and still he chose to stand within their midst. 'They revile me, scandalise me, and try to holler me down on all sides,' he said. 'That's all right. It's okay. Let them continue.'

He would not budge from his commitments as he understood them. As a result, he lost his wealth, the best years of his career and, eventually, his sanity.

The snow was falling more heavily and the cold was starting to bite. I had to get back to my room. I needed to pack, to ready myself for the long trip. But before that, I wanted to see the Dzerzhinsky statue, the monument around which the whole garden had grown.

It wasn't far away — a few hundred metres from where I'd been sitting. A huge and surprisingly modernist work, the statue presented the Cheka founder in a long robe standing atop a column as sleek and functional as a piston. His name, the date of his birth, and the date of his death were given in gold Cyrillic script. Below the text was a sword garlanded by laurels: a recognition, I assumed, of Dzerzhinsky's role in organising repression. A little sign explained in Russian and awkward English: *This work is historically and culturally significant, being the memorial construction of the Soviet era, on the themes of politics and ideology.*

Unlike the Stalin piece, the Dzerzhinsky statue hadn't suffered structural damage during its removal. But a sprayed slogan remained visible on the column — a painted echo of the protests. Looking at the graffiti, I found myself imagining those demonstrations: the electric moment when the first, brave individual defaced a personification of the regime at the very gates of the regime's dungeons.

Yet I also knew that the sentiment painted by that anonymous protester was no longer universal. A campaign had been launched to restore the statue. Nationalists were lobbying for its re-erection outside the Lubyanka so that Dzerzhinsky would again decorate the building he'd guarded for so many years.

Popular enthusiasm for such an obvious symbol of past cruelties seemed unthinkable, even perverse. But it was entirely in keeping with what I'd learned about contemporary Russia. The optimism of 1991 had long since receded, leaving in its wake a deep cynicism, in which repression appeared preferable to disorder.

I found myself thinking, quite unexpectedly, about Paul's return to the United States after his breakdown, about how at the airport a reporter had buttonholed him, asking if he intended to join the civil-rights movement.

His old fire had momentarily flared. 'I've been a part of the civil-rights movement all my life,' he snapped.

Which, of course, was perfectly true. 'Sometimes I think I am the only Negro living who would not prefer to be white,' he'd said, way back in the 1930s. 'Frankly, years ago, I would not have said — as I do now — that I am proud to be a Negro.'

In that passage, I heard Malcolm X and Huey Newton and Eldridge Cleaver and the generation of African-American radicals emerging in the Sixties. I heard Steve Biko and the Black Consciousness Movement in apartheid South Africa, and the anti-colonial rebellions arising all across the Third World. And I also heard a roll call of politicised entertainers, from Harry Belafonte to Nina Simone, from James Brown to Bob Marley, from Chuck D. to Kendrick Lamar.

I thought, too, of Muhammad Ali's celebrated 1967 refusal to participate in the draft for the Vietnam War. 'My conscience won't let me go shoot my brother,' the boxer had said, 'or some darker people, or some poor hungry people in the mud, for big, powerful America. And shoot them for what? They never called me nigger, they never lynched me, they didn't put no dogs on me, they didn't rob me of my nationality, rape and kill my mother and father.'

That was at the height of the anti-war movement. Paul had made exactly the same point in his *Freedom* magazine in 1954, back when Vietnam was barely an issue for most Americans. 'Shall Negro sharecroppers from Mississippi be sent,' he asked, 'to shoot down brown-skinned peasants in Vietnam — to serve the interests of those who oppose Negro liberation at home and colonial freedom abroad?'

Paul's illusions about Soviet Russia had been used, it seemed to me, by those who'd defended the structural injustices of the United States to obscure his extraordinary prescience about some of the most profound questions about American politics.

The Soviet Union that Paul had championed was grotesquely different in reality from the claims he made for it. But that didn't mean that he was mistaken to agitate against the evils of the America he'd known. It didn't mean he was wrong to suggest that ordinary people could unite against racism and oppression. And it didn't mean that a better kind of society wasn't a worthy goal for which to fight.

I remembered the clip from Sydney: Paul's performance for the Opera House construction workers. In that old footage, you could glimpse why he had mattered so much. Singing to the unionists amid their scaffolding and the tools, he'd presented the men with an implicit promise of a different and better order.

I was very cold now, and the light was starting to fade. In the encroaching darkness, the indistinct shapes in the garden felt like a metaphor for what I'd encountered almost everywhere I'd travelled: a past that was immediately present, but no longer seen or understood.

Paul's hero Frederick Douglass had once compared African-American history to a wounded man weaving through a crowd: it was, he said, traceable in blood. True enough. But, as I'd found in Russia and Spain and America, suffering was, in and of itself, no guarantor of remembrance.

Someone had once assured the French general Charles de Gaulle that the gore spilled during Algeria's long war for independence would not easily be forgotten. 'Nothing,' the general scoffed, 'dries quicker.'

The sculpture garden illustrated, I realised, how the dead lived only through the promise of the future. Without a narrative of hope, without some confidence as to what tomorrow could bring, the past — the triumphs and tragedies that constituted the twentieth century — became a sequence of empty signifiers to be shuffled around for any purpose whatsoever.

In 1952, an American trade unionist named Jerry Tyler had briefly met with Paul. Afterwards, he struggled to explain to a friend what he called the 'warmth and love' he'd experienced during the fleeting encounter. '[Paul Robeson] stands like a giant,' Tyler had written, 'yet makes you feel, without stooping to you, that you too are a giant and hold the power of making history in your hands as well.'

Wasn't that the secret of Paul's charisma? There were lots of singers with beautiful voices; there were plenty of good-looking movie stars. But Paul, at his peak, personified the century's great struggles and, as a result, carried with him something of their promise.

The disintegration of the movements for which Paul had been such an icon had left behind a profound void from which we were yet to recover. We did not believe ourselves giants; we did not feel capable of making history. On the contrary, the developed nations were gripped with a sullen disaffection, an apathetic detachment from politics of all kinds.

That despair, that absence of power in our hands, was what permitted demagogues to rally support behind discredited symbols of repression. It was the context in which history became meaningless, and a figure such as Paul became almost incomprehensible.

The Soviet Union, a society in which millions of people had lived lives crossed with barbed wire, deserved to fall. The toppling of its icons — all those stone Lenins and Stalins — was an achievement to be celebrated, not mourned. But that didn't invalidate the old yearning for a different kind of world. If you believed in nothing, you'd fall for anything. Without a vision of a better future, without the sort of hope that Paul had given voice, the dictators would always return.

We urgently need to exorcise the ghosts of the recent past. We need an exhumation of what has been repressed; we need to remember all that we've tried to forget.

I stood up and I dusted the snow from my shoulders.

Paul Robeson was dead, but his story wasn't over.

REFERENCES

Prelude

'This morning …': Foner, 1978, p. 413. See also Goodman, 2013, Ch. 15.

Introduction

'clip of Paul Robeson …': Spontaneous45, 2010; 'Robeson's first and only trip …': the best account comes from Ann Curthoys' chapter in Peters-Little et al., 2010; 'best known American in the world': Horne, 2016, p. 3; 'agents from the Australian Security Intelligence Organisation': Paul Robeson's ASIO file is accessible at the National Archives of Australia; 'are weeping …': Curthoys in Peters-Little et al., 2010; '"Paul Robeson!"': quoted in Goodman, 2013, p. 196; 'Robeson played basketball professionally …': Horne, 2016, p. 3; '"The artist must …"': Foner, 1978, p. 118; 'sometimes called "the poets' war" …': see Cunningham, 1986; '"the light spills intemperately …"': 'The Harbour' in Langford, 2009; 'The famously tortured construction …': see Dellora, 2013; 'Even the modern name …': see Clendinnen, 2003; '*Spotlight*': ABCSplashTV, 1960; '"He was so angry …"': Curthoys in Peters-Little et al., 2010; 'In a famous passage …': Freud, 2003; 'Alfred Hayes published …': Adler, 2011, p. 19.

PART ONE: GENESIS

1 A Peculiar Institution

'In 1963, Williamston …': see Carter, 1999; 'Later that year …': see Carter, 1999, and Cunningham, 2013, p. 48; 'Robason family': the Roberson family maintain a website at http://www.robersons.us; 'I appear before you ...': McNeese, 2007, p. 76; '[I]t was easy to tell ...': Mebane, 1983, p. 13; 'There are five things ...': see Ball, 1998, p. 7; '"Was I ever beat bad?"': see Andrews, 2016 (I've modernised the original phonetic spelling); '"The glory of my boyhood ..."': Robeson, 1958, p. 14; 'William Drew Robeson ...': my primary source here is Brown, 1997; 'The rate of mortality ...': see King, 1995, and Fraser, 2007; '"Every modern method ..."': Baptist, 2014, p. 141; '"I am sure that ..."': Robeson, 1958, p. 21; 'I explained to them how ...': Brown, 1997, p. 12; 'In 1845, William Robason ...': the will is reproduced in Brown, 1997, p. 9; '"Blacks never became ..."': see Carter, 1999, p. 23; 'a curious passage in Paul's memoir ...': see Robeson, 1958, p. 22; 'The second variant ...': Duberman, 1988, p. 284; 'a third version ...': Robeson, 2010, p. 67; 'The J. Douglas Galyon Depot': Greensboro Library, 2016; 'In 1866, William had ...': see Boyle and Bunie, 2001, p. 5; 'I have cousins ...': Foner, 1978, p. 142; 'Indeed, the census of 1870 ...': Brown, 1997, p. 14.

2 In My Father's House

'"You were born here ..."': Brown, 1997, p. 133; '"spiritually located in Dixie"': Robeson, 1958, p. 18; '"The action of President Roosevelt ..."': Norrell, 2009, p. 246; 'David Bryant was ...': Knapp, 2014; '"I don't have a mother ..."': Beekman, 2013; 'but in 1850 ...': Mulvaney, 2016; '"Even while demonstrating ..."': Robeson, 1958, p. 28; '"bridge between the Have-Nots ..."': Robeson, 1958, p. 19; 'Frazier Baker ...': Finnegan, 2013, p. 50; '"the proud people"': Finnegan, 2013, p. 51; 'Later that year ...': 1898 Wilmington Race Riot Commission, 2006; 'The Wilmington coup ...': Tolnay and Beck, 1995, p. 29; 'Paul always maintained ...': Brown, 1997, p. 26, but note also the alternative explanations given in Boyle and Bunie, 2001, p. 20; '"so bad it should have ..."': Boyle and Bunie, 2001, p. 21; '"Not one word ..."': Robeson, 1958, p. 20; 'The Bustills could trace ...': Smith, 1925; 'The Bustills barely ...': Boyle and Bunie, 2001, p. 14; '"Stand up to them ..."': Robeson, 1958, p. 21; '"I never remember ..."': Brown, 1997, p. 37; 'The Princeton cemetery ...': Princeton Cemetery of Nassau Presbyterian Church, 2016; '"all honey and persuasion"': Duberman, 1988, p. 125; '"rendition whose excellence ..."': Brown, 1997, p.39; '"There was always ..."': Robeson, 1958, p. 27; "'Pop was pleased ..."': Robeson, 1958, p. 26; "'My father was always ..."': Robeson, 2001, p. 165; "'Pop's quiet confidence ..."': Robeson, 1958, p. 33; "'the militant policy ..."': Robeson, 1958, p. 26; "'I don't care ..."': Boyle and Bunie, 2001, p. 69; "'the tallest tree ..."': Duberman, 1988, p. 285; 'Nassau Street took ...': Historical Society of Princeton, 2016; 'Wilson understood that ...': see O'Reilly, 1997; "'There's a big darky ..."': Boyle and Bunie, 2001, p. 49; "'Send him out ..."': Kaiser, 1998, p. 18; "'I didn't know ..."': Foner, 1978, p. 154; "'I wanted to kill ..."': Foner, 1978, p. 154; "'Robey, you're on the varsity"': Foner, 1978, p. 154; "'Robeson of Rutgers ..."': Brown, 1997, p. 78; "'I can honestly tell you ..."': Brown, 1997, p. 77; "'The theology was Calvin ..."': Robeson, 1958, p. 18; "'coloured people were not ..."': Brown, 1997, p. 64; 'police had killed ...': see McCarthy, 2015; 'If there should be disloyalty ...': Goldstein, 1985, p. 107; 'word of his seditious ...': Green, 2006, p. 203; 'a nice, placid, kind guy ...': Duberman, 1988, p. 21; 'We wear the mask': Dunbar, 1975; 'Don't you so much ...': Duberman, 1988, p. 23.

3 The Great Future Grinding Down

"'So here we have Harlem ..."': Johnson, 1968, p. 4; "'a mahogany bed ..."': Robeson, 2001, p. 53; 'The Harlem Renaissance ...': see Hillstrom, 2008, p. 26; "'land of plenty ..."': 'The City of Refuge' in Locke, 1992, p. 57; "'seeing that they could not ..."': Huggins, 1976, p. 67; 'the place for a Negro to be ...': Hillstrom, 2008, p. 74; 'prophetic': Locke, 1992, p. 7; 'That was why the poet ...': Wintz, 1996, p. 395; 'Throughout the so-called Red Summer ...': see McWhirter, 2011, and Krugler, 2014; 'All hats off to "Robey" ...': Boyle and Bunie, 2001, p. 74; 'Mine is the future ...': Claude McKay quoted in Locke, 1992, p. 12; 'But Essie lacked ...': see, for example, Brown, 1997, p. xiv; 'Essie's grandfather ...': Ransby, 2013, p. 15; "'He would belong to the world ..."': Robeson, 2001, p. 46; 'In another essay ...': 'The New Negro' in Locke, 1992; "'I'll git de hide ..."': O'Neill, 1941, p. 5; "'This was America ..."': Robeson, 2001, p. 56; "'I don't take dictation ..."': Duberman, 1988, p. 55; "'I knew little ..."': Boyle and Bunie, 2001, p. 105; 'white actress kisses Negro's hand': Duberman, 1988, p. 58; "'Robeson," wrote the critic ...': Duberman, 1988, p. 64; "'redeemed Africa"':

Hillstrom, 2008, p. 31; '"a lunatic or a traitor"': Du Bois, 1996, p. 129; '"One of the great measures ..."': Foner, 1978, p. 69; '"books began to happen to me"': Hughes, 1993, p. 16; '"The Negro Speaks of Rivers"': Locke, 1992, p. 141; '"[I]f I do become ..."': Foner, 1978, p. 68; '"Nigger Jim Harris ..."': O'Neill, 1941; 'In the rancorous debate ...': see Duberman, 1988, p. 65; 'In North Charleston ...': *The New York Times*, 2015; 'In Europe, the 369th ...': Huggins, 1971, p. 55; '"We return ..."': McWhirter, 2011, p. 32; '"I am a Negro ..."': Robeson, 1958, p. 9; '"This is fabulous ..."': Rhodes-Pitts, 2011, p. 31; '"hold this choice bit ..."': Locke, 1992, p. 308; '"Now as then ..."': Rhodes-Pitts, 2011, p. 107; 'In Charleston, Essie's ...': see Ransby, 2013, p. 16, and Burke, 2002; 'necessary evil': Roberts and Kytle, 2012; '"look to the uneasy ..."': Paul Robeson quoted Douglass in Robeson, 1958, p. 35; 'Denmark Vesey had led ...': Roberts and Kytle, 2012; 'Charleston conservatives ...': for example, Hunter, 2010; '"Lift up yourselves ..."': Jacobs, 2014, p. 165; 'In the 1930s ...': see Kayton, 2003, pp. 182–202; 'The church traced ...': Moore and Dolkart, 1993; 'On 27 January 1976 ...': Duberman, 1988, p. 549; '"My brother's love ..."': Robeson, 1958, p. 9; '"less harmful than drugs ..."': Locke, 1992, p. 223; '"a honey of a show"': Hughes, 1993, p. 223; '"an overture to an era ..."': Hillstrom, 2008, p. 61; '"Why don't you fellows ..."': Seton, 1958, p. 35; '"the sorrow songs"': Du Bois, 1994, p. 117; '"the dignity that has come ..."': Allen, Ware, and Garrison, 1995, p. x; '"the audience was very ..."': Robeson, 2001, p. 81; '"[A]ll those who listened ..."': Robeson, 1930, p. 89; '"The American Negro ..."': Locke, 1992, p. 231; '"hold in them a world ..."': Robeson, 2001, p. 87; '[T]he time was fast approaching ...': Tragle, 1973, p. 310; '"the embodiment of the aspirations ..."': Duberman, 1988, p. 80; '"Harlem is a ruin ..."': Ellison, 1964; '*We are men!*': Wicker, 2011, p. 29; 'Kids Who Die': Hughes, 1995, p. 210; 'In Chicago, the total population ...': Alexander, 2012, p. 189; 'In Ferguson ...': Graeber, 2015; 'Across America, ex-felons ...': this is the central thesis of Alexander, 2012; 'Tillman was personally ...': Moreduck, 2014; 'a bronze sculpture honoured ...': Curtis, 2013.

PART TWO: EXODUS

4 An English Gentleman

"'I shall never forget ...'": Seton, 1958, p. 9; "'find a nice cozy place ...'": Duberman, 1988, p. 87; "'bivouacking ground for art ...'": Ransome, 1907, p. 33; 'For Essie, the location ...': see Richardson, 2003; 'Giant Negro Actor': Seton, 1958, p. 39; "'People went out of their minds ...'": Boyle and Bunie, 2001, p. 192; "'A sorrow that seemed ...'": Seton, 1958, p. 44; "'They stomped, cheered and applauded ...'": Boyle and Bunie, 2001, p. 193; "'charming, well-built English ...'": Robeson, 2001, p. 154; "'more ozone than ...'": Hunt, 2009, p. 243; "'She was like a schoolgirl ...'": Boyle and Bunie, 2001, p. 208; 'The delight of it ...': Boyle and Bunie, 2001, p. 162; "'deliberate attempt ...'": Duberman, 1988, p. 114; "'In Soho ...'": Seton, 1958, p. 63; "'Of course, I think ...'": Foner, 1978, p. 67; "'be something monstrous ...'": Kolin, 2002, p. 32; "'to find the part ...'": Swindall, 2011, p. 30; "'black and white blood ...'": Swindall, 2011, p. 12; "'kind of culmination'": Foner, 1978, p. 67; "'She can't even get ...'": Duberman, 1988, p. 134; "'As Othello I walk ...'": Swindall, 2011, p. 28; "'The blow on Desdemona's ...'": Boyle and Bunie, 2001, p. 227; "'I took the part of Othello ...'": Seton, 1958, p. 54; "'every time white folks ...'": Swindall, 2011, p. 98; "'There has been no Othello ...'": Seton, 1958, p. 54; "'You mean that someone ...'": Robeson, 1930, p. 133; "'Everyone [in the Village] dated ...'": Boyle and Bunie, 2001, p. 158; "'tremendously interested'": Robeson, 1930, p. 136; "'He leaves a trail ...'": Robeson, 1930, p. 146; "'like a plantation hand ...'": Foner, 1978, p. 152; "'How could one not ...'": Swindall, 2011, p. 31; "'That Paul Robeson ...'": Boyle and Bunie, 2001, p. 215; "'If the Negro was ...'": Seton, 1958, p. 52; "'Paul is not any different ...'": Duberman, 1988, p. 140; "'just one more Negro musician ...'": Duberman, 1988, p. 140; "'You will do these things ...'": Duberman, 1988, p. 141; "'a free spirit ...'": Duberman, 1988, p. 143; "'I had a talk with NC ...'": Duberman, 1988, p. 146; "'beautiful English woman ...'": Boyle and Bunie, 2001, p. 248; "'[Othello] was a general ...'": Boyle and Bunie, 2001, p. 220; "'My husband and I ...'": Ransby, 2013, p. 77; 'Paul was devastated ...': see in particular Boyle and Bunie, 2001, pp. 261–65; "'*Othello* has taken away ...'": Duberman, 1988, p. 137; "'She loved me ...'": Act I, Scene III;

'"Paul and I understand …"': Ransby, 2013, p. 80; '"Am terribly happy at No 19 …"': Robeson, 2001, p. 200.

5 Proud Valley

'By accident, he'd encountered …': see Robeson, 2001, p. 156; '"summer of soups and speeches"': Davies, 1994, p. 343; '"Some fifty years later …"': Robeson, 2001, p. 348; 'Before the year was out …': see Cope, Robeson, and Jones, 2003; 'Yet not so far from …': Carradice, 2014; '"punching out the doorman"': Boyle and Bunie, 2001, p. 279; 'Yolande, he said …': Duberman, 1988, p. 166, and see also Boyle and Bunie, 2001, p. 266, and Seton, 1958, p. 59; '"This man said he …"': Seton, 1958, p. 73; '"the eternal music of common …"': Cope, Robeson, and Jones, 2003, p. 58; 'Down there in the dark …': Williamson, 1999, p. vi; 'It's from the miners …': Cope, Robeson, and Jones, 2003, p. 55; 'By the early decades …': see Fryer, 1984, p. 295; '"to keep respectable homes …"': Fryer, 1984, p. 357; 'In his poem "Heritage" …': Locke, 1992, p. 250; '"So long, / So far away …"': Hughes, 1995, p. 122; '"do a lot towards …"': Duberman, 1988, p. 179; '"a million mad savages …"': Duberman, 1988, p. 180; '*Sanders of the River* was regarded …': Sinclair, 1993, p. 39; '"Mr Robeson, do you remember"': Cope, Robeson, and Jones, 2003, p. 57; 'In the nineteenth century …': see Pincombe, 2011; '"We are happy …"': Cope, Robeson, and Jones, 2003, p. 87; '"My warmest greetings …"': Cope, Robeson, and Jones, 2003, p. 89; '"To die," he'd said …': Cope, Robeson, and Jones, 2003, p. 62.

6 What Fascism Was

'"Keep on talking …"': Seton, 1958, p. 82; '"I never understood …"': Seton, 1958, p. 84; '"Everything seemed to be centred …"': Low and Breá, 1937, p. 20; '"you put yourself …"': Dessaix, 2008, p. 30; 'Under the so-called …': see Tremlett, 2006, especially Ch. 3; 'Once a great empire …': see Preston, 2006, Preston and Preston, 1996, and Fraser, 1979; 'The Republic founded …': Lloyd, 2015, p. 43; 'For the Nationalists …': see Preston, 2012; '"our blunt ideals …"': 'I Remember Spain' in Cunningham, 1986, p. 355; '"Nothing," he said later …': Boyle and Bunie, 2001, p. 376; '"was the great man …"': Townsend and Forge, 1976, p. 40; '"Fascism," he told …': Foner, 1978, p. 118; '"I have been criticised …"': Boyle and Bunie,

2001, p. 380; 'But, for the first time …': see Boyle and Bunie, 2001, p. 381; 'As we crossed …': see Lloyd, 2015, Part 4.2; '"I am essentially a practical …"': Duberman, 1988, p. 215; 'Alan and I found …': see Lloyd, 2015, Part 11.5; 'The façade was the same …': Bessie, 1975, p. 38; 'At the very highest point …': see Lloyd, 2015, Part 13.2; '"The anti-aircraft guns bark …"': 'Air raid: Barcelona' in Nelson, 2002, p. 121; 'From the very beginning …': see Collum and Berch, 1992; '"driving past orange …"': Robeson, 2001, p. 298; '"Negro soldiers from Chicago …"': Robeson, 2001, p. 298; '"I felt like a human being …"': Carroll, 1994, p. 134; '"the wrong word for negro"': Carroll, 1994, p. 133; '"Here for a little …"': 'Benicasim' [sic] in Cunningham, 1986, p. 242; '"the only ugly landscape …"': Haldane, 1951, p. 129; '"much more homesick …"': Martin, 2016, p. 150; '"so-called Grand Hotel"': Robeson, 2001, p. 299; '"You don't get people …"': Duberman, 1988, p. 218; '"secularised"': Haldane, 1951, p. 130; '"Saw lots of Negro comrades …"': Robeson, 2001, p. 299; '"there was no other man …"': Yates, 1989, p. 132; '"the men stomped …"': Robeson, 2001, p. 299; '"the colour of beetroot …"': Haldane, 1951, p. 130; '"I doubt if they really care …"': Duberman, 1988, p. 219; '"We hear artillery …"': Ransby, 2013, p. 130; '"We came to wipe out …"': Carroll, 1994, p. 136; '"Like men we'll face …"': 'If We Must Die', Huggins, 1971, p. 71; '"the heroic atmosphere …"': Foner, 1978, p. 126; '"I often think Paul never …"': Boyle and Bunie, 2001, p. 387; '"Franco is coming …"': Rhodes, 2015, p. 222; '"They had week-old beards …"': Carroll, 1994, p. 173; '"*Rojos!*"': Hochschild, 2016, p. 302; 'In Spain …': Tremlett, 2006, p. 1; 'In Madrid …': Mathieson, 2014, and O'Keefe, 2013, were both helpful here; 'The Valle de los Caídos …': Tremlett, 2006, Ch. 2; 'Alongside the bones …': Preston, 2012, p. 450.

PART THREE: REVELATIONS

7 You Cannot Imagine What That Means

'"old Abe Lincoln"': Duberman, 1988, p. 236; '"probably the most famous …"': Horne, 2016, p. 3; 'In 1944, when Paul turned …': Duberman, 1988, p. 284; '"We are going to get along …"': Heale, 1990, p. 130; '"one hell of a people"': Lieberman, 2000, p. 34; '"I hesitated to come"': Seton, 1958, p. 95; 'The hotel had been built …': Hotel National, n.d.; 'He had arrived in the midst …': Fitzpatrick, 1999, p. 7; 'The Moscow metro': O'Mahony, 2003, was helpful here; '"We were born to …"': Fitzpatrick, 1999, p. 68; '"They have never been told …"': Seton, 1958, p. 89; '"spurred the Negro citizens here …"': Duberman, 1988, p. 256; '"Before I came, I could hardly believe …"': Seton, 1958, p. 95; 'Yelena was a Russian-born …': see Khanga and Jacoby, 1992; 'community of black expats': see Carew, 2010, and Baldwin, 2002; 'That child was Lily …': see Golden, 2002; '"an old friend of mine …"': Foner, 1978, p. 348; 'In the 1930s, the building was …': see Holmes, 1999; 'Upon his return …': see Horne, 2016, especially Ch. 5; '"[T]he electricians had decided …"': Foner, 1978, p. 123; 'Uta Hagen, the Desdemona …': see Swindall, 2011, p. 104; '"a highly desirable tomorrow …"': Duberman, 1988, p. 285; '"VDNKh"': see Kurkovsky, 2007; 'During one grim day in Georgia …': see Wexler, 2003; '"We will not go back …"': Buhle and Dawley, 1985, p. 104; '"That sounds like a threat"': Robeson, 2010, p. 111; '"I think …"': Duberman, 1988, p. 676; 'But in 1948, the FBI …': Paul Robeson Jr notes that from 1943 the FBI classified Paul Robeson as a dangerous subversive. See Robeson, 2010, p. 53; '"something like a triumphal …"': Duberman, 1988, p. 339; '"We shall not make war …"': Robeson, 2010, p. 143. See also Goodman, 2013, Ch. 3; '"Nuts to Mr Robeson …"': Duberman, 1988, p. 687; '"declare his disloyalty …"': Goodman, 2013, p. 56; '"I have said it before …"': Foner, 1978, p. 253; 'It was only when the journalist …': Robeson, 2010, p. 213; '"contrary to the best interests …"': Goodman, 2013, p. 200; 'The more I walked …': see Shaw, 2014; '"an avowed disciple …"': Goodman, 2013, p. 119; '"Lynch the fucking niggers!"': Horne, 2016, p. 124; '"preview of American stormtroopers …"': Duberman, 1988, p. 367; '"You'll get in …"': Duberman, 1988, p. 369; 'After the Paris speech …': see Robeson, 2010, p. 158; 'The playwright Lillian Hellman …': Hellman, 2000; '"very silly"': Goodman, 2013, p. 106; '"a bewildered man …"': Ransby, 2013, p. 190; 'With the support …': see Goodman, 2013, p. 165; '"I want everybody …"': Duberman, 1988, p. 411; '"How different this was …"': Crossman and Koestler, 1950, p. 130; '"a rather dark Mongolian …"': Duberman, 1988, p. 211; '"When we attempted …"': Robeson, 2010, p. 222; '"I don't know anybody …"': Duberman, 1988, p. 412; 'He developed a fascination …': Duberman, 1988, p. 438;

'"Are you …"': Foner, 1978, from p. 413. See also Goodman, 2013, Ch. 15; 'Three years earlier …': see Greer, 2011, p. x; 'A thin-lipped Democrat …': see Miller, 1994–1995; 'Mr Robeson is Right': Robeson, 2010, p. 254.

8 Crossed with Barbed Wire

'Russia — My Story': see Gilbert, 2016; 'On the morning of 27 March …': Duberman, 1988, p. 498; '"You are our children …"': Robeson, 1958, p. 109; 'In defiance of his critics …': see Duberman, 1988, p. 467; '"I am overwhelmed …"': Swindall, 2011, p. 176; '"[H]e was sure he would …"': Swindall, 2011, p. 186; '"depressive paranoid psychosis"': Duberman, 1988, p. 498; '"Please …"': Robeson, 2010, p. 314; '"You don't know …"': Duberman, 1988, p. 502; 'By virtue of his patrimony …': Sullivan, 2015, p. 230; 'Paul had been briefed …': Robeson, 2010, p. 247; 'For instance, Memorial's project …': Tavernise, 2015; '"The Topography of the Terror"': see Kravchenko, 2015; 'I'd used her map …'; Bondarenko, n.d.; 'Perm-36': see Shmyrov, 2003; '"Glory to the heroes …"': Danilovich and Coalson, 2015; 'Pauli was very critical …': see Robeson, 2010, p. 326; 'In 1963, Essie organised …': Duberman, 1988, p. 512; '"much thinner …"': Duberman, 1988, p. 523; '"I'm just putting …"': Robeson, 2010, p. 369.

Epilogue

'The garden emerged …': see 'Beauty Will Save', n.d.; '"I have made …"': Foner, 1978, p. 118; 'Spain': Cunningham, 1986, p. 1; 'From very early …': the classic account of this remains Morrow, 1963; '"I am a radical …"': Foner, 1978, p. 221; '"I am well …"': Robeson, 2010, p. 152; '"Never say that you …"': Robeson, 2010, p. 154; '"You have been so greatly …"': Foner, 1978, p. 429; '"Auden's brand of amoralism"': Orwell, 1981, p. 238; '"They revile me, scandalise me …"': Foner, 1978, p. 230; '"A campaign had been launched …"': Clark, 2015; '"I've been a part …"': Duberman, 1988, p. 522; '"Sometimes I think I am the only Negro …"': Foner, 1978, p. 91; '"My conscience won't let me go shoot …"': Bingham, 2016, p. 18; '"Shall Negro sharecroppers …"': Foner, 1978, p. 378; '"warmth and love"': Duberman, 1988, p. 709.

FURTHER READING

BOOKS

Adler, William M., *The Man Who Never Died: the life, times, and legacy of Joe Hill, American labor icon*, Bloomsbury, New York, 2011.

Alexander, Michelle, *The New Jim Crow: mass incarceration in the age of colorblindness*, The New Press, New York, 2012.

Allen, William Francis; Pickard Ware, Charles; and McKim Garrison, Lucy, *Slave Songs of the United States: the classic 1867 anthology*, New York, Dover, 1995.

Baldwin, Kate A., *Beyond the Color Line and the Iron Curtain: reading encounters between black and red, 1922–1963*, Duke University Press, Durham, 2002.

Ball, Edward, *Slaves in the Family*, Farrar, Straus and Giroux, New York, 1998.

Baptist, Edward E., *The Half Has Never Been Told: slavery and the making of American capitalism*, Basic Books, New York, 2014.

Bessie, Alvah Cecil, *Spain Again*, Chandler & Sharp, San Francisco, 1975.

Bingham, Clara, *Witness to the Revolution: radicals, resisters, vets, hippies, and the year America lost its mind and found its soul*, Random House, New York, 2016.

Boyle, Sheila Tully and Bunie, Andrew, *Paul Robeson: the years of promise and achievement*, University of Massachusetts Press, Amherst, 2001.

Brown, Lloyd L., *The Young Paul Robeson: on my journey now*, Westview Press, Boulder, 1997.

Buhle, Paul and Dawley, Alan, *Working for Democracy: American workers from the Revolution to the present*, University of Illinois Press, Urbana, 1985.

Carew, Joy Gleason, *Blacks, Reds and Russians: sojourners in search of the Soviet promise*, Rutgers University Press, Brunswick, 2010.

Carroll, Peter N., *The Odyssey of the Abraham Lincoln Brigade: Americans in the Spanish Civil War*, Stanford University Press, Stanford, 1994.

Clendinnen, Inga, *Dancing with Strangers*, Text Publishing, Melbourne, 2003.

Collum, Danny Duncan and Berch, Victor A., *African Americans in the Spanish Civil War: 'This ain't Ethiopia, but it'll do'*, G.K. Hall, New York, 1992.

Cope, Phil; Robeson, Marilyn; and Jones, Nia, *Gadewch I Paul Robeson Ganu!: dathlu bywyd Paul Robeson a thrafod ei berthynas a chymru* (*Let Paul Robeson Sing!: celebrating the life of Paul Robeson and his relationship with Wales*), Pwyllgor Paul Robeson Cymru, Aberystwyth, 2003.

Crossman, R. H. S., and Koestler, Arthur, *The God That Failed: six studies in communism*, Hamilton, London, 1950.

Cunningham, David, *Klansville, U.S.A.: the rise and fall of the civil rights–era Ku Klux Klan*, Oxford University Press, New York, 2013.

Cunningham, Valentine, *Spanish Front: writers on the civil war*, Oxford University Press, New York, 1986.

Davies, Idris, *The Complete Poems of Idris Davies*, University of Wales Press, Cardiff, 1994.

Dellora, Daryl, *Utzon and the Sydney Opera House*, Penguin Books, Melbourne, 2013.

Dessaix, Robert, *Arabesques: a tale of double lives*, Picador, Sydney, 2008.

Du Bois, W. E. B, *The Souls of Black Folk*, Dover Thrift Editions, New York, 1994.

Du Bois, W. E. B., et al., *African American Political Thought, 1890–1930: Washington, Du Bois, Garvey, and Randolph*, M.E. Sharpe, Armonk, 1996.

Duberman, Martin B., *Paul Robeson*, Knopf, New York, 1988.

Dunbar, Paul Laurence, and Lida Keck Wiggins, *The Life and Works of Paul Laurence Dunbar*, Kraus Reprint Co, Millwood, 1975.

Finnegan, Terence, *A Deed So Accursed: lynching in Mississippi and South Carolina, 1881–1940*, University of Virginia Press, Charlottesville, 2013.

Fitzpatrick, Sheila, *Everyday Stalinism: ordinary life in extraordinary times — Soviet Russia in the 1930s*, Oxford University Press, New York, 1999.

Foner, Philip Sheldon (ed.), *Paul Robeson Speaks: writings, speeches, interviews, 1918–1974*, Brunner/Mazel, New York, 1978.

Fraser, Rebecca J., *Courtship and Love Among the Enslaved in North Carolina*, University Press of Mississippi, Jackson, 2007.

Fraser, Ronald, *Blood of Spain: an oral history of the Spanish Civil War*, Pantheon, London, 1979.

Freud, Sigmund, *The Uncanny*, Penguin Books, New York, 2003.

Fryer, Peter, *Staying Power: the history of black people in Britain*, Pluto Press, London, 1984.

Golden, Lily, *My Long Journey Home*, Third World Press, Chicago, 2002.

Goldstein, Robert J., *Political Repression in Modern America from 1870 to the Present*, G.K. Hall, Boston, 1985.

Goodman, Jordan, *Paul Robeson: a watched man*, Verso, London and New York, 2013.

Green, Howard L., *Words That Make New Jersey History: a primary source reader*, Rivergate Books, New Brunswick, 2006.

Greer, Bonnie, *Langston Hughes: the value of contradiction*, Arcadia Books, London, 2011.

Haldane, Charlotte Franken, *Truth Will Out*, Vanguard Press, New York, 1951.

Heale, M. J., *American Anticommunism: combating the enemy within, 1830–1970*, Johns Hopkins University Press, Baltimore, 1990.

Hellman, Lillian, *Scoundrel Time*, Little Brown, Boston, 1976.

Hillstrom, Kevin, *The Harlem Renaissance*, Omnigraphics, Detroit, 2008.

Hochschild, Adam, *Spain in Our Hearts: Americans in the Spanish Civil War*, Houghton Mifflin Harcourt, Boston and New York, 2016.

Holmes, Larry E., *Stalin's School: Moscow's Model School No. 25, 1931–1937*, University of Pittsburgh Press, Pittsburgh, 1999.

Horne, Gerald, *Paul Robeson: the artist as revolutionary*, Pluto Press, London, 2016.

Huggins, Nathan Irvin, *Harlem Renaissance*, Oxford University Press, New York, 1971.

—— *Voices from the Harlem Renaissance*, Oxford University Press, New York, 1976.

Hughes, Langston, *The Big Sea: an autobiography*, Hill and Wang, New York, 1993.

——, *The Collected Poems of Langston Hughes*, Vintage Books, New York, 1995.

Hunt, Tristram, *Marx's General: the revolutionary life of Friedrich Engels*, New York, Metropolitan Books, 2009.

Jacobs, Nancy Joy, *African History Through Sources*, Cambridge University Press, New York, 2014.

Johnson, James Weldon, *Black Manhattan*, Arno Press, New York, 1968.

Kaiser, Ernest, *Paul Robeson: the great forerunner*, International Publishers, New York, 1998.

Kayton, Bruce, *Radical Walking Tours of New York City*, Seven Stories Press, New York, 2003.

Khanga, Yelena and Jacoby, Susan, *Soul to Soul: a black Russian-American family, 1865–1992*, W.W. Norton, New York, 1992.

King, Wilma, *Stolen Childhood: slave youth in nineteenth-century America*, Indiana University Press, Bloomington, 1995.

Kolin, Philip C., *Othello: new critical essays*, Routledge, New York and London, 2002.

Krugler, David F., *1919, the Year of Racial Violence: how African Americans fought back*, Cambridge University Press, New York, 2014.

Langford, Martin (ed.), *Harbour City Poems: Sydney in verse 1788–2008*, Puncher and Wattmann, Glebe, 2009.

Lieberman, Robbie, *The Strangest Dream: communism, anticommunism and the US peace movement 1945–1963*, Syracuse University Press, New York, 2000.

Lloyd, Nick, *Forgotten Places: Barcelona and the Spanish Civil War*, CreateSpace, 2015.

Locke, Alain (ed.), *The New Negro*, Maxwell Macmillan International, New York, 1992.

Low, Mary, and Breá, Juan, *Red Spanish Notebook: the first six months of the revolution and the civil war*, M. Secker & Warburg, London, 1937.

Martin, Sylvia, *Ink in Her Veins: the troubled life of Aileen Palmer*, UWA Publishing, Crawley, 2016.

Mathieson, David, *Frontline Madrid: battlefield tours of the Spanish Civil War*, Signal Books, Oxford, 2014.

McNeese, Tim, *The abolitionist movement: ending slavery*, Chelsea House, New York, 2007.

McWhirter, Cameron, *Red Summer: the summer of 1919 and the awakening of black America*, Henry Holt & Co, New York, 2011.

Mebane, Mary E., *Mary, Wayfarer*, Viking Press, New York, 1983.

Morrow, Felix, *Revolution and Counterrevolution in Spain*, New Park, London, 1963.

Nelson, Cary (ed.), *The Wound and the Dream: sixty years of American poems about the Spanish Civil War*, University of Illinois Press, Urbana, 2002.

Norrell, Robert J., *Up From History: the life of Booker T. Washington*, Belknap Press of Harvard University Press, Cambridge, 2009.

O'Neill, Eugene, *Nine Plays*, Modern Library, New York, 1941.

Orwell, George, *A Collection of Essays*, First Harvest, New York, 1981.

Peters-Little, Frances, et al., *Passionate Histories: myth, memory, and Indigenous Australia*, Aboriginal history monograph no 21., ANU Press, Acton, 2010.

Preston, Paul, *The Spanish Civil War: reaction, revolution and revenge*, Harper Perennial, London, 2006.

——, *The Spanish Holocaust: inquisition and extermination in twentieth-century Spain*, Harper Press, London, 2012.

——, *A Concise History of the Spanish Civil War*, Fontana, London, 1996.

Ransby, Barbara, *Eslanda: the large and unconventional life of Mrs Paul Robeson*, Yale University Press, New Haven, 2013.

Ransome, Arthur, *Bohemia in London*, Dodd, Mead & Company, New York, 1907.

Rhodes, Richard, *Hell and Good Company: the Spanish Civil War and the world it made*, Simon & Schuster, New York, 2015.

Rhodes-Pitts, Sharifa, *Harlem Is Nowhere: a journey to the mecca of black America*, Little, Brown, New York, 2011.

Richardson, John, *The Chelsea Book: past and present*, Historical Publications Ltd, Whitstable, 2003.

Robeson, Eslanda Goode, *Paul Robeson, Negro*, Harper & Brothers, New York, 1930.

Robeson, Paul, *Here I Stand*, Othello Associates, New York, 1958.

Robeson, Paul, Jr, *The Undiscovered Paul Robeson: an artist's journey, 1898–1939*, Wiley, New York and Chichester, 2001.

——, *The Undiscovered Paul Robeson: quest for freedom, 1939–1976*, Wiley, Hoboken, 2010.

Seton, Marie, *Paul Robeson*, Dennis Dobson, London, 1958.

Sinclair, Neil M. C., *The Tiger Bay Story*, Butetown History & Arts Project, Cardiff, 1993.

Sullivan, Rosemary, *Stalin's Daughter: the extraordinary and tumultuous life of Svetlana Alliluyeva*, Harper, New York, 2015.

Swindall, Lindsey R., *The Politics of Paul Robeson's Othello*, University Press of Mississippi, Jackson, 2011.

Tolnay, Stewart Emory, and Beck, E. M., *A Festival of Violence: an analysis of Southern lynchings, 1882–1930*, University of Illinois Press, Urbana, 1995.

Townsend, William and Forge, Andrew, *The Townsend Journals: an artist's record of his times, 1928–51*, Tate Gallery Publications, London, 1976.

Tragle, Henry Irving (ed.), *The Southampton Slave Revolt of 1831: a compilation of source material, including the full text of* The Confessions of Nat Turner, Vintage Books, New York, 1973.

Tremlett, Giles, *Ghosts of Spain: travels through a country's hidden past*, Faber and Faber, London, 2006.

Wexler, Laura, *Fire in a Canebrake: the last mass lynching in America*, Scribner, New York, 2003.

Wicker, Tom, *A Time to Die: the Attica prison revolt*, Haymarket Books, Chicago, 2011.

Williamson, Stanley, *Gresford: the anatomy of a disaster*, Liverpool University Press, Liverpool, 1999.

Wintz, Cary D., *Remembering the Harlem Renaissance*, Garland Publishing, New York, 1996.

Yates, James, *Mississippi to Madrid: memoir of a black American in the Abraham Lincoln Brigade*, Open Hand Publishing, Seattle, 1989.

ARTICLES, PAMPHLETS, AND REPORTS

1898 Wilmington Race Riot Commission, *1898 Wilmington Race Riot — Final Report, May 31*, North Carolina Office of Archives, 31 May 2006, http://www.history.ncdcr.gov/1898-wrrc/report/report.htm

Andrews, Cornelia, 'Interview with Cornelia Andrews — North Carolina Digital History', 2016, http://www.learnnc.org/lp/editions/nchist-antebellum/5326

Bondarenko, Sergei et al., *A Topography of the Terror: Lubyanka and its surrounding*, Moscow, Memorial, n.d.

Burke, W. Lewis, 'Post-Reconstruction Justice: the prosecution and trial of Francis Lewis Cardozo,' *South Carolina Law Review* 53, no. 2, 2002.

Carradice, Phil, 'Albion Colliery Explosion,' 2014, http://www.bbc.co.uk/blogs/wales/entries/7bca678b-6153-3b63-8a95-934049bf4b3d

Carter, David C., 'The Williamston Freedom Movement: civil rights at the grass roots in eastern North Carolina, 1957–1964,' *The North Carolina Historical Review* 76, no. 1, 1999.

Clark, Fiona, 'Iron Felix Rears His Ugly Head in Moscow', *DW.com*, 26 June 2015, http://www.dw.com/en/iron-felix-rears-his-ugly-head-in-moscow/a-18541985

Curtis, Mary C., 'Strom Thurmond's Black Daughter: a symbol of America's complicated racial history,' *The Washington Post*, 5 February 2013, https://www.washingtonpost.com/blogs/she-the-people/wp/2013/02/05/strom-thurmonds-black-daughter-a-flesh-and-blood-symbol-of-americas-complicated-racial-history/?utm_term=.c48b5c363525

Beekman, Dan, and Matthew Lysiak, 'Bronx Judge Vacates Conviction in 1975 Rape', *New York Daily News*, 12 April 2013, http://www.nydailynews.com/new-york/bronx/new-york-city-judge-vacates-conviction-1975-child-rape-death-article-1.1314857

Danilovich, Mikhail and Coalson, Robert, 'Revamped Perm-36 Museum Emphasizes Gulag's "Contribution to Victory"', *Radio Free Europe*, 25 July 2015.

Ellison, Ralph, 'Harlem Is Nowhere', *Harper's*, August, 1964.

Gilbert, Paul, 'New Permanent Exhibit Dedicated to Russian Tsars Opens in Moscow', *Russia Insider*, 15 February 2016, http://russia-insider.com/en/

culture/new-permanent-exhibit-dedicated-romanov-and-rurik-dynasties-opens-moscow/ri12329

Graeber, David, 'Ferguson and the Criminalization of American Life', *Gawker*, 19 March 2015.

Greensboro Library, 'City of Greensboro, NC: 303 E. Washington J. Douglas Galyon Depot', 2016, http://www.greensboro-nc.gov/index.aspx?page=1016

'Historical Society of Princeton', 2016, http://www.princetonhistory.org/collections/historic-sites.cfm

Hotel National, 'Hotel National, a Luxury Collection Hotel', *National.ru*, accessed 5 October 2016, http://www.national.ru/en/history

Hunter, Jack, 'Denmark Vesey Was a Terrorist', *Charleston City Paper*, 10 February 2010, http://www.charlestoncitypaper.com/charleston/denmark-vesey-was-a-terrorist/Content?oid=1756179

Knapp, Krystal, 'NY Judge Sends Princeton Man, Freed Last Year, Back to Prison', *Planet Princeton*, 1 July 2014, http://planetprinceton.com/2014/07/01/ny-judge-sends-princeton-man-freed-last-year-back-to-prison

Kravchenko, Artem, 'Topography of the Terror: Moscow's memory of repression', *Digital Russia*, 2015.

Kurkovsky, Diana, 'Monumentalizing Wheat: Soviet dreams of abundance', *Gastronomica* 7, no. 1, 2007.

McCarthy, Tom, 'Police Killed More Than Twice as Many People as Reported by US Government', *The Guardian*, 5 March 2015, https://www.theguardian.com/us-news/2015/mar/04/police-killed-people-fbi-data-justifiable-homicides

Miller, Adam, 'The Pioneer Fund: bankrolling the professors of hate', *The Journal of Blacks in Higher Education*, no. 6, Winter 1994–1995.

Moore, Christopher, and Dolkart, Andrew S., *Mother African Methodist Episcopal Zion Church Designation Report*, New York City Landmarks Preservation Commission, 1993.

Moredock, Will, 'Ben Tillman Was a Racist, Terrorist, and Murderer: it's time to take down his statue', *Charleston City Paper*, 5 February 2014, http://www.charlestoncitypaper.com/charleston/ben-tillman-was-a-racist-terrorist-and-murderer-its-time-to-take-down-his-statue/Content?oid=4857402

Mulvaney, Katie, 'Brown U. Student Leader: more African-American men in prison system now than were enslaved in 1850', *PolitiFactRhodeIsland*, 2016, http://www.politifact.com/rhode-island/statements/2014/dec/07/diego-arene-morley/brown-u-student-leader-more-african-american-men-p/

'Museon Park of the Fallen Heroes in Moscow', *Beauty Will Save*, n.d., http://viola.bz/museon-park-of-the-fallen-heroes-in-moscow

O'Keefe, Ken, *International Brigade Sites in Central Madrid: the Spanish Civil War*, Madrid, Asociacion de Amigos de las Brigadas Internacionales, 2013.

O'Mahony, Mike, 'Archaeological Fantasies: constructing history on the Moscow metro', *Modern Language Review* 98, no. 1, 2003.

O'Reilly, Kenneth, 'The Jim Crow Policies of Woodrow Wilson', *The Journal of Blacks in Higher Education*, no. 17, Autumn 1997.

Pincombe, Ian, 'From Pit to Paradise: Porthcawl's changing identity, from the eighteenth to the twentieth century', *Welsh History Review* 25, no. 4, 2011.

Princeton Cemetery of Nassau Presbyterian Church, Nassau Presbyterian Church, 2016.

Roberson, Mike, 'Roberson Family', *Robersons.Us*, 2016, http://www.robersons.us

Roberts, Blain, and Kytle, Ethan J., 'Looking the Thing in the Face: slavery, race, and the commemorative landscape in Charleston, South Carolina, 1865–2010', *Journal of Southern History* 78, no. 3, 2012.

Shaw, Charles, 'The Most Soviet Park in Russia', *The Appendix* 2, no. 1, 2014.

Shmyrov, Victor, 'The Gulag Museum', *Museum International* 53, no. 1, 2003.

Smith, Anna Bustill, 'The Bustill Family', *The Journal of Negro History* 10, no. 4, 1925.

Tavernise, Sabrina, 'Russian Project Honors Stalin's Victims and Stirs Talk on Brutal Past', *The New York Times*, 20 September 2015, http://www.nytimes.com/2015/09/21/world/europe/russian-project-honors-stalins-victims-and-stirs-talk-on-brutal-past.html?_r=0

VIDEOS

Spontaneous45, 'Paul Robeson Sings for the Workers at Sydney Opera House', 14 November 2010, https://www.youtube.com/watch?v=Eg7bPgrosAE

'Walter Scott Death: video shows fatal North Charleston police shooting', *The New York Times*, 7 April 2015, https://www.youtube.com/watch?v=XKQqgVlk0NQ

ABCSplashTV, 'Paul Robeson: on colonialism, African-American rights (*Spotlight*, ABC, 1960)', YouTube, 20 August 2013, https://www.youtube.com/watch?v=puOIdh944vk

ACKNOWLEDGEMENTS

A book is always a collective project. The idea took shape from conversations with Stephanie Convery, who was one of the book's earliest readers and a constant source of support and suggestions. Jacinda Woodhead, Rjurik Davidson, and Alison Croggon all provided valuable feedback on early drafts, as did my agent, Jenny Darling. I owe a debt to those who assisted with my travels, as well as to the Sidney Myer Foundation for its generous support through a creative fellowship, which aided in the production of this book. I also thank Julia Carlomagno at Scribe for her enthusiasm for the manuscript and for the editorial advice that greatly improved it.